MODERNIST FORM

MODERNIST FORM

Pound's Style in the Early Cantos

JOHN STEVEN CHILDS

Selinsgrove: Susquehanna University Press
London and Toronto: Associated University Presses

Associated University Presses
440 Forsgate Drive
Cranbury, NJ 08512

Associated University Presses
25 Sicilian Avenue
London WC1A 2QH, England

Associated University Presses
2133 Royal Windsor Drive
Unit 1
Mississauga, Ontario
Canada L5J 1K5

Excerpts from Canto I, Canto II, Canto IV, Canto VII, Canto IX, Canto XIV, Canto XVI, Canto XVII, Canto XIX, Canto XX, Canto XXI, and Canto XXX are from Ezra Pound, *The Cantos of Ezra Pound*. Copyright 1934 by Ezra Pound. Reprinted by permission of New Directions Publishing Corporation.

The paper used in this publication meets the requirements of the American National Standard for Permanence of Paper for Printed Library Materials Z39.48-1984.

Library of Congress Cataloging-in-Publication Data

Childs, John Steven, 1947–
  Modernist form.

  Bibliography: p.
  Includes index.
  1. Pound, Ezra, 1885–1972. 2. Pound, Ezra,
1885–1972—Style. 3. Modernism (Literature) I. Title.
PS3531.O82C2837 1986 811'.52 85-62781
ISBN 0-941664-15-5 (alk. paper)

Printed in the United States of America

To Ben D. Kimpel—
1915–1983

CONTENTS

ACKNOWLEDGMENTS

THE GERM OF this book was sprouted in the unlikely atmosphere of closed rooms filled with the accumulated smoke of Ben Kimpel's endlessly burning, perpetual Camel. If the facts herein concerning Pound's poetry or his life are accurate, such accuracy is entirely owing to the razor-edged precision of Kimpel's mind (a mind, by the way, which fitted Pound's like a key in a well-made lock—a rarity perhaps in the relations between poets and their critics). If there are failures in precision here, they are my own when I have parted from Kimpel's passionate dispassion. I, like my fellow Poundians, await T. C. Duncan Eaves's completion of the work that he and Kimpel had nearly finished at Ben's death in the spring of 1983.

This study also is the result of the acute scrutiny of J. R. Bennett, whose command of current stylistics and critical practice insured that many of my more ill-thought-out notions died aborning. When, as it frequently did, my reasoning strayed or my common sense failed, Dick Bennett's commentary was a sure remedy and tonic. Most importantly, the impatience with impressionistic or unconsidered literary opinion which this book reflects is Bennett's direct legacy, as is his corollary humanity and faith in literature as a revivifying influence in a culture that too often turns from humanity.

I wish as well to extend my thanks to L. E. Guinn for what must have seemed to him his thankless efforts in keeping my linguistic theory and practice honest.

Finally, I wish to express my gratitude to James C. Cowan for his heartening moral support throughout this endeavor.

1

THE CANTOS AND MODERNISM

TWO BASIC FACTS about *The Cantos* of Ezra Pound strike most first readers.

The Cantos are monumental: the physical weight of the fourth edition is substantial, especially compared to the proverbial "slim volume of verse." *The Cantos*, considered as a whole, are simply one of the longest poems in world literature.

The Cantos are difficult: the hapless amateur opens the volume at random, and finds, to his dismay, that he is unable to "construe" a given page, much less determine the relation of that page to the one which follows or precedes it. The one unifying factor, in fact, seems to be a bewildering variety of symbols and languages, and the peculiar insertion into the poem of tracts of prose.

The professional reader, the critic, has a slightly different reaction depending on his attitude about modern literature, and his patience. His first response may well be that the monumentality of *The Cantos* is misplaced (might not much of this have been excised without anyone's noticing?), and the difficulty gratuitous (does one really want to achieve proficiency in economics, Confucianism, or Chinese ideograms merely to read a poem?). The critic may legitimately ask whether the returns are worth the effort.

I will of course argue in the pages that follow that the effort is doubly repaid; *The Cantos*, even if partly understood, offer up treasures of esthetic beauty proportionate to their monumentality; apart from the necessary acknowledgement of sources, learning to understand *The Cantos* is itself a heuristic process of great utility in coming to terms with other difficult Modernist works like *The Bridge*, *Paterson*, or *Finnegans Wake*.

But if *The Cantos* are long and difficult, they are also coherent. They cohere structurally in a fashion which may be unapparent only because the devices which link line to line, verse paragraph to verse paragraph, and canto to canto are often extremely exiguous, and because those devices are by and large peculiar to twentieth-century poetry (although many of these devices can occasionally be found elsewhere in the literary traditions of Europe and the Orient).

Literary coherence—despite critics' pronouncements to the contrary—is probably *sui generis;* a reader's perception that a work hangs together may in part be the outcome of convention, but each successful literary work more generally establishes its own unity. Like Stephen Dedalus's paradigmatic basket, a poem "is first luminously apprehended as self-bounded and self-contained upon the immeasurable background of space or time which is not it."[1] Stephen, the reader will recall, calls this wholeness *integritas*, and coupled with *integritas* is *consonantia*, the harmony of the work's parts. It is, however, the *quidditas* of a poem, its "suchness," which lends ambiguity to all definitions of literary coherence, for, although we may easily distinguish that which is a poem from what it is not and though we may set up standards of proportion and harmonic balance, we can neither predict nor even objectively deduce a work's "suchness." Whatever had been its standards in previous eras, in the nineteenth century at least coherence in literature usually involved, in terms of the novel, the "well-made" plot and consistent characterization (this latter trait usually is manifested by plausible psychological development). In that century, the shorter literary genres too, the short story and the lyric poem, had their standards of unity: in the short poem, a poet like Browning aimed at a "satisfying" (satisfying for the reader) union of verbal concision and cameo-like psychological portraiture; in the story, James and Maupassant were as concerned with what was unsaid as with what was said.

The great literary works of the twentieth century are responses to both kinds of coherence. Since Flaubert (and, with Pound and Joyce, we may use Flaubert as the origin of many Modernist impulses), the management of discourse as a whole and precision on the level of the line or sentence (the *mot juste*) have been combined into a basic literary standard.[2] Unfortunately, it is all too easy to lose sight of the greater whole in pursuing the sometimes tortuous difficulties of the individual instance. If the reader is involved in deciphering pun after pun in *Finnegans Wake,* or if he is puzzling over the sense link between two juxtaposed lines in *The Cantos,* how is he ever to discover the meaning of the larger whole? One answer may be that to decipher the pun or to discover the link is to begin to understand the greater armature which animates the work as a whole.

In fact, the attempt to understand a Modernist work by the modes of reading one brings to most pre-twentieth-century works is doomed to failure. The defeat of readerly (see Glossary) expectations in Modernism is itself a vexed question, to which I shall return in a later chapter. To revert, however, for a moment to my well-intentioned but perplexed reader: what else does he notice besides the length and difficulty of *The Cantos?* He may at first be hard put to discover a plot (the poem is, after all, according to its author, an epic). He may have trouble discovering who is speaking to him, and whether that speaker remains the same throughout the work. He may be disconcerted by visual form; what is he to make of shifts in orthography, of the insertion of lengthy prose passages into verse, or, taking into consideration the fact that *The Cantos is* a poem, of the absence of any regular pattern of meter or stanza? I shall assume that my reader has by his side a good handbook like the *Annotated Index* of Edwards and Vasse, or Terrell's *Companion,* to help him with sources, and a half-a-dozen foreign language dictionaries, to help him through passages in Latin, Italian, or Greek (I will assume he has some French).[3] His difficulties, then, are basically with form.

By "form" I mean, first of all, stylistic properties, and, secondly, those elements of a literary work (I shall call these semiotic "codes") which have not traditionally been the concern of stylistics. In *The Cantos,* for example, the reader may observe definite repeated stylistic traits which arise in a relatively circumscribed area of the discourse; that is to say, he may observe Pound doing some characteristic things with the ordering of his words within particular lines, or he may note a certain level of diction inhering in certain passages. On the other hand, the reader will also be concerned with the kinds of effects Pound is deploying throughout large groups of cantos, or even through *The Cantos* as a whole; these include the use of several language systems, for example, and the employment of Pound's famous "ideogrammic" method. Certainly, these last effects are elements of Pound's style in a broad sense, but stylistics, understandably, does not as yet have the tools to deal with these.

Negatively, my discussion of form will have little to do with interpretative strategies. I might frame the definition of my approach in structuralist terminology and say that *The Cantos* (and Modernist works in general) do not often demonstrate strict referentiality. Of course, it is becoming commonly understood today that all literature has no real reference to the objective world, that literary works (the "poetic Sign") refer to themselves. Much twentieth-century literature, however, foregrounds this "self-referential" property of literature in general; it is not, for example, the historical Confucius or the cultural history of China to which *The Cantos* refer, but the Confucius-of-*The-Cantos* and the Poundian concept of "Chineseness." The problem of Pound's translations is closely allied to this question, and persons having difficulty with Pound's role as translator will have difficulty with the concept of self-referentiality. One may of course adopt the stance that a translation of the *Seafarer* should reflect certain psychological and cultural attitudes of Anglo-Saxon Britain; but one may also, with Pound, adopt the stance that such a translation should not be of the "content" of the *Seafarer,* but of the peculiar phenomenon which is the unique text of the poem. Of course, this latter stance inevitably implies "departures" from the meaning of words in the original, but the reference of the translation is to its source-as-text, not to the source-as-artifact.

In saying above that many critics currently assume that "literature has no reference to the objective world," I am not forwarding the nonsensical claim that literature has no *relation* to the world. That relation is however very problematic. Certainly, literature is in the world, it is part of objectivity; and yet, unlike most objects, it is at once *about* the world in which it exists, and, at the same time, creates its own world. It is in the different ways that literature can be "about the world" and in the intensity of the worlds it creates that we may see a partial distinction between twentieth-century literature and the literature which precedes it. The fictional worlds of Shakespeare and Balzac, for example, are more "unitary" than Pound's or Joyce's; this fact can be clearly seen in Balzac's paradoxical attempt, in the *Comédie humaine* for instance, to balance the conflicting demands of, on the one hand, a social world becoming increasingly fragmented, increasingly various, and, on the other, a literary structure which imposes formal cohesion on that fragmentation. If, for example, the pre-twentieth-century fictional or poetic narrative attempts in the interests of a spurious plenitude to mirror to some extent what was seen as the linearity of time, the form of twentieth-century narrative, like *The Cantos,* is dictated by a poetics of absence (stylistically evident in deletion and fragmentation) and superimposition (the stylistic indicator of which is condensation). Experience in the modern world is portrayed by the writer as alternately broken, lost, and unknown, or full beyond the capacity of the individual consciousness.

The Cantos' reader's search for plot and speaker, then, is not pointless, but misdirected. He looks for an "active" character, for example, where he should be looking for the outlines of character which are left when the illusion of plenitude is withdrawn. In the Malatesta cantos, for example, the character of Sigismundo is accrued through the medium of a palimpsest whereupon letters to and from him, chronicles of his times, and the "speaking" voices of his contemporaries, friends and enemies, are superposed. Where then is Sigismundo? He, like the rose in the steel dust, is created in the formal forces enacted by *The Cantos* themselves.

Hence, to study what *The Cantos* are "about" is to study those formal forces. This activity does not involve shifting the traditional paraphernalia of characterization, of plot action, of theme, to form. Form does not mean in the same way that a personality or a situation means. Form implies a predictable series of absences (signalled in *The Cantos* by deletion), recurrences, and other relations between its component parts. In fact, it is not even in the absences or recurrences that meaning resides, but in the relations themselves. This, finally, is what I meant above when I argued that the poetic sign does not have reference to objectivity, to isolable units (whether human or otherwise) in the world; rather, modern literature is unconcerned with the colors of the threads in the carpet; it values instead the tension produced by the loom.

My emphasis on form, however, is not the critical corollary to "l'art pour l'art," any more than is Pound's concern with formal devices in *The Cantos* an aesthetic outcome of that stance. "L'art pour l'art" is after all a political or social slogan:

> Nonconformists rebel against the handing over of art to the market. They gather around the banner of "l'art pour l'art." This slogan springs from the conception of the total artwork, which attempts to isolate art from technology. The solemnity with which it is celebrated is the corollary to the frivolity that glorifies the commodity. Both abstract from the social existence of man.[4]

Walter Benjamin is here writing of mid-nineteenth-century France, where the slogan arose. By 1915 or 1916, when *Cathay* and *Lustra* appear and when the plan of *The Cantos* is germinating, Pound has absorbed the lessons of the nineties, of Imagism and Vorticism and Symbolism, of the first terrible battles of the First World War. It is specious to speak of the Modernist concern with form as an instance of "art for art's sake." The new interest with modes of writing as opposed to "subjects" is indebted as much to the renewed interest in myth, in the structure of the unconscious, or the nonrepresentative in the visual arts, as it is to the nineteenth-century "musical" theories of poetry forwarded by Poe, Swinburne, or Lanier.

Akin to Modernist interest in form is the modern critic's interest in structure, the relations between elements in the literary text. The importance of these relations is not peculiar to literature. Contrary to popular belief, structuralists do not hold up an eviscerated collection of flimsy outlines, like a Calder mobile, and say: "This is the heart of the poem." Rather, they see in structural relationships the dynamism, the kinesis, of the *individual* literary work. Because music is clearly an art of relationships, of tonal or temporal intervals, it lends itself easily to structural analogy; it is in *this* sense of musical relationship, and not in the sense of some vague impression of individual tones, that Modernist writers (initially prompted by Pater and instanced by T. S. Eliot in "Ezra Pound: His Metric and Poetry" and "The Music of Poetry") use formal analogies based in music.

But poetry, of course, has verbal reference, and music does not. Even poetic rhythm is dictated by linguistic stress and not by the exigencies of a time signature. Pound and Joyce, in their "fugal" uses of literary form, are not attempting pure musicality, a use of words for their sounds. The sound of words, in any case, is only one aspect of linguistic, and thereby necessarily poetic, form. The Modernists were influenced by many formal spheres; they drew from the formal dynamism of the machine, from the dialectical dynamism of history, or from the psychic dynamism of the unconscious. The Modernists dismissed the pure and solitary Idea, the Word, and sought to place value on the relation between words: that relation would by its very nature be transitory, useful, like language itself, only for the moment.

The Cantos, then, imply that it is by the movement of words (what Pound termed "logopoeia") and idea/images ("phanopoeia"), as well as by the sounds of words ("melopoeia") that we are moved.

Another way in which a Modernist text may refer to itself as form is through the use of "intertexts". Michael Riffaterre (see below) uses the term "intertext" to define portions of a work which are "quoted," which do not originate with the author of the text. Near the end of this study I shall take up the complicated subject of an author's originality, but for the time being I should like to draw the reader's attention to an important characteristic of Modernist literature: the insertion of borrowed phrases, sentences, and longer units of discourse into the syntagm (see Glossary) of the work. Actually, a major reason that even experienced readers of Modernist texts occasionally have need of one of the many "handbooks," "companions," or "notes to" the modern classics is this very insertion of older texts into the discourse. Such texts may not always be purely literary—the snatches of popular song in *Ulysses* or the letters in *Paterson*; moreover, the quoted intertext is freqently not in any way signalled. *The Cantos*, especially, comprise lengthy passages of quoted material: the Malatesta and Adams cantos are merely obvious examples; hardly a page of the *Draft of XXX Cantos* goes by without the insertion into the poem of a word or phrase drawn from an author other than Pound. When an alien syntagm appears in a text, when the reader is aware that a passage in a text is not his author's, the result will be a deferred referentiality; the quoted or "stolen" text will signify itself and its origin elsewhere. The original meaning of the intertext will become secondary; it will be deferred, in other words, until its source, and the significance of that source, is identified. In the intertext, then, the reader of the Modernist work has the clearest example of Modernism's tendency to foreground "literariness" itself rather than some idea or sequence of events in the objective world. Finally, the use of intertexts contributes to the already fragmented syntagm of the text: the disjunctiveness commonly remarked of Modernism is a function not only of the linguistic markers proper to Modernist style but also of the "disruption" of the form by alien intertexts.

Pound and His Critics

Pound criticism of the last thirty years, beginning with Hugh Kenner's *The Poetry of Ezra Pound*, has been dominated by the techniques of traditional explication. Great resources of patience, diligence, and ingenuity have quite rightly been brought to bear on *The Cantos*; the sort of formal description proposed here quite simply could not be done without the painstaking source-hunting which is the staple of much Modernist criticism in general, and especially of Pound criticism, for reasons just stated in the preceding section. The sheer wealth of allusion alone in the great Modernist works makes such groundwork essential. In what follows I shall be repeatedly indebted to scholars like Kenner, Christine Brooke-Rose, K. K. Ruthven, Edwards and Vasse, Kimpel and Eaves, Donald Gallup, D. D. Paige, Carroll Terrell, and Dilligan, Parins, and Bender.[5]

This is not to say that a certain amount of structural and thematic interpretation has not had a significant place in Pound scholarship; here I might mention as only one example among many Donald Davie's *Poet as Sculptor*.[6] Nonetheless, very little interpretative work has been done along the more or less semiotic and linguistic lines proposed here. There are obvious reasons for structuralists' reluctance to tackle Modernist verse. For one thing, the tools of structuralist and semiotic analysis, owing perhaps to structuralism's origins in Formalism, have most often been employed on fictional narrative. One need only think of the best-known works of the most influential structuralists (here I might cite as diverse a collection as Barthes's *S/Z*, Propp's *Morphology of the Folk-Tale*, or Heath's *The Nouveau Roman*) to recognize structuralism's emphasis on fiction. Secondly, again owing to its origins in Formalism, structuralism has insisted on the need to understand simple plot structures (folk-tales, medieval literature, and, with Umberto Eco, even comic books) before tackling the staggering complexity of modern classics. It is doubtful that, at least in terms of its structure, poetry is ever as simple as the simplest fictions. Although, as Barthes has shown in *S/Z*, even relatively short fictional narrations can show evidence of extreme polysemy, nonetheless, poetry by its very nature encourages variety of signification on all levels.

In the structuralist analysis of poetry (or in the analysis of poetry, as opposed to prose, in any critical school), the situation can be confused. An excellent example of the kind of heated dispute about the nature of poetic interpretation which may develop even among structuralists who share essentially the same suppositions can be seen in Riffaterre's well-known attack on Jakobson's and Lévi-Strauss's analysis of Baudelaire's "Les Chats."[7] A consensus about the principles of poetic analysis, however, has been slowly growing among post-structuralists (see Glossary) over the past decade. The contributions of Riffaterre are partly responsible for this tentative rapprochement, but other critics, like Christine Brooke-Rose and a variety of younger analysts, have also lent cohesiveness to post-structuralist poetic interpretation. I will take up these specifically technical and methodological developments below.

In Pound criticism itself, one of the few analysts to adopt a more or less structuralist outlook is Herbert Schneidau. In *The Image and the Real* and "Wisdom Past Metaphor," Schneidau offers readings of *The Cantos* which are neither, on the one hand, overgrown with terminology and needless pedanticism, or, on the other, diffusively metaphysical and subjective. Schneidau believes that "Pound's remarkable poetics argues a revolutionary break-away from metaphorical habits in composing poems," and that, even before *The Cantos*, the poet "had already determined to use similarity devices i.e., metaphor only with great discipline, and to cross-fertilize them with the tendencies of a metonymic 'drive.' "[8] I shall defer an analysis of the Jakobsonian principle of metonymic-metaphoric polarity until the next chapter. I would like to suggest, instead, the critical results which Schneidau achieves through his use of Jakobson's ideas:

> I am tempted to identify Jakobson's metonymic pole with true creativity in modern literature. I base this point on the following train of thought: the decay and overthrow of the representational theory of art in our time will no longer allow us to think of the process of poetic gestation as simply a matter of selecting a subject and deciding what one wants to say about it. . . . The work does not "imitate" or describe or make a point about something external in so simple a way. . . . Rather it would seem the work is more nearly a product of wanting to say things *in a certain demanding way:* not the "hunt for a subject to accommodate a certain stock vocabulary" which Pound denounced, but rather a process of being pressed toward the work by the force of a certain stylistic drive. What the serious artist does is try to lead himself almost to the aphasic barrier. . . . And which kind of aphasic is it that the artist's struggle is like? Mostly it would seem, the metonymic kind, with similarity disorder; it is he who would be unable to "select" a subject, especially in the case of the Flaubertian type of writer . . . the search for the mot juste is the struggle. . . .[9]

Schneidau goes on to argue that Pound's is a "poetry of ellipsis"; the discontinuity and "jaggedness" with which every reader of *The Cantos* is familiar is the reflection of Pound's attempt to approach "rough speech" and the concision of prose. The result of ellipsis, Schneidau says, is that Pound's "luminous details" thus "stand out jaggedly, reaching toward each other everywhere, making everything the context of everything else; they are not muffled in redundant linguistic padding" (Schneidau, 1976: 25). In Chapter 3, in fact, I shall attempt to demonstrate that ellipsis or deletion is a verifiable trait, with recurrent linguistic markers, which is central to Pound's style.

Another point which Schneidau makes in the long quotation above, and one to which I will, again, return later in this study, concerns the idea that the work does not "imitate or describe or make a point about something external." The Modernist poem signifies in much the same way as any twentieth-century nonrepresentational visual artwork: it not only is non-mimetic, it also actively destroys in its perceiver the attempt at establishing a reference to any immediate sense perception in the objective world. In the same fashion as we can say that a painting by Klee is not *about* anything, at any rate in the sense that Brueghel's paintings are about Dutch peasant life, so can we say that *The Cantos* are not about some literary "subject," in the sense that Browning's *The Ring and the Book* is about certain historical characters involved in a given situation. In this regard, Schneidau cites Kenner's remark that the Pound canon after *Lustra* is "the longest working-out in any art of premises like those of cubism" (Schneidau, 1976: 26).[10]

A natural question may well have arisen in the reader's mind at this point: If a theme, a point of view, authorial intent, cluster of images, or central symbol doesn't hold together *The Cantos*, what on earth does? I shall undertake the answer to this highly legitimate query in the chapters which follow. I might suggest at this point, however, that such an answer will be based on the supposition that an entirely novel species of poetic organization is created by Pound and reflected in *The Cantos*, a form of organization revealed by Christine Brooke-Rose in an explication which is exemplary of many of the procedures which I shall bring to bear here.

In *A Structural Analysis of Pound's Usura Canto*, students of Pound have the only full-scale semiotic interpretation of *The Cantos* available.[11] As her subtitle *(Jakobson's Method Extended and Applied to Free Verse)* indicates, Brooke-Rose deploys the wide-ranging linguistic tools developed by Roman Jakobson, but with an alert eye to the subsequent reservations of his pupils. In fact, besides her cogent demonstration of current techniques of semiotic method, Brooke-Rose does a Herculean (perhaps an Augean) job, in her first chapter, of making sense of the critical confusion which seems to attend contemporary post-structuralist criticism.

Brooke-Rose's method is deductive: proceeding from general traits on the levels of grammar, "parallelisms on the level of convention" or rhetoric, the levels of prosody and phonemics, and the level of semantics, her analysis moves "inward" evermore exiguously, examining finer and finer traits.

Her explication begins by noting the most visible features in Canto 45 in a fashion roughly similar to my remarks on the reader's immediate perception of *The Cantos* in general. Some of the most obvious traits include the fact that the poem is a "block of some fifty lines in free verse," that there are "a lot of cultural allusions," and that there is an abundance of "grammatical parallelism." In all, Brooke-Rose notes forty-nine "very visible features" which she submits to increasingly closer analysis.

The core of Brooke-Rose's study is Chapter Six, the detailed analysis of her four levels. There is no reason (nor is there space) to summarize this chapter here, even were summary possible with so thorough an analysis. Fortunately, Chapter Five offers a general overview of the features Brooke-Rose goes on to discuss in considerable detail. Again, these features lie on the levels of grammar, rhetoric, and semantics, and are generally as follows: the canto possesses a "preponderance of nouns which helps to give the static effect"; "non-determination (lack of determiners, use of negatives)" is foregrounded; there are few metaphors; "colorless" verbs lend a "non-temporal" effect and "particular" verbs lend an effect of precision;

parallelisms are achieved by relatively unchanging verb "pivots" surrounded by alternating nouns; finally, "non-grammatical features such as the litany form with its repetition are countered by the active function of the verbs" (Brooke-Rose, 1976: 29). Consequently, the canto reflects an "action which affects everything" (that is, usury), and there is thus "a very real tension between the static surface and the dynamic action of usury which underlies the surface" (Brooke-Rose, 1976: 30). It is the structural foundation of this tension which Brooke-Rose goes on to analyze exhaustively.

Unfortunately, for the purposes of creating a definition of form in *The Cantos*, Brooke-Rose's nearly faultless analysis of Canto 45 has one serious shortcoming: the Usury canto is simply not statistically typical of the style of most of the remaining cantos. Curiously, Brooke-Rose fails to explain why she did choose Canto 45 for analysis: the choice, in fact, seems random. Admittedly, her aim is a thorough analysis of structure, and such exhaustiveness could not be applied to long stretches of *The Cantos* without a corollary expansion of her text into a multivolume work. And, quite candidly, I have not attempted here to remedy her lack. I have, in fact, confined my remarks to the structure of *A Draft of XXX Cantos*, limiting my investigation to passages which seem to me paradigmatic of Pound's style. Nonetheless, this is not to say that my perceptions are impressionistic; the reader will find a statistical appendix corroborating my remarks at the end of this study. The findings which appear in that appendix will sufficiently illustrate that, although Pound's style is generally characterized by a high percentage of fragmented structures, Canto 45 possesses only a very few fragments; although ambiguous or ambivalent lines appear frequently in *The Cantos*, they are nearly absent in Canto 45; and although Pound's lexicon is largely "Imagistic" (a characterization I shall explain in Chapter 2), the vocabulary in Canto 45 is, as Brooke-Rose points out, "archaic."

The Stylistic Foundation

I shall not here rehearse in detail the debate over the nature and ends of stylistics which has arisen over the last forty years. Obviously, what follows here assumes the existence of stylistics as a fairly well-defined discipline; that the actual practice of stylistics, like that of its parent field, linguistics, is eclectic in its methods should be apparent to nearly everyone now working in the critical vineyards. There is nothing inappropriate about eclecticism per se in any method of analysis. When hostile critics complain about disparate and conflicting stylistic approaches, however, they usually call into question stylistic theory rather than practice. In any discipline, from physics to philosophy, a wide variety of tools (drawn from methodologies themselves perhaps obsolete) is used in analysis: physicists still argue over the elements of the model of the material universe, but they are in agreement about the processes needed to induce nuclear fission. Unfortunately, criticism is quite often infected with the odd notion that certain practices are inseparable from the theory which supposedly supports them. We need not, for example, wholeheartedly subscribe to Freudian theory in order to see the validity of psychoanalysis in the interpretation of reader response. By the same token, we need not be Marxists to accept some of Marxism's insights into the production of literature as a commodity. If criticism is not to descend into the obscurantism and peculiarities of, for example, outmoded systems of thought like metaphysics, then it will have to adopt what it can of proven practices without overmuch concern with the theoretical provenience of those practices.

At the outset of this chapter I discussed very generally a few of my assumptions about style and form. I should like now to make these assumptions firmer. Style, as it is used here, assumes a dichotomy between Norm and Deviation. The older dichotomy, that between Form and Content, has been to an extent discussed above, and I will return to the Form-Content opposition later; suffice it to say, for the moment at least, that in Modernist poetry, form is homologous with content. The question thus arises of what I intend by the term "deviation." I shall be assuming two kinds of deviation from a norm, one synchronous and the other diachronous. As following chapters will indicate, *The Cantos* do deviate to some extent from the spoken language, a characteristic commonly, although debatably, assigned to poetry as a genre. On the other hand, the much-noted "conversational" quality of *The Cantos* would seem to militate against such deviation, and, in fact, twentieth-century poetry *does* seem to depart less from spoken language (in, for example, word order or lexicon) than the poetry of any preceding period. The problem is compounded by the addition of another species of deviation, one which cannot simply be classified as either diachronous or synchronous (see Glossary). This is the thoroughgoing "defamiliarization" which, as Victor Shklovsky has noted in his well-known remarks, is a property of all literary language.[12]

In its putative capacity as information-bearer, ordinary language tends to "automatize" its structure in order to convey its meaning efficiently. Literature, on the other hand, involves, as Jakobson terms it, a "set to the message," a predisposition to call attention to itself. Consequently, defamiliarization entails by definition a necessary and constant deviation from the spoken language. Defamiliarization does not only characterize the movement from ordinary to poetic language; it may be said also to characterize the movement from literary period to literary period; devices become automatic in one school of poetry and are thrown over by the succeeding school. This process is of course evident in the shift from late-nineteenth-century poetry to that of the early twentieth century; one very obvious example of defamiliarization in this period is the advent of free verse. In fact, free verse is also an excellent example of a novel form of defamiliarization in modern poetry which extends beyond period boundaries; twentieth-century poetry not only departs from the regular metrics of nineteenth-century verse, but also from the regular metrics which characterizes most verse in the English-language tradition. My point here is that twentieth-century poetry, unlike poetry of literary periods before it, is not content with overthrowing the poetic conventions of the period immediately preceding it, but is actually intent on dismantling the very conception of the structure of poetry. Free verse is only a very obvious instance of this tendency; more complex deviations from previously assumed standards of poetic structure, regardless of period, include conscious obstruction of reference, a high degree of syntactic "non sequitur," and even, in the case of *The Cantos* and many other long Modernist poems, the insertion of prose in what is otherwise assumed to be verse form.

The result of defamiliarization may entail "foregrounding." Foregrounding is the process whereby those features which are deautomatized become central devices in poetic language. Actually, foregrounding is less a "result" of defamiliarization than an element which stands in reciprocal relation to it; defamiliarization, after all, would go unnoticed if foregrounding did not call attention to the presence of its action. Thus, the terms "deviation" and "foregrounding" are to an extent equivalent. At any rate, at this point it should be obvious that deviation, defamiliarization, and foregrounding all take place not so much in the text as in the reader's perception of it. Consequently, we are brought to the point where we must face one of the most vexing questions in the theory of stylistics: Where does style lie? in text, author, or reader?

I shall here adopt several stylistic strategies which Riffaterre has advanced throughout various stages of his career, beginning with his essay "Criteria for Stylistic Analysis."[13] In this early essay, Riffaterre argues that, whether or not style features are consciously imposed on a text by an author, those devices, in terms of the practical work of stylistics, only have reality insofar as they are perceived by the reader.[14] Throwing the burden of recognition of style features onto the literary capacity of a reader has inevitably led to debates about the nature of that reader, but for the present I shall not pursue these. Even though Riffaterre himself later became embroiled in the conflicts over the construction of that critical Frankenstein's monster, the "super-reader," his earlier, more general, remarks on the role of readership in style studies still hold. In "Criteria" he argues that the reader is "the consciously selected target of the author" in that a style feature (Riffaterre terms this an "SD," stylistic device) "is so contrived that the reader cannot overlook it." Riffaterre continues:

> This interdependence between the SD and its perception is, in short, so central to the problem that it seems to me we may use this perception to

locate stylistic data in the literary discourse. Unfortunately, taste changes and each reader has his prejudices. Our problem is to transform a fundamentally subjective reaction to style into an objective analytic tool, to find the constant . . . beneath the variety of judgments, in short to transform value judgments into judgments of existence. The way to do it is, I believe, simply to disregard totally the content of the value judgment and to treat the judgment *as a signal only.*[15]

Foregrounding, then, constitutes that "signal" which points to a stylistic feature in a given text.

One problem with the designation of stylistic features in *The Cantos*, however, is the very high degree of foregrounding that the poem presents. As I argued above, Modernist poetry offers so radical a departure from the conventions of the poetic past that nearly every line seems to be in some sense foregrounded. Consequently, I would like to forward in the chapter which follows a tentative idiolectic (see Glossary) norm for Pound's later poetry in his earlier Imagist practices; Imagism, it seems to me, creates a relatively simple matrix on which the devices of *The Cantos* expand. Expansion, of course, implies some essential structural relation with a norm. Although foregrounding *may* take the form of a thorough departure from some aspect of automatized language (although even this implies a relation of opposition), it probably more often employs a systematic expansion of particular aspects of the norm. In this latter insight I am again indebted to Riffaterre.

In his *Semiotics of Poetry,* Riffaterre forwards a bundle of terms which will recur throughout this study: "matrix," "model," "hypogram," "expansion," and "conversion." Definitions are in order. The matrix of a poem is its semantic import, which is, he contends, realizable as a literal sentence, and later, in Chapter 5, I shall suggest some "realized" matrices for the *Draft.* The model is the initial manifestation of the matrix in the poem as variant; other variations succeed the model, producing the text. Text production occurs either through the rule of expansion, which "transforms the constituents of the matrix sentence into more complex forms," or the rule of conversion, which "transforms the constituents of a matrix structure by modifying them all with the same factor."[16] Now, it is obvious that poetry operates by indirection; although most poems make some sort of mimetic statement, the intent of that statement is in the form of semiotic meaning governed by sign production. Sign production, here the metamorphosis of mimetic signs into poetic signs, is derived on the basis of the hypogram. Riffaterre argues that hypograms are preexistent forms consisting of clichés, intertexts, the semantic features of a word (its "semes"), or descriptive systems associated with a word ("usury" in Pound, for example, is associated with devaluation of cultural standards and the corruption of natural processes).

More generally, style, for Riffaterre, simply comprises those aspects of a text to which the reader's attention is drawn (that which is foregrounded); style is not a fixed commodity, neither ornament nor meaning, but a dialectic between a semantic matrix and the transformation of that matrix into a given text. Foregrounded elements are, at face value, mimetic signs; they would remain mimetic (and, in fact, they *do* remain mimetic for readers without literary competence or an interest in poetry) if it weren't for the reader's participation in the more or less conscious activity of "reading a poem." Actually, and here I depart from Riffaterre, the very fact that a sign is foregrounded suggests that that sign is probably literary rather than mimetic. At any rate, the reader perceives a hypogram in the sign and scans his literary and linguistic competence for previous associations in the form of semes, clichés, and so on. Collectively, hypograms produce a tentative matrix (very generally, the poem's "meaning") in the reader's mind. In the text, the matrix is producing actual models in the form of phrases, lines, and stanzas: in other words, text production is under way. The reader interprets the text unconsciously by testing its signs for conversion or expansion. He explores the possibility that the poem is a kind of "fugal" repetition of or variation on a theme. Linguists will perhaps recognize here something very similar to the way listeners interpret sentences. In other words, sentences can be produced either through addition (rhetorical parataxis) or embedding (rhetorical hypotaxis).

Why All Those Terms?

It is doubtful that anyone involved in any of the current avenues of criticism would seriously argue that the use of terminology is not often abused. And every reader of criticism, I am sure, has at one time or another had the distinct feeling that a given critic has coined a given term merely out of the sheer joy of creation. Many of the terms in linguistics and semiotics overlap, and I shall try to point out where such duplication occurs. Many older terms, like "tenor" and "vehicle," are still useful. And, often, as in Brooke-Rose's substitution of "underlying" and "actual" for the "deep structure" and "surface structure" of linguistics, technical terms stand in need of more direct and less complex usages in the discussion of literature. Nonetheless, as William Beauchamp points out, the purpose of an abstract terminology is precision:

The purpose of abstraction, of "jargon," is to develop models sufficiently precise and sufficiently broad so as to account for multiple instances of literary phenomena. The experience of the act of literature is usually a private, subjective, solitary one; but the systematic study of that experience is a legitimate object of scientific inquiry—and that's what literary semiotics is about.[17]

Although the words and phrases used by semioticians are not themselves sacrosanct, consistency in usage should be a major goal in criticism (as yet such consistency is a remote ideal). I should like to make two important points in this regard: 1) despite the terms criticism uses, there must be widespread agreement (as measured, perhaps, by sheer quantity of use) upon their meaning, and 2) meaning, obviously, is a direct outcome of the care critics are willing to lend to definition. Consequently, I shall only be using terms which have enjoyed fairly widespread approval through the efficacy of their descriptive precision, and their use at the hands of critics like Barthes, Jakobson, and Riffaterre.

Further, I shall here be concerned largely with the linguistic sign, the word: *The Cantos* however employ other types of signs and this unusual practice (for poetry) is what makes semiotic analysis valuable. The possible dependence of all signs on some sort of linguistic foundation need not occupy us here except to say that all artifacts produced by culture signify; as Barthes states, "as soon as there is a society, all usage is converted into a sign of itself."[18] I certainly will not argue that all signs in *The Cantos* are not in some sense language, but, on the other hand, certain very important signs used there (the ideograms come immediately to mind) do not operate through the same process of linguistic signification as do English, French, or Latin words and phrases.

In fact, when I come to analyze the nonlinguistic signifier I may say that certain of these signs are, unlike words, motivated (see Glossary). The Pound-Fenollosa theory of the ideogram is an exellent example of one manifestation of motivated signification. I should like to remark at this point, by the way, that, as with Pound's "theory" of translation, the purely linguistic accuracy of the theory of the ideogram is unimportant in understanding his poetry. Fenollosa's well-known explanation (by way of Pound) of the ideogram for "East" ("the sun entangled in the branches of a tree") implies that this Chinese sign is exactly motivated. Again, the fact that Chinese characters are in reality often phonetic, and therefore unmotivated, is inconsequential insofar as *The Cantos* are concerned; in the poem, ideograms are to be read as motivated in precisely this "Imagist" manner. Used in this fashion, the ideogram is an iconic sign: that is, a sign in which the signifier in some sense resembles its signified. Other icons in *The Cantos* include Egyptian hieroglyphs and the "Off Limits" poster of Canto 22. One further type of sign is the index, which signifies through a process wherein the signifier is in some sense causally provoked by its signified. If, with Barthes, we are willing to view the index as a "trace," we might consider Canto 75 (the "music" canto) as a whole a form of indicial sign. I shall return to the classification of signs in *The Cantos* below.

The expressions which I have up till now discussed can be seen as "working" terms, concepts which will have general applicability throughout the following discussion. I should like to finish my discussion of terminology, however, with mention of a group of terms which will have specific application in the chapters which immediately follow. These are expressions designating, I shall argue, the major stylistic devices of *The Cantos:* fragmentation and deletion, condensation, and coupling. One other trait, "free rhythms," is well enough known under the expression "free verse" that I shall defer discussion of it until a later chapter. All five of these terms have already seen some service at the hands of the critics who have conceived them: William E. Baker in *Syntax in English Poetry,* S. R. Levin in *Linguistic Structures in Poetry,* and David Lodge in *The Modes of Modern Writing.*[19] I shall, of course, deal with each of these works as the concepts to which they give rise present themselves in the following discussion.

An Illustration

In the interests of suggesting the general strategy which my study will adopt, however, I shall here offer a brief demonstration of the term's applicability by way of analyzing the concluding lines of Canto 1:[20]

1	And I stepped back,
2	And he strong with the blood said then: "Odysseus
3	"Shalt return through spiteful Neptune, over dark seas,
4	"Lose all companions." And then Anticlea came.
5	Lie quiet Divus. I mean, that is Andreas Divus,
6	In officina Wecheli, 1538, out of Homer.
7	And he sailed, by Sirens and thence outward and away
8	And unto Circe.
9	Venerandam.
10	In the Cretan's phrase, with the golden crown,
	Aphrodite,
11	Cypri munimenta sortita est, mirthful, orichalchi,
	with golden
12	Girdles and breast bands, thou with dark eyelids
13	Bearing the golden bough of Argicida. So that:[21]

I should first like to consider the English-language sentence structure here, ignoring, at present, the role Latin syntax plays. Although it is perhaps not immediately apparent, the syntactic structures of the first eight lines are all identifiable sentences. Lines 9 through 13, on the other hand, contain a variety of structures, none of which is a complete English sentence. We might "parse" this latter group of lines as: 1) a modifier ("Venerandam") followed by 2) an explanatory prepositional phrase ("in the . . ") 3) after which another prepositional phrase characterizes 4) the proper noun "Aphrodite"; line 11 continues the characterization of the goddess with 5) a truncated relative clause in Latin (the only nearly complete clausal structure

in this passage), 6) two adjectives, and 7) an adjectival prepositional
phrase. After the caesura of line 12, there occurs 8) an apostrophe begun
with the "thou" which refers to Aphrodite and concluded with another
prepositional adjective phrase linked in line 13 with a participial phrase.
The entire passage ends with 9) a subordinating conjunction. The oddness
of the passage is made apparent when I diagram it (arrows represent
modification, brackets indicate syntagmatically linked structures performing the same purpose, and the $\emptyset$ points to a missing structure):

$$\text{a) } 1\text{- } 2 \rightarrow 4$$
$$\text{b) } 3 \rightarrow 4 \leftarrow [5,6,7]$$
$$\text{c) } 8 \rightarrow 4 \leftarrow [\text{"thou"}]$$
$$\text{d) } 9 \rightarrow \emptyset$$

I have rather arbitrarily segmented the syntagm of this passage into four
units; my organization of these relationships, however, is unimportant
since it is clearly evident that, no matter what system I use to schematize
them, the basic relationship is the same: modification of a central proper
noun. Aphrodite serves as "pivot" to a syntactic bundle of prepositions,
adjectives, and relative clauses. The identifying "aside" which follows
"Venerandam" and the concluding conjunction form a residue which I shall
discuss in a moment.
     In most traditional written (not spoken) discourse, the sentence, ob-
viously, is the basic unit of communication, and when, as here, the reader
is confronted with a written chain which is clearly not a sentence, she will
immediately assume that something has been deleted. This passage, of
course, lacks an "apparent" or "surface" verb phrase (hereafter, "VP"); there
is a subject noun phrase ("NP"), "Aphrodite," and a number of syntactically
unnecessary modifiers which qualify the NP. In other words, the VP has
undergone the stylistic device which I referred to above as "deletion." I
should like to note in passing that feature "9" ("So that:") also has quite
clearly undergone deletion: in this case, of both NP and VP. Individual
deletions produce the more general trait of "fragmentation." Deletion and
fragmentation are, in a sense (in *what* sense, I shall make clear in Chapter
3), figures of absence; condensation, which also appears in this passage,
may be said to be a figure of presence (condensation occurring when a
syntactic structure is made to serve formally the purposes of what would
normally be two structures).
     The "artificial" order of "with the golden crown, Aphrodite" may be
explained in two ways: either the prepositional phrase ("P-phrase")/NP
structure is a concession to the Homeric hymn which forms the intertext of
these lines, or the P-phrase is associated with the "Venerandam" which
precedes it. Neither of the explanations, however, need be exclusionary;
the action of condensation allows both possibilities. In fact, another aspect

of the dual articulation of condensation is evident in "Venerandam" itself, since the word's etymology suggests not only a literal meaning ("worthy of veneration"), but also an earlier evocation of the goddess herself (Venereus/Aphrodite). And, on yet another level, this initial "transformation" of Aphrodite on the verbal level forms a model for the various guises the goddess adopts throughout *The Cantos*. Finally, the contrast between the Latin "Venus" buried in "Venerandam" and the Greek "Aphrodite" of the following line echoes the Latin translation of the *Odyssey* referred to in the preceding verse paragraph. Condensation, in one form or another, is arguably one of the major devices of both Modernist poetry and prose; irony, the use of multiple points of view, and, on the semantic level, valuational ambivalence all employ one signifier as a relatum of two signifieds.

In the first verse paragraph, Pound translates Divus's version of the *nekuia* by way of the "Seafarer" poet. The use of languages here foreshadows the employment of the "ply over ply" motif in succeeding cantos, and seems to reinforce the "ply over ply" juxtaposition of the verse paragraphs at hand. The "I" of line 1 refers to Odysseus, and then, four lines on (line 5), to Pound himself. Again, the discourse confronts the reader with condensation: here, of personae. The point of view in this handful of lines is kaleidoscopic, although, as we shall see, the multiplicity here is fairly limited compared to that which manifests itself in some of the cantos which follow. To recapitulate, there are a number of speakers here: Homer, Divus, the Anglo-Saxon poet, Odysseus, Tiresias, and a fussy, mock-scholarly commentator who is only one of the several specifically Poundian personae. This last speaker, by the way, reappears five lines down citing the origin of "Venerandam": "In the Cretan's phrase." Further, a new persona, whom one might call the "real" Pound, surfaces in the canto's final, fragmented "So that:"; this reading depends on one's agreement with the generally shared assumption that the first speaker in Canto 2 is Pound. Finally, I should like to draw attention to the "Lie quiet Divus" of line 5 before I leave the question of personae. Here Pound (perhaps in the mask of the scholiast, perhaps not) reiterates in literary terms the mimesis described by Homer, which is translated by Divus himself. In other words, as Odysseus symbolically and literally lays the dead to rest, so Pound lays *his* precursor to rest.

Except for the slight deletion which lends the verse paragraph its "Anglo-Saxon" tone in line 4 (" 'Lose all companions' "), syntax is regular here, and fragmentation is absent. Condensation occurs in line 7 with "he sailed"; the referent of "he" is apparently Odysseus, but, since lines 5 and 6 in their role of commentary interpose between the last mention of the Greek hero, the reference is made to a degree unclear. The uncertain status of the pronoun sanctions other readings, but what these may be is, at this stage, not signalled.

In summary, then, the devices discussed above appear as follows: *fragmentation* in verse paragraph one, line 6 ("out of Homer"), and in verse paragraph two throughout, especially in line 13; *deletion* of VP or NP associated with the P-phrase of line 6, verse paragraph one, and in verse paragraph two, absence of VP; *condensation* in the "he sailed" of line 7, the "Venerandam" of line 9 ("semantic" condensation), and the "with the golden crown" of line 10. In addition to these devices, the passage also contains multiple shifts in point of view. Each of these factors is foregrounded to the extent that each departs from normal usage. On the other hand, since some of the devices are not unusual in poetic usage (especially the fragmentation and condensation of verse paragraph one), foregrounding in the sense I discussed above is evident only in verse paragraph two. Actually, the devices of verse paragraph one all arise from the fact that this passage is largely a translation from Divus "out of Homer" in pseudo-Anglo-Saxon style. Hence, if any element is truly foregrounded here, it is the use of translated material itself. And, indeed, Pound's liberal use of intertexts is one of the most clearly marked traits of *The Cantos*. Furthermore, this trait seems to be closely connected with rapid shifts in point of view.

Verse paragraph two is also to a degree translated, however, and since it employs all three traits in an unambiguous manner, it will be viewed by most readers as the more typically "Poundian" of the two passages. Moreover, the entirety of the first canto, with the exception of the last verse paragraph, is devoted to the *Odyssey* intertext; consequently, this final verse paragraph is semantically, as well as stylistically, anomalous. In other words, the syntagm of the canto as a whole has been disrupted by the conversion of the final strophe. The reader may seek a semantic connection between this unit and what precedes it on the level of deep structure, but the discovery of such a connection would be at best dubious. Rhetorically, too, this concluding verse paragraph is aberrant; most of the canto, with the exception of the abovementioned comments on Divus, is devoted to a discourse involving the travels of Odysseus. When I take into consideration the many deletions and the compounding attributes of the final lines, however, this section seems to fulfill the role of a rhetorical apostrophe. The troublesome "So that" of the concluding line exacerbates the problem since it does not seem to belong to the apostrophe or to the discourse which precedes the apostrophe; hence, the syntagm is disrupted a second time.

I have not here attempted an analysis of the canto as a whole, but the interested reader will note that such an analysis would not resolve the dilemma. The Odyssean intertext might supply clues to one or two problems which arise before the final verse paragraph, but that intertext clearly does not provide models for the verse paragraph in question. In the next chapter, I shall advance the argument that the juxtaposition of semantically and stylistically anomalous units is a central characteristic of Pound's style from his Imagist period on.

The underlying matrix of Canto 1 comprises hypograms having to do with Odysseus-as-wanderer, poet-as-wanderer, and poet-as-worshipper. In fact, if we are willing with Riffaterre to accept matrices as shared cultural and literary conventions, then the last of these hypograms, poet-as-worshipper, will go a long way toward explaining the concluding apostrophe; the poet, in time-honored fashion, is simply invoking the goddess at the commencement of his epic. The Odyssean *nekuia* which precedes the apostrophe may then be seen as a sort of preface to the "voyaging outward" which begins properly in Canto 2. On the rhetorical level, the articulation of discourse/lyrical apostrophe forms the model for succeeding paradigms, and, on the level of the "microcontext" (see Glossary for macro- and microcontext) of the canto itself, the three traits I have been discussing will provide the model for their own continual recurrence which generates Pound's style.

Obviously, I have not resolved the question of the relation of the bulk of Canto 1 to its final five lines. Such resolution is in fact impossible within the context of Canto 1 alone; since this canto presents paradigms as models which generate the text which follows, no one element is explicable outside the larger context of the generated text. Just as the elements of a complex sentence such as "shifters" (pronouns like "he," for example), subordinating conjunctions (like "So that"), and even common nouns and verbs are not definable without recourse to paradigms (antecedents for shifters, the clauses bracketing a subordinating conjunction), so elements of a "complex" poetic syntagm cannot be explained until sufficient elements have been generated to enable the reader to generate stylistic and semantic paradigms for the poem as a whole. Consequently, the apostrophe to Aphrodite of Canto 1, and, for that matter, the canto's "second-order" translation of Homer, are akin to a sentence only partly read; certainly, some sense may be drawn from it, but complete coherence awaits a total reading. The chapters which follow constitute a prolegomenon to such a reading.

2

METONYMY, IMAGISM, AND THE FOUNDATIONS OF POUND'S STYLE

I SHOULD IMAGINE that there are very few readers of contemporary criticism who are unfamiliar with the term "metonymy." Those readers of the not-so-old school who, with James Thurber, recall their high school English teacher's love of figures of speech will remember that Miss Groby (Thurber's name for the archetypal high school literature teacher) set her students "night after night, for homework, to searching in *Ivanhoe* and *Julius Caesar* for metaphors, similes, metonymies, apostrophes, person-ifications, and all the rest." Eventually, Thurber says, "it got so metonymies jumped out of the pages at you, obscuring the sense and pattern of the novel or play you were trying to read."[1] It is probably with a sense of déjà vu that a number of middle-aged literary critics repeat this ordeal. These persons will, with Thurber, remember that Miss Groby defined a metonymy as the use of the Container for the Thing Contained (the capitals are Thurber's). Consequently, confusion arises because "metonymy" in recent criticism appears to be a kind of rhetorical philosopher's stone, far more complicated that Miss Groby's humble Container for the Thing Con-tained. In fact, contemporary rhetoric seems to be experiencing something new under the sun: fervent partisanship over a figure of speech.

Such partisanship is not surprising since it was Roman Jakobson himself who "re-discovered" metonymy. When Jakobson, in a now-famous essay discussing the linguistic impediment of aphasia, suggests that not only aphasics tend to view the linguistic world either metaphorically or metonymically, but that writers, too, tend to do so, a critical Pandora's box was broached.[2] Briefly stated, Jakobson's conception of metonymy involves a predisposition by speakers (or writers) toward the "axis of the combina-tion." The aphasic with a "selection disorder," in other words, cannot think of single-word synonyms, or more loosely "metaphors," for a word and thus he employs words which are semantically associated with a term to define that term: instead of defining a "hut" as a "cabin" or "hovel" (and therefore *substituting* synonymically equivalent terms), the aphasic defines "hut" as "poverty" or "thatched roof." Widening his range of application,

Jakobson hypothesizes that certain writers tend to favor metonymy (which is combinatory and associative) over metaphor (which is selective and substitutable). The realist novelist, for example, "metonymically digresses from the plot to the atmosphere and from the characters to the setting in time and space"; Jakobson cites *Anna Karenina* as a prime example of a metonymic novel.[3]

Jakobson's original concept has been considerably refined during the last decade, and the recent career of the term is itself an intriguing chapter in the history of ideas. Nonetheless, the definition of metonymy has achieved some precision, initially at the hands of the rhetoricians belonging to Group μ, and more recently in the refinements of Peter Schofer and Donald Rice.[4] Schofer and Rice have clarified Group μ's rather idiosyncratic view of metonymy (the underpinnings of which are too complicated to be gone into here), and have arrived at the definition which I shall employ henceforth:

> Metonymy is a trope characterized by a semantic and referential relationship of causality made possible by the presence of the category of semantic feature *cause*.[5]

For Schofer and Rice, the microcontext of a passage is established within the syntagm occupied by a trope, and the macrocontext (see Glossary) comprises that portion of the syntagm necessary to infer the sign *in absentia*. The authors then list a number of subcategories of metonymy, all of which are in some way based on spatial or temporal causality: cause for effect, effect for cause, agent for instrument, and so forth. Schofer and Rice avoid *pure* contiguity as a basis for metonymy for reasons stated below.

When the mythical Miss Groby instructs her class, then, to take out their Shakespeares, she is using the metonymy "author for his work" or "producer for product." Such metonymy is based on causal contiguity. When she refers to the "Crown" of England, meaning Henry IV, she employs a spatial metonymy (since crowns are associated with kings). The reader may object that this last illustration is in fact a synecdoche, but Schofer and Rice contend that "the trope *crown* for *king* can be read either as a metonymy or a synecdoche, depending on whether the crown is simply associated with the king . . . or whether it is considered an integral part of the concept of monarch" (Schofer and Rice, 1977: 128). Actually, overlapping between tropes, these authors judiciously point out, is inevitable, and they argue that "awareness of the problem and of the fact that tropes can be analyzed in two different manners is solution enough." Further, Michel Le Guern, to whose insights on metonymy and metaphor I shall return, says on this score "Il ne faudrait pas . . . accorder trop d'importance à cette différence entre métonymie et synecdoque: il s'agit d'une différence de degré plus que d'une différence de nature."[6]

The relationship between metonymy as a way of articulating a literary text and the Imagist movement of poetry is based on the extension of the concept of metonymy past the limits of the one-word trope. It is not the object of this study to prove that literature as a whole may be divided along the axes of metaphor and metonymy; nevertheless, a metonymic organization relying on causal and spatial contiguity does seem to animate Pound's Imagist poetry. Moreover, as I shall argue throughout this chapter, Imagism provides a crucial part of the stylistic model for *A Draft of XXX Cantos*. In this regard, Joseph Riddel contends that Imagism uncovers "the possibility of the long poem" in the modern tradition.[7] Such a possibility occurs because of the "freedom from the commanding origin" which a play of "originating forces," brought about through Imagism and Vorticism, offers:

> The praxis of the moving Image puts in question the idea of the unified or autotelic text, or the thought of poetic closure. It also resists the possibility of a text commanded by any one of its elements: a controlling theme, a privileged point of view, authorial intentionality, image cluster, or central symbol.[8]

What Riddel says of the nature of the Image could easily be applied to a good deal of Modernist poetry: "It displaces time linearity (and succession) into a figural space ('a moment of time'), producing a formal mirage (a *sens*). The unconscious has no time, nor any object. It is displaced as time, as consciousness, and thus as a movement of images" (Riddel, 1979: 341). Riddel's "linearity" is merely that narrative movement which I noted in Chapter 1 as a signal of the pre-Modernist text, and which is "displaced" by the metonymic organization of *The Cantos*. In fact, *The Cantos* are that "figural space" which produces the "formal mirage" which comprises the cantos themselves.

Riddel continues:

> The Image is curative, then, only in the sense of interpreting, of bringing to consciousness (as form, visibility). The force of writing disseminates by radical displacement, by condensation, staging, transcribing. Thus [the first and second tenets of Imagism] suspend the notions of both immediacy and mediation, and suggest a poetics that precedes the thinking of the play of presence and absence. Pound's Image recapitulates, by reproducing the primordial event of a writing without origin, a writing at the origin. (Riddel, 1979: 342)

The tenets of Imagism to which Riddel refers are well-known:

1. Direct treatment of the "thing," whether subjective or objective.
2. To use absolutely no word that did not contribute to the presentation.

3. As regarding rhythm: to compose in the sequence of the musical phrase, not in the sequence of the metronome.[9]

In augmenting these principles, Pound defined the Image itself: "An 'Image' is that which presents an intellectual and emotional complex in an instant of time." For the critic concerned with the formal structure of Modernist literary texts, the essentially linguistic framework of the Imagist project and its implied metonymic foundation are intriguing. Each of the "points" is susceptible of "translation" into linguistic features articulated along an axis of combination. Further, the manifestation of such articulation is empirically verifiable in the structural analysis of individual Imagist poems which act as stylistic predecessors of the first thirty cantos. Before I embark on such verification it is worth noting in passing that, as Riddel points out, "Pound's theory of the Image is not simply a postulate of form or style, but a theory of generative and dislocating force—in a sense, a theory of translation" (Riddel, 1979: 340). I differ with this observation only in that this very "generative and dislocating force" is itself productive of stylistic traits (as I shall argue in detail in subsequent chapters).

But to return to the linguistic elements of Imagist doctrine: the central issue here is one of referentiality. The Imagist poem seeks to superimpose two or more signifiers, with their accompanying signifieds, in order to create a unitary sign having an overall signified, the Image. At first glance, this process seems merely to be a description of the construction of an extended metaphor, but it is in the "direct treatment" of the "thing" signified that the true nature of the process is made clear. The contrast between a poetic system which is animated by metaphor and one which is animated by metonymy is conveniently illustrated by the contrary projects of Symbolism and Imagism. Although Symbolism may have had a passing influence on the early stages of Imagism, Pound was at pains to distinguish Imagism from the earlier movement. As Stanley Coffman notes, Pound "was uninterested in the philosophy of Symbolism"; this lack of interest arose in part from the purposeful inexactitude of the Symbolists' use of metaphor which, in turn, is related to Pound's more general antagonism toward "ornamental" figures.[10] In fact, Imagism is distinguished from Symbolism partially by the former's predominant use of metonymy which results in the "condensation" which plays so large a part in later definitions of Imagism. David Lodge says of metonymy and synecdoche that they are "*condensations* of contexture," and that these are produced by "a transformation of a notional sentence . . . by means of deletion" of portions of the syntagm.[11]

Finally, the referential differentiation between metaphor and metonymy is outlined by Michel Le Guern:

La relation métonymique est donc une relation entre objets, c'est-à-dire entre réalités extralinguistiques; elle est fondée sur un rapport qui existe dans la référence, dans le monde extérieur, indepéndamment des structures linguistiques qui peuvent servir à l'exprimer.[12]

Metaphor, on the other hand, operates so that "la relation entre le terme métaphorique et l'objet qu'il désigne habituellement est détruite" (Le Guern, 1973: 15). Le Guern illustrates the metaphorical "destruction" of reference with the following quote from Pascal: "Le noeud de notre condition prend ses replis ses tours dan cet abîme." Le Guern comments that the entire figure designating the convolutions of a knot in no way designates a real "knot" in "notre condition." The true signified of Pascal's remark is that "la complexité de notre condition a ses éléments constitutifs dans ce mystère." Metonymy, conversely, *does* refer to "real" elements in its designations. Thus, the use of "le *vase,* la *coupe,* le *calice,* pour la liqueur contenue dans le vase, dans la coupe, dans le calice" in no way "destroys" the strict referential meaning of *vase, coupe,* or *calice.*

That privileged text of Imagism, "In A Station of the Metro," illustrates the linguistic character and the metonymic articulation of Imagist verse:

> The apparition of these faces in the crowd:
> Petals on a wet, black bough.[13]

Pound's account of his condensation of the original thirty-line poem, of which this two-line haiku is the result, is well-known. His process of deletion is mirrored by the reader's reconstruction of the terms of the metonymy upon which the poem hinges. On one level "Metro" seems to operate through a substitution relation; the "apparition of these faces" is *like* "petals." But even on this level, deletion is apparent in the absence of the marker of the simile "like." Are we meant to "recover" this deletion of similitude, a substitution relation, or, rather, are we meant to perceive the two lines in a spatial juxtaposition? The syntactically parallel construction of the two lines (NP, P-phrase/NP, P-phrase) emphasizes the integrity, and not the transposition of each. Pound does not merely intend us to conceive that "faces" *are like* "petals," but that, through contiguity of "a thing outward and objective" and a "thing inward and subjective," the two elements are spatially juxtaposed. That which is therefore recovered by the reader is the "intellectual and emotional complex in an instant of time." Schneidau raises much the same point in asking whether it is "not more illuminating to say that the second line . . . acts as some sort predication about the first line . . . than as a mere analogy of it."[14]

Imagist poetry handles physical movement in a fashion which is ingenious; since "presentation" is spatial, that is it juxtaposes images caught in an instant of time, the presentational structure must either avoid the representation of movement, or cause action to be seen as "sculpted." In "Metro," for example, stasis is achieved simply through the absence of verbs. In "Gentildonna," published in November 1913, eight months after "Metro," it is as if movement has been incorporated in a pastoral frieze or in the Modernist ballet movements of Nijinsky's *Petrouchka*. The relatively complex embedding of "Gentildonna" (which itself will be discussed in the next section) retards the motion which the poem ostensibly presents:

> She passed and left no quiver in the veins, who
> > now
> Moving among the trees, and clinging
> > in the air she severed,
> Fanning the grass she walked on then, endures:
>
> Grey olive leaves beneath a rain-cold sky.[15]

Of course, the emphasis lent to "now" in the second line reinforces this sense of retardation (as does the tension established between the participials "Moving" and "clinging" in line three). The poem suggests a remembered perception, a fixed memory, which has been recovered and made stationary; the woman, after all, only "endures" in the present; it was only in the past, which is necessarily removed from activity, that she "passed." It is, in fact, the present vision of the "olive leaves" which seems the more kinetic of the poem's two images, although it, too, is a "sculpted" view.

The heuristic problem presented to the reader here, of course, is to reestablish the link between the memory of the woman and the objective sight of the olive leaves. Readers would tend, in the Romantic or Symbolist poem for example, to seek a clue to the thematic deletion in metaphor: they might, for instance, try to determine what portions of the matrix within the hypograms (see Glossary) of "grey" leaves and "rain-cold" sky lie within the portion of the matrix involving a woman who "left no quiver in the veins." The result might well be the determination of a rather standard overall matrix: "the woman I once loved has left me, and nature mirrors my distress." Certainly, the Pound of *A Lume Spento* had been quite capable of developing such a theme, but such is not the case in "Gentildonna." Imagism, through its accentuation of the precise word, the well-constructed signifier, encouraged its practitioners not to concern themselves overly with distinct thematic signifieds. Part of this impulse away from referential content no doubt arose through Imagism's desire to separate itself from (if not to react to) the excess of Symbolist "associations," the result of which was, according to Pound, that the symbol "was degraded to the status of a word."[16] Curiously, then, it is Symbolist verse which is "readerly" and Imagist verse which is "writerly" (see Glossary). It is not unlikely that the exhaustion of Imagism within a fairly short time is in part owing to this unconcern with "meaning" in the traditional, propositional sense. On the other hand, the use of spatial juxtaposition as itself productive of meaning (as opposed to the use of metaphor to "suggest" meaning) would be salvaged, and later turned to use in *The Cantos*.

"Gentildonna," then, records an experience, the perception of a memory coupled with a vision of the natural world, but makes no attempt to comment upon that experience. Of course, the very adoption of personae insures this lack of authorial comment, and, too, Pound had by this time begun to embody in his poetry the lessons he had learned from modern prose. To this experience I shall turn next.

Logopoeia

The second of the three points is the most accessible to traditional linguistic examination; the stricture "to use absolutely no word that did not contribute to the presentation" is clearly traceable to the Flaubertian doctrine of the *mot juste*. Indeed, Imagist poetry is syntactically one of the most prose-like of verse styles. Browning, Gautier, and Laforgue had reinforced in Pound the certainty that verse could be "good writing" free of "the opalescent word, the rhetorical tradition."[17]

In the two poems discussed above, the lexical component of each is largely free of ornate, evaluative modification and noncolloquial words. The adjectives in each, however, seem to perform a purely descriptive role; "grey" and "rain-cold" in "Gentildonna" and "wet" and "black" in "Metro" do not seem to serve the quasi-metaphoric purpose of, for instance, "petals" in "Metro." The "faces" (or more exactly their "apparition") may arguably be metaphorically substituted for "petals"; and, in turn, the "petals" share the hypogram of "wet/black" in the context of "bough." But is "on a wet, black bough" merely a species of prepositional modification of "petals" or does the image serve some additional structural purpose within the poem? Surely, Pound, following tenet two, would not add such a figure merely for "atmosphere." In fact, the reader must recover a great deal of the referential context which underlies line one in order to establish the importance of the final P-phrase. It is interesting to note that "nonprofessional" readers (in this case undergraduates), in discussing this poem, commonly resolve the dilemma presented by the image through a metaphorical reading: the "wet, black bough" symbolizes, more or less, a line of rain-drenched subway passengers standing on a gloomy platform. On analysis, such a resolution is really quite remarkable; it calls upon a curious shared cultural experience that somehow juxtaposes subway-riding with being rained on. Actually, this ingenious interpretation of the matrix *is* the only metaphoric explanation for the image in question. The Gordian knot is sliced, however, when one realizes that the concluding phrase is not metaphoric at all.

In two printings of "Metro" the components of the poem are carefully spaced:[18]

> The apparition (hiatus) of these faces ( ) in the crowd ( ):
> Petals ( ) on a wet, black ( ) bough ( ).

The linkages between the components are, in line one, syntagmatically related in the poet's mind, and, in line two, related contiguously in space. The pivots around which the poem turns, in the absence of verbal structures, are "The apparition" and "Petals." In "Metro" the P-phrases (two of which locate objects in space) are dissociated, here literally by the device of spacing, from the pivots. Hence, "on a wet, black," for example, preserves its independence as "presentation." Like "real" petals on a "real" bough, the poetic "petals" and "bough" exist contiguously, not sequentially. The point is made even clearer by the separation of "on a wet, black" from "bough," further establishing the spatial juxtaposition of the real objects. "Wetness" and "blackness," then, become here not merely the accidents of substance, but substance itself.

The relative clause and modifying participial phrases of "Gentildonna" present a more difficult problem. Additionally, the right-branching structure (see Glossary) of the first five lines, which employs the relative pronoun "who" as the subject of the concluding "endures," further complicates the structure. Finally, the sequence of tenses adds yet another layer of linguistic ordering (shifting from present to past to present to past to present). The recovery of the deleted verb in the last line, like the recovery of verb structures in "Metro," would be questionable at best; either the "leaves" "exist" or they "endure" (although many of the preceding verbs would offer just as propositional a predication). Indeed, the absence of verbs in a poem filled with verbal structures foregrounds deletion, and plausibly forces the reader to recover all the verbs contiguously as predications about the "leaves." Of course, such predication is central to the poem if the image in the concluding line is in a substitution relation to the preceding lines. This is to ask, are the "olive leaves" a metaphor for the "gentildonna"? The answer to this question lies, again, as it did in "Metro," in the matrix, here, the hypogram of the "leaves beneath a rain-cold sky." Some of the predications attributed to the woman are indeed at least plausible predications about the "olive leaves"; the leaves "mov(e) among the trees," certainly, and may be said to "cling . . . in the air," and, moreover, olive trees (if not their leaves) are well-known for their "endurance." Consequently, the leaves are, like a graceful woman, not an unremarkable figure. The leaves, however, are not juxtaposed to the woman, but to the "rain-cold sky," which latter phrase possesses no distinct referent in the model introduced by the preceding lines. And, again as in "Metro," the linkage of the images in the last line is established by a preposition indicating spatial relation.

A final problem is presented by the "quiver in the veins." We would normally attribute such a sensation to the human persona of the poem, although the leaves, too, possess "veins," and, additionally, might be more reasonably expected to "quiver." Reinforcing the linkage between "quiver/ veins/leaves" is the possible predication, noted above, of many of the poem's verbs in association with "olive leaves." But the reader needn't select attributions along a paradigm as he would in a poem relying on metaphor. Rather, Pound has skillfully arranged the predications arising from the poem's verbs in a relation of contiguity which bifurcates both toward the woman and the leaves; hence, an excellent example of condensation presents itself. As we have seen in "Metro," "Gentildonna"'s pivots, "she" and "olive leaves," are perhaps, taken alone, in a substitution relation, but the adumbration of Janus-faced verbs creates a tension between this metaphoric structure and the deleted, but highly complex, metonymy established by the interior four lines of the poem. This tension creates a spatial form which does not seek to compare, but to juxtapose.

The reader has, in a sense, Pound's own sanction for the above "anti-metaphorical" reading in favor of a metonymic interpretation arising out of spatial juxtaposition, in his "note" to "The Jewel Stairs' Grievance":

Jewel stairs, therefore a palace. Grievance, therefore there is something to complain of. Gauze stockings, therefore a court lady, not a servant who complains. Clear autumn, therefore he has no excuse on account of weather. Also she has come early, but has soaked her stockings.[19]

The poem, from *Cathay*, was viewed as a model for much of what he was attempting to do in his own Imagist verse. He has recovered for his English-speaking reader the deletions understood by the original Chinese reader: note that these are thoroughgoingly metonymic. The "stairs" are a synecdoche (part for the whole), as are the "gauze stockings." The lady's having "come early" is a direct metonymy (effect for cause). K. K. Ruthven says of Pound's attitude toward this poem that the poet could readily appreciate its virtues for it "appeared to confirm the validity of imagist aesthetics." Ruthven goes on to quote Pound himself: in the poem "every-thing is there, not merely by 'suggestion' but by a sort of mathematical process of reduction" (Ruthven, 1969: 156).

The critical history of "Papyrus" is in some ways as interesting as the poem itself (indeed, the very terming of this "fragment" as "poem" is likely still to raise critical hackles). The two main reservations about the little work are that it is a "satire on H.D.," or that it is yet another example of Pound's playing fast and loose with the translation of ancient texts. This is not the place to rehearse such disputes. But whether "Papyrus" be comic, and its inclusion among numerous wry *vers de société* might support this characterization, or whether it be unwarranted as strict translation is irrelevant to the poem-as-artifact. And Pound does present "Papyrus" as artifact; the tiny fragment represents for him a touchstone of lyrical condensation alloyed with an attrition which at once signifies great age and the efficacy of time in purifying form.

It is a commonplace that the translator's act is a complex one. Invention and disposition, in the senses of traditional rhetoric, have already been accomplished by the original poet before the translator sets to his task, but it is wrong to say that translation chiefly involves a species of stylistic resuscitation. In fact, some quite successful translations, among them some of Pound's, employ at least a redeployment of disposition. Moreover, it is doubtful whether invention can in any realistic sense be said to be solely the independent creation of topoi (if so, all poets are translators). The ancients, as a matter of fact, never conceived invention as originality arising from genius, but as the intelligent selection and gifted use of subjects at hand (see Aristotle, *Rhetoric*, 2, 23). And such a conception, of course, fits Pound's notion of translation nicely. Moreover, this view coincides with the poststructuralist view (notably, in Riffaterre) that all texts are composed on the basis of intertextuality, an earlier text providing hypograms for a later one. Thus, "Papyrus" may be seen as either the result of the topos (the hypogram) presented by Sappho's verses, or, on the other hand, as the Sapphic verses themselves, but modified, "translated," by time and tradition.

Deletion is the salient device of the poem. The fact that such deletion, and its result, fragmentation, is heavily foregrounded disconcerts many readers:

> Spring . . .
> Too long . . .
> Gongula . . .[20]

The two most obvious readings of the poem accrete along the metaphoric and metonymic axes. Metaphorically, the "lines" of "Papyrus" depend upon the reader's ready substitution of a vast number of signifieds for each of the highly charged individual signifiers: it goes without saying that the matrix of "Spring" within universal poetic tradition is vast. Three or four of the more important hypograms, however, are easily delimited. On the most basic level, "spring" signifies "annual time," and, on a more specific level, time of "renewal." A more complex level lends the hypogram, "renewal through love." As the reader moves to the next phrase, "Too long," he or she selects from the broader field one or more of the above regions; hence, since all the hypograms have the seme (see Glossary) "time period," he will associate that seme with the same seme in "Too long," and proceed to move on to one of the more specific hypogams, namely, "time appropriate for love," and, since the adverb has the feature "excess," he will quite probably come up with the proposition "something is in excess of the time appropriate for love." Finally, of course, "Gongula" is substituted for "something." It is not surprising that the preceding explication seems a labored way·of getting at the very simple meaning of a very simple poem. In fact, if the metaphoric process describes the way in which the reader "deciphers" "Papyrus," why does Pound insert the ellipses after each line? Arguably, he wishes by this device to assert the fragmentary nature of the original. But the ellipses also are themselves signifiers whose signified is "attrition." Such attrition points both to the wearing away of cultural dross in the poem itself as well as to the attrition which might reasonably be experienced in the poet/lover's expectations. The "excess" signified by "Too long," then, and the "annual" (as well as annular) time of "spring" are brought together under the reigning sign of "attrition." The paradox afforded by the poem is that, although it is "about" the wearing away, the weariness, induced in the lover by longing, it is also susceptible of being reconstructed nearly three millenia later.

In fact, time (which is the subject of the poem) has a dual operation; on the one hand, it is destructive of individuality, and, on the other, it hones, and thereby creates, artistic perfection. That which remains in "Papyrus" is the succession of Images. Further, those Images have been purified by an excision which is, since it is not the work of one man but of history itself, perfect. Here, then, are two of what will later be Pound's main preoccupations in *The Cantos:* the salutary revivification of culture through the awareness of past perfection, and the ability of history itself to effect a tangible and impersonal molding of human consciousness.

Imagism in *The Cantos*

I noted above that the Imagist poem "presented a semantic domain achieved by the deletion of certain elements of the constituting signifieds and the elevation, through the interaction of signifiers, of a resulting signified, the 'complex,' " and that it is in the "direct treatment" of the thing signified that the nature of this process is made clear. I should like to argue that, on one level at least, the "thing" being directly treated in "Papyrus" is the poem, "Papyrus," itself; the poem's ellipses represent the deletion of certain "constituting signifieds," and the words which remain, the signifiers, through not merely their metaphoric interaction and substitution, but through their metonymic conjunction with the deletions, create the "complex." The very fact that this poem, unlike the others I have examined, is resistent to recovery of a syntactic underlying structure indicates a watershed between the Imagist practices of *Lustra* and the more complex processes of *A Draft of XXX Cantos.*

Kenner has in fact said of Canto 2 that

The style is Imagist. The brevity of Imagist notation seized phenomena just on the point of mutating . . . Misrepresented as a poetic of stasis, it had been poetic of darting change; for a whole page, in the Canto, perception succeeds perception like frames of film. . . .[21]

Canto 2 marks the continuation in *The Cantos* of Imagist practices first begun in *Lustra* and *Cathay*. Since Canto 1 is largely given over to discourse in its retelling of a portion of the *Odyssey*, the devices of Imagism are largely absent, and, in fact, *The Cantos* seem to alternate between the two poles of Imagist "lyricism" and discursive "historicism"; Cantos 1 and 2 are representative of such alternation. Pound has been careful, however, to provide a link between the two cantos in the purposive subordinating conjunction which ends Canto 1 (and which recurs in Canto 17). The reader will recall that in my explication of the concluding verse paragraphs of Canto 1 I suggested that the final "So that:" points forward not only to the repeated "So that" which begins Canto 17, but also to Canto 2, without, however, elaborating on the suggestion except to say that the conjunction evidenced extreme deletion and fragmentation. I should like now to examine this fragment more closely.

Most grammars assign the conjunction "so that" to the role of introductory link to an adverb clause of purpose which modifies, in turn, a verb in a main clause, but the final verse paragraph which precedes "So that:" is itself an example of deletion and fragmentation in that a VP is nowhere in evidence in those lines. Consequently, a further deletion has obviously taken place: the verb which normally would be modified by the conjunction has been removed. If we go forward to Canto 2, on the other hand, we may be able to recover the adverbial clause which "so that" introduces. I would argue that line 2, "there can be but one 'Sordello,' " is that clause, giving us the following structure: "∅ so that there can be but the one 'Sordello.' " The problem, then, is to recover the structure underlying ∅. There is a similar case of extreme deletion, as I pointed out above, in "Papyrus," and perhaps my analysis of that poem may suggest a solution to the present dilemma. There is a matrix for Canto 1, albeit a complex one involving the *Odyssey* and a Homeric hymn, and which is something like the Sapphic matrix of "Papyrus," but, as with "Papyrus," deletion in the final verse paragraph of Canto 1 may have little to do with the hypograms of the matrix "original." The major hypograms of Canto 1 involve two rhetorical types; the bulk of the canto, having to do with Odysseus's "voyaging out," acts as a discursive "preface," and the concluding verse paragraph acts as a traditional epic apostrophe to Aphrodite. In other words, I might say that one set of signifieds in Canto 1 is rhetorical, signifying a matricial sentence which might be made apparent as "structural commencement of an epic." I noted above that the adverbial clause which is begun by "So that:" modified a VP which I represented as the deleted "∅." In what sense, then, can the rhetorical signified, "structural commencement of an epic," be said to be a VP? Perhaps the rhetorical situation of the opening lines of Canto 2 may suggest a solution: "Hang it all, Robert Browning, / there can be but the one 'Sordello.' / But Sordello, and my Sordello?" Clearly, the persona here is the speaker whom I termed, in Chapter 1, the "real" Pound, Pound-as-epic-poet (as opposed to the "scholiastic" Pound, for example). The lines are spoken in the first person: we may conclude this from the "je/tu" situation (as Brooke-Rose calls it) here, and from the "my" of line 3. If, then, the latter part of the complex sentence, the adverbial clause, is in the first person, the former half very well may have the poet persona as subject; the rhetorical signified of Canto 1 seems to confirm this conclusion.

I have arrived at the final missing piece of the puzzle: what is predicated about the underlying "I" of Canto 1 which would give me my deleted VP? Actually, the entire canto acts as a predication about the poet-as-maker. Canto 1 is an "overture" (as Hugh Kenner calls it) to the initial sixteen cantos while Canto 2, on the other hand, constitutes the actual beginning of the theme: the poet amidst the artistic, cultural, economic, and political debacle of the twentieth century. In Chapter 1, I put forward a caveat about the use of musical analogies in discussing Modernist form, and in the use of the term "overture" to describe Canto 1 the critic is likely to mislead the reader in one important sense; Canto 1's overture has the curious property of being an intertextual summary, rather than an epitome of the motifs which follow. It is the *Iliad*, for example, rather than the *Odyssey* which we see introduced in the page which begins Canto 2. Canto 1, then, posits a donnée which is linked to what follows by the conjunctive "So that:" which, in turn, functions as a quasi-conditional linkage; Pound uses "so that" here in a colloquial mode often employed by storytelling speakers who wish to indicate that the whole of a preceding narrative, not simply an immediate element of that narrative, is the cause of what follows. Consequently (or so that), the relationship between Canto 1 and 2 is one of cause-and-effect. The "∅" then represents a matrix which might be very simply rendered as "the Odyssean poet voyages out on the project of his epic and invokes the aid of Aphrodite," while the opening lines of Canto 2 reflect the poet's initial frustration over the difficulty of that project.

What has the above discussion of the relation between the first two cantos to do with metonymy? First of all, I would like to reiterate Schneidau's remarks on the Modernist writer and aphasia. The reader will recall that Schneidau likens the Modernist's Flaubertian struggle to that of the aphasic suffering from a contiguity disorder; "it is he who would be unable to 'select' a subject." Secondly, I would like to point up the role of causation in metonymy. Most rhetoricians argue that cause-and-effect relations supply the largest group of metonymies;[22] such relations involve signifier-signified conjunctions wherein cause signifies effect, or effect signifies cause. Under the former signification, the much-quoted Fontanier groups the following typical relations: divine cause for effect ("Christ" for the Church, as in "brothers in Christ"); active, intelligent, or moral cause ("pen" for writer); physical or natural cause ("sun" for heat); abstract and metaphysical cause ("charity" for acts deriving from charity); objective or archetypal cause. In Canto 1, the reader is concerned with this last relation in combination with "intelligent" cause: Pound employs "Homeric" as a metonymy for "epic" for the purpose of enunciating the project which is *The Cantos*. Moreover, if "Homeric" is posited as a signifier for "epic," then, in the same sense, Canto 1 is so articulated that it becomes a metonymy for *The Cantos* as a whole.

The link between Cantos 1 and 2 is not an isolated instance; similar links occur in the first thirty cantos alone between Cantos 2 and 3, 4 and 5, 8 and 9, 18 and 19, and 20 and 21. Some of these connections perform a simple paratactic union (2 and 3, 8 and 9, through "and"); others create some form of parallelism (18 and 19, "Also sabotage . . . / Sabotage," and 20 and 21, "Peace! Borso . . . , Borso! Keep the peace, Borso!"); and still another has a vaguer, and more strictly figurative relationship (4 and 5, the "arena" may in some sense be equivalent to the open places of "Ecbatan"). I shall return to the question of paratactic and parallel linkages between cantos in Chapter 5.

I should like now, however, to turn to the obviously Imagistic style of Canto 2, and to trace out similar Imagist passages in many of the cantos among the first thirty which follow it. I shall pass over the first half of the canto which, in its retelling of Ovid's story of Acoetes and Bacchus, mirrors the Homeric intertext of Canto 1. Page 10 might well be Kenner's "whole page" wherein "perception succeeds perception" (although the canto's Imagist portion actually begins on page 9, line 20):

1	Black azure and hyaline,
2	glass wave over Tyro,
3	Close cover, unstillness,
4	bright welter of wave-cords,
5	Then quiet water,
6	quiet in the buff sands,
7	Sea-fowl stretching wing-joints,
8	splashing in rock-hollows and sand-hollows
9	In the wave-runs by the half-dune;
10	Glass-glint of wave in the tide-rips against sunlight,
11	pallor of Hesperus,
12	Grey peak of the wave,
13	wave, colour of grape's pulp.

14	Olive grey in the near,
15	far, smoke grey of the rock-slide,
16	Salmon-pink wings of the fish-hawk
17	cast grey shadows in water,
18	The tower like a one-eyed great goose
19	cranes up out of the olive-grove,
20	And we have heard the fauns chiding Proteus
21	in the smell of hay under the olive-trees,
22	And the frogs singing against the fauns
23	in the half-light.
24	And . . .

The reader will note the passage's most obvious features: the absence of finite verbs in the first fifteen lines; fourteen compound nouns (and two compound adjectives); a large number of descriptive adjectives (mostly having to do with color) in the first two verse paragraphs; four classical references; with the exception of "hyaline," a relatively simple lexicon; parataxis in the final verse paragraph. I have already noted Pound's use of nonfinite verbs in my discussion of the *Lustra* poems and the final verse paragraph of Canto 1; their function here is not substantially different from that noted above. Three of the features—compound nouns, proliferation of color adjectives, simple lexicon—are related. The classical references are in keeping with the motifs raised in the preceding bulk of the canto, and the concluding use of parataxis, as I have noted, will be examined in a following chapter.

What role, then, do the compound nouns, color adjectives, and simple lexicon play? The reader will note, to begin with, that the compounds fall into three classes (not including the compound adjectives). The largest class comprises, on the level of the deep structure, possessive/NP structures ("wave-cords" = "cords of the wave"); "wing-joints," "sea-fowl," "rock-hollows," "sand-hollows," and "olive-grove" all belong to this class. The second class comprises simple modifier/NP structures; "half-dune," "glass-glint," "fish-hawk," "olive-trees," and "half-light" belong to this class. Finally, the third class has for its deep structure an NP/VP relationship; "wave-runs," "rock-slide," and perhaps "tide-rips" are equivalent to "the wave runs," "the rock(s) slide," and "the tide rips" (this last assumes the derivation of "rips" from "ripples"). Each of these classes, in other words, involves a complex structure, which has undergone deletion, underlying a simple surface structure: "class-one" structures undergo deletion of the possessive "of" and reversal of position; class-two structures (with the exception of "fish-hawk" and "olive-trees" which do not necessarily need hyphenation) undergo deletion of an adjective marker ("glass-glint" = "glassy glint"); class-three structures simply suppress the VP function of the second unit in the compound. The Imagist practice of fragmentation is, again, clearly evident.

In advancing my argument that the lexicon is fairly straightforward here, I would simply cite the fact that, in examining a list of the words making up the passage, several groups of undergraduates found only "hyaline" and "welter" unfamiliar (they were, of course, utterly baffled by the classical references). In other words, "hyaline" and "welter" were, for them, foregrounded.

The reader is left, finally, with an abundance of color adjectives. I noted above that in "In A Station of the Metro" and "Gentildonna" color adjectives were included among the few instances of modification in those poems. In fact, a short survey of types of single-word modification in Pound's Imagist poetry seems to demonstrate that color adjectives play an important role in description. There appears to be a general semantic motivation in the use of color-words in Imagism generally; differentiation of objects by color seems to lend those objects greater specificity, although, on analysis, color adjectives are no more "objective" than other descriptive modifiers. The importance of color to the reader probably arises from the psychological fact that, since color is often the first attribute of an object which a viewer perceives, coloration seems subjectively to be the most basic quality of a substance. Additionally, the syntactic nature of color adjectives differs from that of other sorts of descriptive adjectives. Modifiers having to do with size, for example, like "tall," "small," or "long," naturally undergo inflection indicating degrees of comparison: "tall, taller, tallest," for instance. Certainly, we may inflect color adjectives, but most speakers feel the result is, if not unnatural, at least "specialized." In other words, in the sequence "red, redder, reddest," one is comparing the degrees of red against each other; in the sequence "tall, taller, tallest," however, one is not measuring one "tall" against another "tall" (as one *is* comparing one "red" against another "red"), but one "tall *object*" against another "tall *object*." I might accurately simplify my argument by saying merely that colors are psychologically more concrete than spatial qualities, and unlike spatial qualities, seem to have an existence independent of the substance they "modify." In a very real sense, we are dealing here with a class of adjectives which is "nounier" than other adjectives: so much *does* depend upon a *red* wheelbarrow.

Viewing this passage syntactically, the reader will note, as in the *Lustra* poems, the scarcity of verbs; "cast" in line 17, "cranes" in line 19, and "have heard" in line 21 are the only instances of finite structures. If I add the nonfinite participials, "stretching," "splashing," "chiding," and "singing" to the passage's three verbs, I have a total of seven deep structure VPs as opposed to forty-five substantives; this ratio far exceeds any conceivable spoken or poetic norm. The obvious result of the lack of verbalization will be the elevation of the NP as the major unit of discourse. Consequently, those structures which accrete about NPs, substantive modifiers, should tend to proliferate, and the passage actually contains thirteen adjectives and twenty-two P-phrases. I might also point out that most standard grammars would accord the participials, grouped above with the VPs, the status of substantive modifiers; since participials, however, are VPs on the deep structure, and since here they seem strongly to imply action, I have removed them from this class. Nonetheless, the use of participials does point to Pound's reluctance to "commit" himself to absolute verbalization. The reader will note, finally, the specific purpose of the twenty-two prepositions here (quantitatively, the second largest syntactic group); roughly two-thirds of these indicate place, while a third (like all of the class-one and some of the class-two compounds) indicate possession by the use of "of."

A high proportion of nouns, a near absence of verbs, adjectives largely indicating color, and a relatively large number of prepositions specifying placement: all these features point to the heavy nominalization this passage has undergone. In fact, on examination, I have noted nominalization of the same degree in most of Pound's Imagist verse. Conversely, of course, nominalization will necessarily imply deletion of VPs and consequent fragmentation. William E. Baker, on whose study of poetic syntax I shall rely in Chapters 3 and 4, says of such nominalization that

> the noun, among all the parts of speech, retains a distinctly sensuous—and especially visual—quality. And the noun, of course, is commonly the kernel of a fragment in twentieth-century poetry. The great number of noun fragments in imagist poetry, as the very name of the school suggests, is surely an attempt to capitalize on this sensuous quality.[23]

Although large stretches of *The Cantos,* especially those having to do with history and the delineation of culture, have the normal complement of VPs, I am concerned in this chapter, however, solely with the Imagist passages of *The Cantos,* and these are characterized by thoroughgoing nominalization (supported by lack of VPs, "place" prepositions, and simple adjectives), the result of which is fragmentation on the syntactic level and metonymy on the rhetorical and semantic levels.

Such metonymy is made evident in the passage from Canto 2 by two factors: physical contiguity between elements within the passage, and a syntagmatic, rather than paradigmatic (see Glossary), relation between this passage and the bulk of the canto which precedes it. The matrix which informs the passage is provided by the Ovidian tale of the rape of Tyro by Poseidon, having to do with transformations of the human into the marine, on page 6, line 23:

> And by the beach-run, Tyro,
>   Twisted arms of the sea-god,

> Lithe sinews of water, gripping her, cross-hold,
> And the blue-grey glass of the wave tents them,
> Glare azure of water, cold-welter, close cover.
> Quiet sun-tawny sand-stretch,
> The gulls broad out their wings,
>   nipping between the splay feathers;

The reader is confronted here, by the way, with a situation with which Riffaterre has not dealt; the *Semiotics of Poetry* chiefly deals with poems which would commonly be termed "lyric." Consequently, most matrices for these examples are intertextual. It may very well be, however, that in epics, dramas, and novels in general, and definitely in *The Cantos* in particular, the poet provides some of his own matrices, and here is such a case. Read apart from its matrix on page 6, the passage on page 10 seems indefinite at best, but, knowing that the above lines involving the rape of Tyro underlie page 10, the reader may make apparent the passage's signified.

The model which creates a transition between the matrix and the text on page 10 begins at line 20 on page 9: the model's hypograms involve the aftereffects of the matrix's transformation ("And of a year later . . . the coral face under wave-tinge"), and a further example of the transformation in "Ileuthyeria, fair Dafne of the sea-bords." The last two lines on page 9, "Lithe turning of water, / sinews of Poseidon," both contain a metonymy (water = sinews) and provoke the extended metonymy of page 10, since the passage begins with a description of the sea's surface, and moves through a syntagmatic progression of elements related to the sea. In Riffaterre's terms, such a progression is characterized as expansion. The syntagmatic elements of the text, then, are related contiguously through expansion transformations: the sea surface leads to waves which lead to the beach on which "sea-fowl" splash and stretch near hollows and dunes; a "half-dune" sits by a "wave-run" which recedes with the "tide-rip" out to waves, both near and far, over which a "fish-hawk" glides, casting his shadow back on the the sea surface. The "olive grey" of the hither sea is related, through the signifier, "olive," to the olive grove where Proteus (himself a god of the sea *and* seashore) is chid by fauns plausibly under the aegis of Bacchus.

Before I leave the question of Imagism in the first thirty cantos, I should like to examine two further examples of Imagist practice. Although the specific style traits I have been discussing recur within individual lines, in verse paragraphs, and in the bulk of individual cantos (like Canto 20) throughout the first thirty, the use of the traits manifests itself in much the same manner and for many of the same purposes as we have seen in the *Lustra* poems and in Cantos 1 and 2. In Cantos 4, 16, 17, 20, 23, and 29, however, Imagist passages are linked by recurrent hypograms; because it is one of several types of articulation lending unity to *The Cantos*, such linkage is noteworthy if we are to understand the complex formal interconnectedness of the total poem. Furthermore, in Cantos 14 and 15 (the Hell cantos), an entirely different semantic species of Imagism, one not usually associated with Imagist "lightness" and "grace," is spectacularly present.

I should like to augment Riffaterre's concept of the matrix with respect to the remarks I made above regarding a poet's use of early passages in an epic as the motivation or reference of later passages. The reader will recall that Riffaterre's matrix has two obvious features: it is intertextual, and it is underlying; clearly, Pound employs very many matrices of this type. But matrices of the type I outlined above, intratextual and surface matrices, are abundant as well. On page 14, Canto 4, there is an instance of such a matrix: the passage concerns the story of Actaeon and Diana:

> The valley is thick with leaves, with leaves, the trees,
> The sunlight glitters, glitters a-top,
> Like a fish-scale roof,
> > Like the church roof in Poictiers
> If it were gold.
> > Beneath it, beneath it
> Not a ray, not a slivver, not a spare disc of sunlight
> Flaking the black, soft water;
> Bathing the body of nymphs, of nymphs, and Diana,
> Nymphs, white-gathered about her, and the air, air,
> Shaking, air alight with the goddess,
> > fanning their hair in the dark,
> Lifting, lifting, and waffing:
> Ivory dipping in silver . . .
> Not a splotch, not a lost shatter of sunlight.

Then seventeen lines interpose having to do with Peire Vidal (who acts as a "subject rhyme" with Actaeon since the troubador suffered a similar fate), the savaging of Actaeon by his hounds, and Ovid's "muttering" about "Pergusa," the pool where Persephone was raped. Some of the models of the matrix passage then recur in lines having to do with light:

> Thus the light rains, thus pours, *e lo soleills plovil*
> The liquid and rushing crystal
> > beneath the knees of the gods.
> Ply over ply, thin glitter of water;
> Brook film bearing white petals.
>
> . . . .
> Forked branch-tips, flaming as if with lotus.
> > Ply over ply
> The shallow eddying fluid,
> > beneath the knees of the gods.

The key signified in both passages is here made apparent in the model "ply over ply" which, Hugh Witemeyer has pointed out, is a "recurrent phrase in the *Cantos*, used to describe dynamic, multi-layered processes." The effect of the Image, Witemeyer says, is to "intensify the reader's perception of each process by distinguishing its constituent elements."[24] Other models of the matrix are closely related to this one, and may be listed as follows: the boughs are layered with leaves, the "fish-scaled" roof is layered, light does not penetrate the layered boughs, light rains down/does not rain down on water, women (here, supernatural ones) bathe. These models appear several times in *A Draft of XXX Cantos*.

Finally, in the matrix passages of Canto 4 and in the passages above one may observe once again the stylistic features of Imagism: the near absence of VPs (with the exception of three instances of "to be," and the active verbs "rains" and "pours"), several examples of participials, a simple lexicon largely drawing from words denoting the natural world, a large proportion of prepositions, and the use of color terms.[25]

Light, water, boughs, bathing: these then are the "kernel" signifieds which animate the passages under discussion. Each signified is literally juxtaposed with its neighbors in the real world, creating a metonymy in which each element signifies the others: the boughs, that is, are "bathed" in light which does or does not pass to the water; the light "rains" down, and so on.

Before I turn to the Hell cantos, I should like to make clear the intent of my remarks on the repeated juxtapositions of Images of light, water, boughs, and bathing: this recurrence is in itself without meaning. Moreover, any appearance of one of these Images is not meant to substitute for any of the Images with which it is associated; substitution, of course, is a property of metaphor. In a sense, each kernel Image acts a a mnemonic device for the others; consequently, the original Imagist intent of the Image, the complex caught in an instant of time, has been supplanted by a new purpose, one which has been called forth by the exigencies of retaining coherence over the lengthy space traversed by *The Cantos*. Moreover, each of the kernels is meant to "stand for" itself; boughs are indeed boughs; light, even in its neoplatonist mode, is light. Even bathing, in its transformation as immersion, does not undergo a "metaphoric" transformation when it signifies the action of light on surfaces. The natural world in *The Cantos*, in other words, possesses its own values. Further, rather than providing a set of signifiers having to do with human signifieds, nature is itself the ground of all human action. Pound's view of objective reality is truly "mythological" in that, like the pre-Christian worshipper, he sees the stream not as a symbol or embodiment of a goddess, but as the goddess herself; Helios is not a "personification" for the sun, but the sun itself. Consequently, each of the kernel Images reciprocally serves to remind the reader of its literal and textual contiguity with the others. The more frequently each of the Images appears, the more tightly bound does the link between it and its associated Images become. Finally, this interlacing network ties to itself other stretches of text which initially have nothing to do with the matrix which provides the network.

Cantos 14 and 15 (pages 61 through 67) perhaps provide Pound's most interesting use of Imagist techniques, especially in light of productions like "Gentildonna." The mimesis (see Glossary) in these early poems and in the cantos which I have examined in this chapter is largely concerned with a natural landscape in which supernatural or heroic figures move. Canto 17, of course, deals with the rise of Venice from the sea, but the city is set in a "paradiso terrestre" as yet unpopulated by the merchants, nobility, and statesmen who will people it in later cantos. In fact, the activity in the Imagist passages I have discussed so far is to a large degree ahistorical. In direct contrast to such timeless "natural supernaturalism," the Hell cantos are set specifically in postwar London. Nonetheless, compared with truly historical portions of *The Cantos* like 8 through 11 (the Malatesta cantos) or 24 (the "Este" canto), 14 and 15 still invoke the preternatural; Pound himself envisioned his nekuia as something of a dream, and Terrell compares the technique here to Niccolo's delirium in Canto 20 (*Companion: 67).* The most striking effect of these cantos, however, and one that sets them off not only from most Imagist poetry but also from the bulk of *The Cantos* as well, arises from Pound's vivid use of scatology. The semantic field (see Glossary) here is informed by semes having to do with defecation, vermin, and various forms of moral and cultural pusillanimity. The matrix for 14 and 15, of course, is provided by Dante, who also drew portions of his semantic field from the same region.

On examination, the reader will observe all of the stylistic devices of Imagism which he encountered above. In Canto 14, for example, there are a mere five finite verbs for eighty–nine lines: the initial "io venni" drawn from Dante, three subordinate clauses ("who dislike colloquial language," "those who had lied for hire," and "petrified turd that was Verres"), and the "placard" reading "THE PERSONNEL CHANGES." The remaining verb structures, once again, are participials. Prepositions indicating place are fewer here than in the above examples, but the reasons for this reduction are fairly apparent; the setting for the cantos is obvious (indeed, it is a "luogo d'ogni luce muto"), and the actual disposition of the "sinners" in this phantasmagoria is unimportant. And, as one might expect in a place where light is "muted," color adjectives are nearly absent. In their stead are a predictable series of adjectives which are nearly as "concrete": wet, bare, soiled, pimply, hairy, dry, stray, stale, sadic, dirty, and decayed give an accurate idea of the semantic field from which Pound draws his modification. Finally, this combination of modifying participials with a high proportion of concrete adjectives supports a syntactic structure which is heavily nominalized. NPs here, however, unlike the substantives in the *Lustra* poems and in the other cantos, refer either to deleted proper names, or to types of sinners: thus, there are the "perverters of language," the "profiteers," the "usurers," the "cowardly inciters to violence," and the "back-scratchers." Each individual or group is surrounded syntactically by its participial or adjectival qualifications. The passage beginning Canto 15 is representative:

> The saccharescent, lying in glucose,
> > the pompous in cotton wool
> > > with a stench like the fats at Grasse,
> the great scabrous arse-hole, sh-tting flies,
> > rumbling with imperialism,
> ultimate urinal, middan, pisswallow without a cloaca,
> . . . . . . r less rowdy, ... Episcopus
> > . . . . sis,
> > head down, screwed into the swill,
> his legs waving and pustular,
> > a clerical jock strap hanging back over
> > > the navel
> his condom full of black beetles,
> > tattoo marks round the anus,
> and a circle of lady golfers about him.

Pound here uses an interesting typographical device to augment his emphasis on nominalization: the name of the individual or group which is verbally scourged is set full to the left margin with the accompanying epithets progressively indented until a new aspect of the subject's perfidy or absurdity is named (for example, "ultimate urinal," "his legs waving"), or a new subject is introduced (the "courageous violent" appear immediately after the above passage). Associated with typographical emphasis in both 14 and 15 are a number of passages exhibiting parallelism; lines are tied paratactically (in 14, for example, lines 22 through 26), or through anaphora ("his legs/his condom" above, or "the courageous violent/the cowardly" in the next verse paragraph), or even through alliteration (page 65, line 14 ff., "beneath one . . . / boredom born out of boredom / british weeklies"). This same device will be used in two of Pound's other signal denunciations, Canto 30, the "Pity" canto, and, of course, Canto 45, the Usura canto.

Before I turn my attention to a final look at the metonymic relations in these two cantos, I should like to draw the reader's attention to the use of two general kinds of typographic manipulation in these cantos. In 14 and 15 the first instances of signifiers occur which, although "standing for" natural language, are not themselves intended to signify a specific signified; these are the ellipses indicating deleted names and the placards of page 62. At face value, the purpose of the ellipses seems to be the obvious one of protecting Pound and his publisher from what would have been inevitable libel suits. Indeed, this *is* one purpose for the deletions. But Pound has a further reason for these excisions, one which should recall my investigation above of the heavily deleted "Papyrus": "Even the XIV-XV has individuals in it, but *not* worth recording as such. In fact, Bill Bird rather entertained that I had forgotten which rotters were there . . . My 'point' being that not even the first but only the last letters of their names had resisted corruption."[26] The reader may recall that I said of the ellipses in "Papyrus" that they were "themselves signifiers whose signified is 'attrition' " Here, too, deletion is itself a signifier of attrition, as Pound's remarks make clear. And, again, there is a metonymic relationship between the "worn-away" letters of the names, and the "worn-away" personalities of the characters once signified by those names. The placards of Canto 14 are also indicated by "non-standard" typography; both are printed in capitals, one (ΕΙΚΩΝ ΓΗΣ) in the Greek alphabet, the other ("THE PERSONNEL CHANGES") in the Roman. Here, however, the foregrounded typography nearly converts the placards to the species of iconic sign (see Glossary) which appears in Canto 22 wherein an "off limits" sign (surrounded by a border and hung by a "string") points to the setting of this portion of the canto (Gibraltar) rather than to the actual content of the sign's message. In fact, the placard reading "eikon ges" is actually a complex pun which comments on its own message.

What, finally, is the metonymic relation of these two cantos to one another and to the first thirty cantos which surround them? To take up the latter relation first: both cantos may be said to constitute the sign, "hell," of course, but to imply that this sign is a metaphorical representation of some state of mind is misleading. Such a view of the Dantean and Poundian infernos is not uncommon: Terrell's comment (*Companion*, 67) is typical. "[T]o both Dante and Pound, hell is a state of mind." And Pound's remark that the Hell cantos reflect "the spiritual state of England in 1919 and following" seems to corroborate this metaphorical reading. Certainly, for Dante, hell is, on one level, mental, but the place has a literal reality for him as well. In other words, although one cannot dismiss the metaphorical applications of either Dante's or Pound's vision of hell, Riffaterre's dictum that all poetry is "deviation from mimesis" points up the poverty of metaphoric explanations of the Hell cantos.

It is within the text of *The Cantos* that this region of hell lies. The "sinners" in Pound's inferno, as in Dante's, persist in their sins; actually, it is just this intransigence that is the real essence of sin for both authors despite Eliot's remark the Pound's hell is a "comfortable" one, "ignorant of original sin."[27] Consequently, the punishments for the sins are not so much figurative substitutions for the "real world" activities of sinners in either Pound or Dante as they are the natural result (the effect for cause) of those activities. Just as the *Inferno* is linked to the *Purgatorio* and *Paradiso* which follow it, so Cantos 14 and 15 are juxtaposed to the "Kung" canto which precedes them and the vision of the modern world in Canto 16 which follows them. The scale of relation, then, is not pinned between the poles "nether world/real world," but between "right actions, healthy effects/culpable actions, unhealthy effects." Once again, substitution of a metaphoric signifier as a means to interpret a portion of *The Cantos* is misleading; a sounder exegesis can be based on a metonymic signification involving effect for cause.

3
DELETION AND FRAGMENTATION

DELETIONS ARE COMMON in ordinary language and simple prose:

a. You want to eat?
b. The thin young man wanted to kiss her, and did.
c. I've worked all day. I don't have the energy.
d. "He's not playing with all his marbles." "I know."
e. If I have to drive it in, I'll drive it in.
   If I have to drive it in, I will.

Dwight Bolinger, whose discussion provides the basis for the above examples, says of deletions that they "are done usually 'under identity,' omitting something from a construction is generally a guarantee that the missing element is somewhere in the context."[1] The contexts which provide sense to the above sentences and interchanges are of varying degrees of complexity. In (a) the auxiliary "do" has been deleted in the context of "question" (probably indicated by intonation pattern and objective situation). The deleted portion of (b) responds to language's tendency to reduce informational redundancy: the reinsertion of the deletion ("kiss her") presents no difficulty for the native speaker. The situation in (c) is more complicated because the listener must establish one logical relation between the two sentences, rejecting other possible relations, before she can mentally reinsert the deleted element. The statement-response of (d) is a variation on (b), one difference between them being that the context for the responder's deletion is provided by the first speaker's statement. Another minor difference is that the deletion involves a full clause rather than a VP/NP. Transformational generative grammarians are likely to say that, once one has recognized the deletions of (a) through (e), one has established the only semantic difference between these sentences and the "full" sentences which they represent: both the surface sentence with deletion and the surface full sentence share the same deep structure.

Many semanticists, however, might argue that all of the example sentences are semantically affected by deletion; the deletion of (a) for instance suggests the use of an informal register, and the laconic response of (d) may imply, with appropriate intonation, a diluted sort of litotes. At any rate, all the above deletions are normal in the sense that they, and many structures like them, occur with great frequency in speech and writing. Consequently, (a) through (d), at least, are not foregrounded, and the fact that the non-deleted sentence of (e) *can* be inferred as being foregrounded only bears out the "natural" role of deletion in many contexts.

This brief discussion of syntactic deletion should suggest that the problem of establishing a variation from a norm is not simple, and in literature the problem is further compounded by the relation of speech to writing. Even in an author like Pound who advances "the simple order of natural speech" as his norm of writing, one must still ask in what that "simple order" consists. Linguists and stylisticians (the latter tending to accept the pronouncements of the former) usually accept the subject-verb-complement sentence as the "norm" for a declarative sentence in English. But we have already seen, in (a) and (b) for example, that sentence type and context may create "norms" which allow disruption of the simple declarative pattern. Moreover, the language competence (see Glossary) of the average listener/reader sanctions a wide range of deletions and substitutions based on her ability to carry semantic elements over long stretches of speech/text. In readers with strong literary competence, this ability is considerably enhanced. For the reader with some literary sophistication, deletion will in fact be so foregrounded that an adequate interpretation of the text must await reconstruction of the deletions. Literary deletions, then, as opposed to "conversational" deletions, are not automatized. Therefore, although we may say that conversational deletion often constitutes its own norm, literary deletion often appears as deviation from the norm. This latter situation is the case probably because, in speech, contexts are provided by a variety of extralinguistic "clues," whereas, in writing, contexts can only be provided by the linguistic syntagm. Additionally, speech is open to "recursive" explanations of deleted material if the listener feels the need for them.

There are, then, two kinds of deletions which occur in literature: since literary competence always comprises linguistic competence, ordinary language deletions will of course appear in literature. The second species of deletion, the foregrounded type, not only is peculiar to literature, but is more likely to be met with in twentieth-century, rather than traditional, literature. As writers increasingly tried to employ a spoken norm (whatever that might have meant to individual authors), the deletion characteristic of speech (which is automatized) was carried over into writing where it was foregrounded, and, thus, deletion became a stylistic device. Deletion, in turn, is the basic motive for fragmentation, which William E. Baker, in his *Syntax in English Poetry*, says "gives primary emphasis to the noun, and that the great majority of fragments are classified as such because they contain a noun or a noun phrase which lacks a finite verb to provide grammatical 'sense' to the structure."[2] The VP, of course, is the deleted element of the fragment.

I have already presented evidence in *The Cantos* of just this form of fragmentation which takes the form of nominalization, and in this chapter I shall examine other instances of this form of VP-deleted fragmentation. Baker, however, outlines other types of fragmentation in poetry: the traditional catalogue, as in Homer or Whitman, is clearly related to the nominalized fragment of Pound, and indeed may even be the direct precursor of the modern type; the disintegrating sentence begins coherently enough, but rapidly fragments into various deletion structures; and the absolute phrase, like the catalogue, is a traditional device "formed by attaching a noun and its participial modifiers to a sentence pattern of which they form no essential part" (Baker, 1967: 72). I might note in passing that the high number of participials the reader finds in portions of *The Cantos* might lead him to suspect the presence of this last type in Pound's style.

I should like now to list some simple formal "markers" (see Glossary) for these types of fragmentation:

1. The catalogue is marked in *The Cantos* in two forms: in one, it is a list of NPs with their modifiers, including P-phrases, having some common semantic field, and wherein VPs are deleted; in the other, less common form (and one not noted in Baker), VPs are present and an NP is absent.
2. The absolute phrase comprises a participial or subordinate clause followed by a full clause or further fragmented structure in which no unit is clearly modified by the preceding unit.
3. The disintegrating sentence is often marked by an initial full clause structure followed by either a catalogue or VPs and verbals exhibiting some form of deletion. Punctuation often plays an important role in this kind of fragment since disintegration may be externally bracketed by dashes or parentheses, and may be internally divided at least by commas, and often by semicolons or dashes. In poetry, typographic manipulation may also segment elements.

Baker argues persuasively that the fragment is the one syntactic structure common to the poetry of all major Modernists, and that this structure sets Modernist poetic style off from the style of Modernism's immediate predecessors. Moreover, Baker states that Pound's use of the fragment is the most frequent among his contemporaries; only Whitman, of all the late nineteenth-century and early twentieth-century poets Baker studied, equals Pound's startling ratio of 1.6 fragments to every full structure in a sample of 502 lines from Cantos 2, 3, and 4 (but see statistical appendix for a less selective survey). Baker traces Pound's use of the fragment to the poet's emphasis on the "simple order of natural speech," and it follows logically that for Pound "simple, emotive speech is by nature more fragmentary and nongrammatical than traditional poetry" (Baker, 1967: 60). Unfortunately, there is no direct corroboration of this insight on Pound's part, and, moreover, there is no telling evidence in linguistics which would confirm that speech is "fragmentary and nongrammatical" as opposed to traditional poetry. On the other hand, the reader has already seen the dominant role that the fragment plays in *The Cantos,* and of this role Baker says that "Pound has attempted what none of his . . . predecessors dared, the construction of poems (or large, unified sections of poems) primarily out of fragments." This high frequency of fragmentation, as Baker contends and as I mentioned in Chapter 1, "demands from the reader the recognition and acceptance of a new way of reading poetry" (Baker, 1967: 55–56).

The origin of the fragment in Pound and other Modernists is not obscure: the structure is in part an outgrowth of "elaboration," one of the most common devices of the Victorians. Elaboration involves a "quantitative change in character, in that an extraordinary number of word groups with the same character function together in one sentence and often, though not necessarily, in the same location" (Baker, 1967: 18). Such elaborations led to "unbalanced" sentences wherein "nouns, weighty with digressive modifiers, assumed a kind of autonomous force" (Baker, 1967: 62). Accompanying this purely syntactic disruption brought about by nominalization was the semantic dilemma which arose in the reader as she attempted to link together the various ideas of an elaboration. Swinburne represents the zenith (or nadir) of this development with forty–three elaborate structures in less than 500 lines sampled, and no less than seven "double" elaborations and even one "triple" elaboration within that forty–three. Finally, another historical contribution to the tendency toward fragmentation, albeit a lesser one, may have been the common traditional use of exclamatory fragments like "O tempora, O mores!"

Fragmentation Type 1: The Catalogue

Because the number of fragments in *A Draft of XXX Cantos* exceeds the number of "full" structures, I shall devote my discussion of fragments to the delineation of types, with accompanying examples, rather than to the noting of frequencies and placements of fragmentation (but see statistical appendix). Suffice it to say for the moment that those passages which are made up of full structures nearly always contain "historical" narratives (of mythic, personal, or world history); Cantos 1, 8 through 11, 13, 18, and 19, for example, thus consist largely of full sentences retelling stories of, respectively, Odysseus, Sigismundo Malatesta, Kung (Confucius), and modern business. I might note a curious fact concerning the "business" anecdotes which tends to militate against the idea that Pound thought of "simple, natural speech" as fragmentary: in all instances wherein a colloquial speaker (one whose speech is marked by dialect spellings, for instance) is quoted, the course of that speaker's story is often related in full sentences. John Quinn's anecdote of the "honest sailor" in Canto 12, and all but the first four lines of Mr. Giddings' "torpedo boat" story in Canto 18 illustrate this tendency.

Most of the cases of fragmentation which I discussed in the preceding chapters embody catalogues. In Canto 1's last verse paragraph, for example, Aphrodite is characterized through a catalogue of her attributes: "Venerandam," "with the golden crown," "mirthful," " with dark eyelids," and so on. In this instance, P-phrases, adjectives, and a participial, as opposed to a series of substantives, constitute the catalogue. A more various catalogue occurs in the passage on Page 10, Canto 2. Here, several nouns create the skeleton of the catalogue (instead of the one-noun "pivot" created by Aphrodite), and these are surrounded by descriptive adjectives and participials. A great deal of embedding by means of prepositions takes place in this passage, and the noun pivots of prepositions often are themselves qualified by catalogues of attributes: "sand-hollows / In the wave-runs by the half-dune" is an example of such embedding.

But of course Cantos 14 and 15 best illustrate the "true" catalogue. As I noted in Chapted 2, there are no real main clauses in Canto 14, and Canto 15 employs its few VPs solely in Pound's interchanges with his cicerone, Plotinus. It should come as no surprise that a description of hell would consist of a roll call of sinners; hence, in Canto 14, the politicians (Wilson, Lloyd George, and Balfour), the profiteers (Zaharoff), the "betrayers of language," the "pusillanimous," the traitors and "agents provocateurs," the bigots, slum owners, academics, and Ingram the bishop of London (who reappears in the first verse paragraph of the canto following) appear successively. Embedded in this succession of infamy are further catalogues describing the attributes of the infernal landscape: on page 62, for example, "the blowing of dry dust and stray paper, / foetor, sweat, the stench of stale oranges, / dung, last cess-pool / of the universe, mysterium, acid of sulphur." And on page 63 this grim litany continues with the "slough of unamiable liars, / bog of stupidities, / malevolent stupidities, and stupidities, / the soil living puss, full of vermin." I suggested above that this fragmented listing of sinners suppresses predications about individual sins, and tends to create predications through the sinners' literal and formal association to each other; thus, the politicians are politically contiguous to war profiteers, and both the politicians and profiteers benefit from the betrayal of language by the "press gang."

Actually, the "comminatory" catalogue occurs at least once before the Hell cantos, in Canto 12, page 55, wherein Pound describes John Quinn's attitude toward the members of a board of directors: "the ranked presbyterians, / Directors, dealers through holding companies, / Deacons in churches, owning slum properties, / *Alias* usurers in excelsis, / the quintessential essence of usurers, / The purveyors of employment, whining over their 20 p.c." Here again there is a list of types of social malefactors in which each type is in some way qualified. The reader will note that such qualification takes either the form of a participial, or an appositive NP; thus, the "deacons" are portrayed as both "owning" slums, and as "usurers in excelsis." Formally, such characterization of individuals is identical to catalogues of praise like the "invocation" to Aphrodite in Canto 1; the difference between the two catalogues is merely that the matrix of the former is marked by the seme " + perjorative." Such a reversal is, of course, common; the device of listing evil-doers and their accompanying vile epithets must originally have followed close on the heels of the panegyric catalogue.

I should like to group a rare type of deletion here under the catalogue, although syntactically it bears little resemblance to a list: this is the otherwise "normal" sentence with a deleted subject NP. Such a structure might with equal justice be grouped under the disintegrating sentence, with the exception that, in the "deleted-subject" type, disintegration occurs at the beginning of the "complete" structure rather than at its end. The first instance of this type of deletion occurs in the first sentence of *The Cantos:* "And then went down to the ship." It is only in line 3 that the reader learns the subject of this predication, the "we" of Odysseus' crew. The reason for the insertion of this partial sentence at the commencement of an epic is clear: Pound is quite literally abiding by the convention of beginning an epic *in medias res*. Another instance of subject-deletion occurs on page 79, Canto 17: "Arm laid over my shoulder, / Saw the sun for three days, the sun fulvid." The only reference in this canto for the "my" of "my shoulder" and for the deleted "seer" occurs in the opening lines on page 76, "Flat water before me," although this pronoun still does not clarify who is speaking here. Kenner advances the ingeniously Kennerian notion that the speaker is "Dionysus' vinestock," and this notion would be hard to dispute since there is no less proof for this interpretation than for any other. We have a strange reverse use of condensation here, I believe; as I hope to show in the next chapter, condensation involves the multiple semantic use of one syntactic structure. Here, an absent structure, the subject NP, is left open in order that the reader may insert any one of several possibilities: the voyager-poet, the participant in an Eleusinian mystery, or even Dionysus' vinestock.

Fragmentation Type 2: The Absolute Phrase

This is the least common of the fragmentation types in *The Cantos*, and it is easily confused with the disintegrating sentence, with the exception that, like the deleted-subject subtype above, the fragmentation of the structure happens at the outset. Conversely, this type represents one of the most common forms of fragmentation in traditional poetry. Baker cites two lines from Scott as an illustration:

> All loose her negligent attire, all loose her
> golden hair,
> Hung Margarot o'er her slaughtered sire.

Baker notes a variation on this structure in the early decades of the twentieth century: "When clearly broken away from a sentence pattern, the absolute phrase may resemble a descriptive fragment of the kind common to catalogues," and such fragments are "concrete, highly visual, static" (Baker, 1967: 74). He goes on to quote an example from Oppenheim:

> Clearing in the forest,
> In the wild Kentucky forest,
> And the stars, wintry stars strewn above.

Browning often employs, as he does many of the stylistic devices later used by Pound, this type of fragmentation. Baker assigns the motive for such use to Browning's desire to "reproduce not only the *spoken* but also the play of the *perceived* and *conceived* material of the mind" (Baker, 1967: 75). Be this as it may, whatever the author's intent in using this fragment, the reader's decipherment of it depends on his ability to defer strict predicational analysis of the fragment. In fact, such deferral may be protracted indefinitely.

An absolute phrase occurs in a text I have examined above (although in an odd position): in "Gentildonna" the last line, "Grey olive leaves beneath a rain-cold sky," offers a paradigm of the syntactic and semantic autonomy of the absolute phrase.

Fragmentation Type 3: The Disintegrating Sentence

In Canto 7 a passage appears which embodies both the two types of fragmentation I have just discussed as well as Type 3, the disintegrating sentence; the types, conveniently enough, occur in the order I have given them:

1   Another day, between walls of a sham Mycenian,
2   "Toc" sphinxes, sham-Memphis columns,
3   And beneath the jazz a cortex, a stiffness or stillness,
4   Shell of the older house.
5   Brown-yellow wood, and the no colour plaster,
6   Dry professorial talk . . .
7   now stilling the ill beat music,

8	House expulsed by this house.
9	Square even shoulders and the satin skin,
10	Gone cheeks of the dancing woman,
11	Still the old dead dry talk, gassed out—
12	It is ten years gone, makes stiff about her a glass,
13	a petrefaction of air.
14	The old room of the tawdry class asserts itself;
15	The young men, never!
16	Only the husk of talk.
17	O voi che siete in piccioletta barca,
18	Dido choked up with sobs, for her Sicheus
19	Lies heavy in my arms, dead weight
20	Drowning, with tears, new Eros,

In the first verse paragraph the catalogue of NPs is clearly evident in the "sphinxes," "columns," "wood," "plaster," and so on. In the second verse paragraph the initial two lines are associated (at least through punctuation) with the "old dead dry talk" of line 3, and yet the semantic relation between the dancing woman and the talk is tenuous; the reader must assume that the woman must be doing the talking, and part of the semantic fields of the two units ("departed" in "gone" and "gassed out") may give substance to this assumption.

It is, however, with the last seven lines of the passage that I am concerned, the first line of which is clearly tied to the "shell of the older house" model in the preceding bulk of the passage. But what of the "young men" of line 15? The VP of the fourteenth line, "asserts itself," might underlie the deleted NP of the fifteenth line in association with the adverbial "never": "The young men never assert themselves." If the reader, on the other hand, allows himself to carry over predications from adjoining lines, then line 16, "Only the husk of talk," could also provide an underlying structure which might be made apparent as something like "The young men never converse, they only talk the husk of talk." This latter reconstruction, however, demands a further deep structure VP to accompany the "husk of talk," and thus is less probable. The problem is to an extent insoluble in that line 15 is not "fixed," but points backward and forward along the syntagm. The reader will note in this regard the lexical markers of the passage, which are equally ambivalent; the "tawdry class" of line 14 has semantic associations with the "sham" of the initial passage, and the setting of that passage may be seen as a metonymy for the class which produced it. The "class" probably comprises the "young men" who, in turn (again metonymically), are signified by the "house" which "expulses" the "older house" of vanished cultural values.

True disintegration sets in with the Dantean "O voi che. . . ," and the reference to Dido which follows it. Certainly, Dante's address to his readers following the "ship" of his narration in the "little boat" is appropriate for insertion in an epic; this is especially the case since the purpose of Dante's line in the original is to caution his readers that he is about to engage in mysteries, and Canto 7 concerns "mysteries" in that it deals with "ghosts" of the past. Yet might not such a pronouncement have justly appeared earlier since ghosts appear throughout the canto? And when we consider the succeeding lines about Dido, Sicheus, and Aeneas, the purpose becomes thoroughly enigmatic. Carroll Terrell here aligns Dante's "voyage" imagery with Pound's textual exigencies: "Pound is picking up the original Odyssean theme of the sea voyage in order to link this canto with the preceding six" (*Companion*, 34). Terrell's insight is undoubtedly correct, as far as it goes: plausibly, other hypograms in this canto could be tied back to preceding cantos; the "thin husks [Pound] had known as men" of line 10, page 26, for example, may be linked to the initial reminiscence in Canto 2 with as much justice, and the reference to Lorenzaccio on page 27 echoes that nobleman's appearance in Canto 5. In fact, the only resolution of the difficulty must rely on imputing psychological motivation to the placement of this and other lines in the passage at hand. On the whole, I am attempting to avoid such imputation in this study, but the very nature of disintegrating sentence fragmentation compels this conclusion. Baker says of this type that "to attempt to force the words into mutually exclusive syntactic molds probably defeats the poet's intention and perhaps weakens the effect of the whole" (Baker, 1967: 70). The reason for this situation is that "such complete disintegration of syntactic forms presupposes more than ingenuity on the part of the reader. A reader must also possess a background of experience similar to . . . the poet's" (Baker, 1967: 72). Consequently, the matrix here is formed "dove sta memoria," and the "movement" of Pound's mind in remembrance is reflected in the shifting fragments of the passage. I should like to take up again below, in the section concerned with the function of fragments, the question of mental representation and its relation to fragmentation srtructures; before I do move on to the various roles of structural fragmentation, one more type of disintegrating sentence needs to be examined.

This subtype of disintegrating sentence may conveniently be grouped with what is traditionally termed the "cento," a "patchwork" of dissociated lines from classics (originally from Homer and later Virgil and Ovid). The cento form with which I am here concerned employs not only single-language excerpts from a single author, but also multiple-language excerpts as well. In the canto from which I drew the above example of all three types of fragmentation, Canto 7, the initial passage provides a good instance of just this species of intermixture of languages and matrices:

1   Eleanor (she spoiled in a British climate)
2   Ἔλανδρος and Ἑλέπτολις, and
3   poor old Homer blind,

4   blind as a bat,
5   Ear, ear for the sea-surge;
6   rattle of old men's voices.
7   And then the phantom Rome,
8   marble narrow for seats
9   "Si pulvis nullus" said Ovid,
10   "Erit, nullum tamen excute."
11   Then file and candles, e li mestiers ecoutes;
12   Scene for the battle only, but still scene,
13   Pennons and standards y cavals armatz
14   Not mere succession of strokes, sightless narration,
15   And Dante's "ciocco," brand struck in the game.

16   Un peu moisi, plancher plus bas que le jardin.

17   "Contre le lambris, fauteuil de paille,

18   "Un vieux piano, et sous le baromètre. . ."

There are directly inserted here portions from Ovid, Bertrans de Born, Dante, and Flaubert, and a reference to Homer's "ear for the sea-surge," *polyphloisboio;* and the passage of course begins with an historical allusion to Eleanor of Aquitaine who is associated with the Greek puns on Helen's name. These interposed quotes, this use of five languages (including the Old French of "e li mestiers ecoutes" and the Provençal of "y cavals armatz") is further intermingled with at least five hypograms: the ambiguously "destructive" force of Eleanor, Homer's skill and Helen's perilous beauty, Ovid's advice on how to meet girls, the craftsmanship of "li mestiers ecoutes," and of Dante, and the *mot juste* of Flaubert's description. Finally, this interfoliation of languages and hypograms is not always homologous; although Helen's presence is implied in line 6, her epithets are applied to Eleanor in line 1; the "sightless narration" of line 14 which seems to be in association with Dante, just as easily and more properly casts back to "poor blind Homer" of line 3.

But the matrix of the passage is not particularly arcane: a succession of exemplary narrators or, perhaps better, types of narration, is paraded before us; each writer, Homer, Ovid, de Born, Dante, and Flaubert, represents a specific manner of precise observation (Homer's "observation," for example, is auditory and Dante's is drawn, like Flaubert's, from a detailed repository of contemporary cultural images), while, at the same time, we witness representative objects of that observation: Homer's sea and old men's voices, Ovid's lovers, the bourgeois commodity-ridden environment of late nineteenth-century France. It is perhaps, however, the languages themselves which signify the observations which are foregrounded here. Translation of the kinds of narrative perfection each author represents is, for Pound, impossible; at the same time, denied translation (and the "levelling" action of a univocal English), Pound is forced to dispose his "exhibits" in a discontinuous syntagm. Consequently, as the reader will undoubtedly notice, not only does this passage manifest all of the traits of fragmentation I have already discussed (lack of VPs, absolute phrases like the initial one concerning Eleanor followed by a remark about Homer), but also it brings to bear a further fracturing of the *langue* (see Glossary) itself, and with it, of the *parole* of the individual lines and parts of lines.

Examples of this sort of fragmentation by insertion of foreign-language matter in *The Cantos*, of course, could be extended almost indefinitely; such insertion is one of the most foregrounded elements in the poem. As Kenner has remarked, and as I have discussed elsewhere, the use of a given language in *The Cantos* is itself a signifier of some trait which Pound has associated with that language, such that Latin signifies precision, Provençal grace, and so on.[3] Another, and perhaps more perplexing instance, for example, occurs in Canto 20, page 89:

> Sound slender, quasi tinnula,
> Ligur' aoide: Si no'us vei, Domna don plus mi cal,
> Negus vezer mon bel pensar no val."
> Between the two almond trees flowering,
> The viel held close to his side;
> And another; s'adora".
> "Possum ego naturae
> non meminisse tuae!" Qui son Properzio ed Ovidio.

where phrases in English, Latin, Greek, Provençal, Italian, and again Latin and Italian stand in a kind of apposition to each other; in fact, the "slenderness" of the sound can be said to be a kind of "ringing," and the ringing a kind of clarity, and the "sound" a song. Further, the ringingly clear song is exemplified by "Domna don plus mi cal." The bonds between each language phrase are tightly drawn, and yet, again, the stylistic effect is fractured, so that, as Baker says, "disintegration . . . presupposes more than ingenuity on the part of the reader . . . he must also possess a background of experience similar to . . . the poet's"; and here that "background" includes knowledge of the languages involved in the passsage.

The Roles of Fragmentation

There is simply no way an interpretative strategy confronted with fragmentation can avoid reference to psychological processes in Pound and his reader. A purely linguistic or syntactic explanation of fragmentation can be advanced, but it suffices little to explain the widespread foregrounding of the fragment. In regard to the use of participials in their function of supplanting VPs, for example, I might say that deletion here is of various forms of "to be," and that, hence, all participials are in reality deep structure progressives, lending to the passages in which they appear the effect of ongoing motion. But then why should deletion take place at all? Of absolute phrases, I might say that Pound here adopts a kind of narrative economy wherein one structure is made to serve a dual purpose. Yet what need has Pound of economy in a poem one hundred and twenty cantos long? And so through all the phases of fragmentation.

When one says that an author's work possesses a certain form, in the sense I discussed in the first chapter, one is speaking of a property greater than that comprising elements on a microcontextual level. It is difficult here to avoid charges of impressionism; in extending style traits to an "overall effect," stylisticians often destroy whatever credibility, in terms of precision and sufficient evidence, they may have created in their arguments. When I say that fragmentation is one of the signal, one of the highly foregrounded, traits of Pound's style in *A Draft of XXX Cantos,* I am stating the obvious. When I go on, as I hope I have done in this chapter, to demonstrate the radical extent to which Pound carries fragmentation and the multiple uses he makes of it, I may have called the reader's attention to a series of facts which may have gone unnoticed. When, however, I attempt to make assertions about the perceived effect of fragmentation in a reading of *The Cantos,* I move on to ground which is neither obvious nor even particularly firm. Baker's assertion in this regard is nearly as far as one can go in attributing a certain effect in the reader brought on by fragmentation, but that assertion does not take us far in understanding the complexity of *The Cantos.* And a question perhaps even more fundamental than the stylistic effect of fragmentation is left unanswered: why *does* fragmentation play so prominent a role, not only in *The Cantos,* but in much of Modernist verse? and why does the device, if it is an effective one, not appear earlier in English poetry?

It seems to me that only one strategy in contemporary criticism is adequate to begin to explain the relation of fragmentation in the text to its effect in the reader's interpretative process, and that strategy is a phenomenological one. In the opening pages of this study, I committed myself to a descriptive stance which would not be undercut by resorting to "thematics" at moments of difficulty (that is to say, at moments in the text wherein purely linguistic evidence seems insufficient or disingenuously self-evident). I am not at this point, then, going to bring nonlinguistic meaning in by the backdoor in the form of an "objective" phenomenological "solution" of the dilemma posed by fragmented structures in Modernist literature. Nonetheless, I should like to suggest to the reader the close coincidence of assumptions about the objective world which both Pound and other Modernists, on the one hand, and phenomenologists, on the other, share. The Imagist "project" and Husserl's "phenomenological meditation" are uncannily similar in many respects; both place great emphasis on the "intentional" consciousness which can only exist, as Husserl himself might have put it, between a thing "outwardly" seen and "subjectively" experienced. Moreover, as Kevin Kerrane explains, in phenomenological meditation:

> A phenomenon under consideration is "bracketed": all presuppositions, inferences, and judgments about it, including the issue of its spatio-temporal existence, are held in abeyance. This purifying phase of meditation frees the phenomenologist [and the poet] to examine the essential structure of the individual phenomenon. As he attends to the residual given, he may describe the object of consciousness in its multiple perspectives and attempt a series of "reductions," focusing awareness so as to intuit whatever reveals itself as essential in the phenomenon (eidetic reduction)—or even in the pure stream of consciousness itself (transcendental reduction).[4]

A paradox presents itself: in seeking to mirror the world phenomenologically, and therefore accurately, the Modernists in, I would argue, *all* the arts constructed "texts" which are in no way mimetic of the world. Such a conundrum is inevitable because, as Riffaterre argues, all literature (and literature here is exemplary of the other arts of the twentieth century) is a conversion away from mimesis. Jakobson's dictum, too, that literature, as opposed to the other modes of discourse, is a "set to expression" is a linguistic argument in favor of the active (even perhaps hostile) antimimesis of Modernism.

The reader will note, too, Kerrane's remark concerning the "eidetic" reduction typical of phenomenological meditation; such reduction is very close indeed to defamiliarization in literature. It would seem to me that there is no more radical way in which to "deconstruct" the phenomenon of a literary text than to fragment that which is usually perceived as whole, be that whole a material object or a literary text like the *Iliad*, the *Ars Amatoria*, or *Un Coeur Simple*; in the poems of *Lustra*, it was objects which were so deconstructed; in *The Cantos*, not only objects, but discourse itself is disassembled. Again, it is not the purpose of this study to pursue Kulturgeisten, but this impulse to reduce phenomena to "essentials" (and mutatis mutandis, "reality") by disintegration implies a profound insecurity on the part of twentieth-century artists and philosophers concerning the evidence of one's eyes and ears.

Be all this as it may, is there not a more "salubrious" light which may be cast on the process of fragmentation? Kerrane goes on to summarize the positive effects of phenomenological poetics by pointing out Sartre's emphasis on the liberating effect of imagination-as-intentional-act, Bachelard's loving examination of material images as lived experiences, and the general phenomenological view that the reading of literature is "fundamentally active." In regard to this last perspective, Kerrane quotes Poulet: "When I read as I ought . . . I am persuaded . . . that I am freed from my usual sense of incompatibility between by consciousness and its objects." Phenomenology, then, sees the act of reading as "participatory." I would further argue that Pound, too, demands shared subjectivity and participation from his reader in that the reader must delve, make intertextual forays, must read backward and forward along the syntagm, to understand *The Cantos*. Furthermore, phenomenology makes of the literary text an ontological absolute (here, Kerrane cites the importance Ransom lends to "irrelevant texture," for example, as a mode of reproducing the richness of the phenomenal world).

If one considers the truly paradigmatic uses of fragmentation in Modernist literature—in the "Circe" chapter of *Ulysses*, in the interior monologues of *The Years*, or even later, in the *Dream Songs* of Berryman—it soon becomes apparent that the uses to which such fragmentation are put cannot solely be offered up under the sign of, as Baker puts it, creating "a realistic transcript of . . . psychic content." At times Pound does use fragmentation for this purpose; in, for example, portraying the disintegrating consciousness of Niccolo d'Este. But passages like the two above which begin Cantos 7 and 20 can certainly not be classified as "transcripts" of someone's "psychic content," especially not that of the razor-edged, polymathic acuteness of an Ezra Pound at the height of his powers. Nor, would I argue, does fragmentation play this psychically disintegrative role in much else of Modernist literature except as a special instance, in the portrayal of dreams or madness for example, and here we may find evidence for the same usage in Browning, and even Shakespeare.

Fragmentation, then, is used stylistically in the interests of accuracy; whether one chooses to view such accuracy as phenomenologically appropriate, or artistically effective, or imaginatively liberating, it is nonetheless a conscious accuracy aimed eventually at coalescence: exactly what species of coalescence I shall examine in a later chapter on the concept of "coupling." For the time being, however, I should like to turn to another important stylistic device—condensation.

4
CONDENSATION AND SPATIAL FORM

IT HAS BEEN over forty years now since Joseph Frank published his well-known essay, "Spatial Form in Modern Literature." Following are some excerpts from that essay[1] (Frank is discussing the accuracy of Lessing's argument in the *Laocoon*):

> Literature . . . makes use of language, composed of a succession of words proceeding through time; and it follows that literary form, to harmonize with the essential quality of its medium, must be based primarily on some form of narrative sequence. Lessing used this argument to attack two artistic genres highly popular in his day: pictorial poetry and allegorical painting.

The eighteenth-century problem has modern affinities since "modern literature . . . is moving in the direction of spatial form. This means that the reader is intended to apprehend [the] work spatially, in a moment of time, rather than as a sequence." Such apprehension, however, presents a dilemma which Frank poses as a question:

> Or was the poem itself one vast image, whose individual components were to be apprehended as a unity? But then it would be necessary to undermine the inherent consecutiveness of language, frustrating the reader's normal expectation of a sequence and forcing him to perceive the elements of a poem juxtaposed in space rather than unrolling in time. This is precisely what Eliot and Pound attempted in their major works.

Frank concludes his discussion of this particular perceptual problem with remarks the gist of which may by now be familiar to the reader of this study:

> The one difficulty of these poems, which no amount of textual exegesis can wholly overcome, is the internal conflict between the time-logic of language and the space-logic implicit in the modern conception of the nature of poetry. Esthetic form in modern poetry, then, is based on a space-logic that demands a complete re-orientation in the reader's at-

titude toward language. Since the primary reference of any word-group is to something inside the poem itself, language in modern poetry is really reflexive: the meaning-relationship is completed only by the simultaneous perception in space of word-groups which, when read consecutively in time, have no comprehensible relation to each other . . . modern poetry asks of its readers to suspend the process of individual reference temporarily until the entire pattern of internal references can be apprehended as a unity . . . this conception of poetic form [which] has left its traces on a whole generation of modern poets, can be formulated only in terms of the principle of reflexive reference.

I have quoted Frank at such length to show that many of the problems with which this study has up till now concerned itself are not novel ones in the criticism of Modernist literature. Crucial to Frank's argument and to my own are three key ideas in the quotations above. These include Frank's observation that Modernist poetry asks of its readers to perceive it "all at once," rather than sequentially; Eliot and Pound, especially, seem to wish to "frustrate" the reader's "normal expectation of a sequence." Modernism's "space-logic," then, alters the referential function of ordinary language because the "primary reference of any word-group is to something inside the poem itself." And, since consecutive reading is a useless strategy in the face of Modernist poetry, the reader must employ what Frank calls the "principle of reflexive reference."

In the present chapter, I should like to consider those elements of Modernist technique which may be characterized as bolstering "spatial form." Actually, it may well appear fatuous to state that Modernist poetry possesses spatial elements; the reader will rightly object that *all* verse depends heavily on "spatial elements" if we count among those elements enjambement, disposition of lines, and types of stanzas (to say nothing of the possibly "spatial" properties of prosody). Clearly, then, what both Frank and I intend by "spatial form" in its modern sense is the use of space as a nearly hostile counterforce, in some poets (here one thinks of the Surrealists) an emetic, to temporal narration. Twentieth-century poets, in this as in a few of the devices discussed in preceding chapters, have forerunners in the late nineteenth century; Browning, of course, makes a conscious and concerted effort to disrupt the linearity of time, as it is commonly conceived, through interior and exterior monologues, and through the juxtaposition of opposing points of view. Whitman, too, seems to disregard sequence in favor of what seems at times to be the visual impact of chunks of verse on the page. But neither the "conventional" uses of space (enjambement, etc.), nor the seminal techniques of Browning and Whitman are what Frank and others intend by this novel use of space in twentieth-century verse.

The Modernists often remind us (here I might mention Yeats's gyres, Joyce's reading of Vico, or Brecht's of Marx) that there are many species of time. Pound's much-repeated remarks about the Schifanoia fresco demonstrate that he assumed a tripartite time: mythic or divine time, historic time, and personal time. In effect, only one of these is sequential, historic time, but even history is badly misread if it is only read linearly. If only syntactically through the absence of VPs, Pound enacts a diminution of "finite" time in *The Cantos*. What is permanent is almost necessarily what is not fixed; it is in its realignment with contemporary modes of perception that cultural permanence retains its permanence; my remarks on "Papyrus," or on Cantos 15, 16, and 17 should make this clear.

Another "exhibit" (albeit a hackneyed one, unfortunately) which elucidates this tendency in the twentieth-century arts to accord a status to simultaneity in space equal to that accorded to sequence in time is Eisenstein's theory of montage. The analogy between Modernist literature and Eisenstein's principle was probably inevitable from the first; early on, critics noted the similarity between the method of film editing as Eisenstein described it, and the techniques of, say, Joyce. One might even argue that recently an entire cottage industry of film/literature criticism has been built on "The Image in Process."[2] The trouble with Eisenstein's "montage principle," as most film editors would agree, is that the theory was the result of an inevitable technical development in film-cutting; that is, the Soviet director's theory (as he himself would probably have admitted in retrospect) grew out of the exigencies of the cutting room, or, to use the jargon of film criticism, out of the qualities of the medium. At any rate, this study is not the place to explore the etiology of montage; my point here is to clarify spatial form in literature through the analogous use of spatial form in film.

Eisenstein describes the montage in, as he puts it, the following "imperative" form:

> *Representation A* and *representation B* must be so selected from all the possible features within the theme that is being developed, must be so sought for, that their juxtaposition—that is, the juxtaposition of *those very elements* and not of alternative ones—should evoke in the perception and feelings of the spectator the most complete *image of the theme itself.* (Eisenstein, 1965: 169)

What is the result of this technique in the viewer? Eisenstein says "that it is precisely the *montage principle,* as distinguished from that of *representation,* which obliges spectators themselves to create . . . ." (Eisenstein, 1965: 169). I doubt that I need argue the pertinence of Eisenstein's remarks to Imagism, certainly, nor to the devices in the first thirty cantos which I have discussed in preceding chapters. Eisenstein's use of the signal terms "juxtaposition," "image of the theme," or "as distinguished from [the principle] of representation," should by now ring familiarly in the patient reader's ears. Of course, the famous essay from which the above quotations are drawn goes on to discuss the psychological basis of the montage principle, and to illustrate the principle with well-known examples concerning the clock face, *Anna Karenina,* and the director's perplexed dealings with the Manhattan street system (which he misidentifies as the "New York" street system). And, of course, we have Eisenstein's own enactment of his principle in the "Odessa Steps" sequence in *Potemkin.*

I should, however, like to explore in a little greater depth the analogy between juxtaposed film shots evoking "the image of the theme itself" and Pound's Images in *The Cantos.* The principles of cinematic spatial form (montage) and spatial form in *The Cantos* (commonly termed the "ideogrammic method") share a common semiotic basis: I might argue that each image/shot bears, besides the signifieds which constitute its autonomy as an image or shot, a signified in the overall theme, and the syntagm of such underlying signifieds is constituted in the perceptions of the reader/viewer. In illustration of this principle, one might easily convert the opening lines of Canto 9, the "Post-Bag" canto, into a cinematic montage:

> One year floods rose,
> One year they fought in the snows,
> One year hail fell, breaking the trees and walls.
> Down here in the marsh they trapped him
>   in one year,
> And he stood in the water up to his neck
>   to keep the hounds off him.
>   . . . .
> And he fought in Fano, in a street fight,
> and that was nearly the end of him;
> And the emperor came down and knighted us . . .

The initial three lines, in fact, closely suggest the much-used device of suggesting the passage of time in films by the flipping pages of a calendar, or the rapid succession of shots of newspaper front pages: actually (I might comment in passing), the history of montage since the twenties is a good example of how an artistic technique, at one time highly foregrounded, becomes quickly automatized. Now, a director might shoot, and an editor dispose, these lines in the following manner: shot one would disclose the turbulent edge of water lapping over the walls of a dyke; a dissolve might reveal a line of weary soldiers tramping through swirling snow which, in turn, would give place to hail in an orchard which, in the next shot, would become a marsh wherein we see a close-up of Sigismundo, the water lapping at *his* face. And so on through the various images of the passage. The concatenation of shots would promote in the mind of the viewer the theme "trials and tribulations of Sigismundo Malatesta," which would be embedded as a signified in each of the shots. But the reader may note that some of these shots, like that of the flood rising, in no way suggest this theme in itself; the signified of the rising flood shot might more properly be simply "tribulation."

In fact, the cinematic quality of the Malatesta cantos is, on examination, startling. Not only do we have the use of the montage principle, but we have the use of documents as icons of themselves much as a director might pan to a letter in the hands of one of his actors, not to indicate the content of the letter, but to establish the result of the letter on its reader. This, of course, is to say nothing of the many wide-angle "action" scenes, a la D. W. Griffith, which permeate this section of *The Cantos*.

But to return to the question of spatial as opposed to temporal art: the student of Pound will by this time undoubtedly be awaiting the introduction of "ideogrammic method" into this discussion of juxtaposition and spatial arrangement. Pound's definition of the method is similar to Eisenstein's explanation of *his* method: the ideogrammic method involves "the examination and juxtaposition of particular specimens—e.g. particular works, passages of literature . . . as an implement for acquisition and transmission of knowledge."[3] And Fenollosa's description of "compounding" in Chinese ideographs supplies the germ of this idea: "In this process of compounding, two things added together do not produce a third thing, but suggest some fundamental relation between them."[4] Later in the essay, Fenollosa advances the notion that the relation between the "two things added together" is "more important and more real" than things "which are related." Finally, Fenollosa's remarks on the whole of the Chinese ideograms themselves could with equal justice be applied to *The Cantos:*

> The manifold illustrations which crowd its annals of personal experience, the lines of tendencies which converge upon a tragic climax, moral character as the very corner of the principle—all these are flashed at once on the mind as reinforcing values with an accumulation of meaning which a phonetic language can hardly hope to attain.

For "phonetic language" above, I might substitute "traditional poetry."

But a caveat is here in order; in the same essay in which the concepts I have just stressed are discussed, Fenollosa argues that "thought is successive, not through some accident or weakness of our subjective operations but because the operations of nature are successive." Consequently, linguistic "reproduction" must follow the "same temporal order." It would be foolhardy to argue that *any* spoken or written syntagm, or for that matter any word (phonemes may or may not be a special case), is not perceived linearly; hence, to state that a literary passage somehow achieves its effect in the reader through simultaneous operations would be quite simply false. And yet, I *have* argued that Pound's poetry must to a degree be read in exactly this synchronic fashion. An extended solution to this dilemma must await a later chapter; I may, however, indicate now very briefly how the reader of *The Cantos* is supposed to hold two or several Images, hypograms, or intratextual references at once in her mind.

The answer quite simply is that *The Cantos,* like all of the great works of Modernism, cannot be read. They must be read, and reread, and read again, as Frank repeatedly makes clear. This process was consciously intended by the authors of these works. Joyce's quip to the harried reader who struggled for months with *Finnegans Wake* about the relation of the lengthy writing time of the novel to its reading time was only partly facetious.

Yet there *is* a stylistic means by which Pound produces at least the perceived effect of simultaneity within the microcontext: condensation. I draw the term from David Lodge, and I shall quote the context in which he uses it in a moment; I must point out, however, that Lodge's is not the only use of the word in more or less the sense I am using it. The intent of "condensation" here is not far different from Freud's in his discussion of the process in dream imagery, and Baker, speaking in terms of syntax, calls condensation a "fused structure" which he defines as "a word or word group whose meaning and/or grammatical form could integrate the word or words into either of two other discrete structures. Such fusion very often has the effect of confusing traditional syntactic relations" (Baker, 1967: 66). Lodge introduces the term in his discussion of contexture and metonymy; he contends, with Jakobson, that the "process" of condensation and contexture is that in which

> "any linguistic unit at one and the same time serves as the context for simpler units and/or finds its own context in a more complex linguistic unit." But "contexture" is not an optional operation in quite the same way as "substitution"—it is, rather, a law of language . . . Metonymies and synecdoches are *condensations* of contexture.[5]

Baker cites two examples from Pound of the device; the first is from Canto 4:

> And by the curved, carved foot of the couch,
>   claw-foot and lion head, an old man seated
> Speaking in a low drone . . .

The other is from *Hugh Selwyn Mauberly:*

> Beneath the sagging roof
> The stylist has taken shelter,
> Unpaid, uncelebrated,
> At last from the world's welter
> Nature receives him.

In the first passage from *The Cantos*, Baker argues, the "claw-foot and lion head" refer primarily to the "couch" and secondarily to the "old man." In the second passage, which Baker admits is a "trivial example," the participials of the third line may with equal justice belong either to the sentence which precedes them, or that which follows them (notably, the first passage consists entirely of fragments, whereas the second comprises two perfectly unexceptional full sentences). Baker comments on the fact that the fragment easily gives rise to "such free and easy rapprochement."

Pound says nothing directly in his criticism on the matter of fragmentation, but there are several references to the processes of condensation; in fact, he may well have automatically subsumed fragmentation under condensation, although there is no evidence, again, that this is the case. At any rate, it is legitimate to view fragmentation as a form of condensation since, obviously, the fragment is a "condensed" version of a more extended deep structure. The fragment, however, in terms of its functions, cannot be comprised under the process of condensation; on the one hand, fragmentation only occasionally (as in the case of the absolute phrase, for example) takes the "dual" form characteristic of condensation, and, on the other, fragmentation frequently aims at great specificity in reference (as in the catalogue). This latter function is opposed to condensation's always ambivalent (if not ambiguous) role.

Consequently, in Pound's concise equation in the *ABC of Reading*, "Dichten = Condensare," his astute play on the dual significance of "dichten," both "to tighten" and "to write (poetry)," calls to mind the second of the Imagist tenets, "To use absolutely no word that does not contribute to the presentation."[6] And in a letter to Hubert Creekmore looking back over what he had so far accomplished in *The Cantos*, Pound writes in 1939 that the "foreign words in the *Cantos*," the ideograms, the "typographic disposition," and the "abbreviations" all contribute to "condensation to maximum attainable" for the purposes, respectively, of indicating "duration from whence or since when" (in regard to foreign words and ideograms), facilitating the "reader's intonation" (typographic disposition), and saving "*eye* effort" (abbreviations).[7] Finally, Pound occasionally makes an important distinction between prose and poetry in his critical essays: "The language of prose is much less highly charged, that is perhaps the only availing distinction between prose and poesy. Prose permits greater factual presentation, explicitness, but a much greater amount of language is needed."[8] Clearly, Pound is here setting up a corollary equation to accompany the "dichten/condensare" equivalence: as signifiers rise in terms of sheer quantity, the "charge" of the individual signification diminishes. In Chapter 3, I asked what need Pound had of economy in a poem the length of *The Cantos*, and in the functions of condensation we may now find an answer.

Simply speaking, there are two forms of "quantitative" literary economy.

Narrative economy is easily illustrated by Chekhov's famous remark on the wall-hung rifle included in a story's opening description, and the later "economic" use of the rifle in a plot function: such economy is syntagmatic. Lyric economy is more complex, although, like Chekhov's narrative economy, it serves to "tighten," to bring together elements of the discourse, and is frequently paradigmatic. In lyric poetry, condensation verges on paronomasia; one early instance, reminiscent of the originary myths which occur in all cultures, appears in Canto 4, page 14, line 1, where the swallows' cry, which echoes Philomela's voicing of her cannibalized nephew's name, also echoes Raymond's answer to Seremonda's question; "It is Cabestan's heart in the dish?" "It is." Ambiguity in the poetic sign (noted so often by New Critics like Empson and Ransom) takes a form wherein the signifier possesses multiple signifieds, no one of which is "privileged" by the poem's macrocontext. In his search for a determinate signified, the reader very often looks to a poem's matrix, models, and hypograms for corroborating signifieds. This process works fairly well in pre-twentieth-century literature (which is, more often than not, the object of Riffaterre's use of hypograms and matrices), or in some twentieth-century literature (including Pound's). In *The Cantos*, however, the reader is often uncertain about both the intent of a signifier and its reference. For example, the Homeric epithet "ἐλέπτολιζ" is applied, as it is in Aeschylus, to Helen (Canto 2, line 11). Yet in Canto 7 "ἐλέπτολιζ," in line 2, seems at first to stand in apposition to Eleanor of Aquitaine in line 1, and then to recur to the original meaning in association with Homer and the "old men's voices" of lines 3 and 6. Actually, this example reflects a very simple use of condensation; obviously, Pound wishes the reader to equate Helen with Eleanor, and he brings about an equivalence between the two politically catalytic women through an identical epithet. A more complex aspect of condensation here is not so readily apparent; since the epithet occurs in the original Greek, it seems probable that the reader is to note the recurrence of this "feminine" trait "from whence and since when" it "began" in Helen.

The reader may note that Chekhov's example of narrative economy in the short story partakes of the same order of "deletion of the unnecessary" which is invoked by the second point of Imagism, and that Chekhov's illustration involves what structuralists interested in prose narrative sometimes call an "instrument" of plot, and not a purely linguistic element. This distinction between economy in plot elements and economy in linguistic elements may be the hinge upon which Pound's according of "charge" to poetry (as opposed to prose) swings. This is not to say, of course, that Pound raises an absolute dichotomy between prose and poetry on the basis of whether or not a text "charges" its linguistic elements: far from it. As Pound's repeated remarks on Flaubert, Hueffer, and Joyce make abundantly clear, the modern poet can learn much from the *mot juste* of contemporary prose writers. In a sense, however, Pound's injunctions against "saying in poetry what could be better said in prose" have something of the tenor of a lament. Important Modernist poetic projects, like Pound's and Eliot's, in one way or another debunk post-Renaissance poetry generally; whether such attacks take the form of Eliot's positing a dissociation of sensibility in the seventeenth century or Pound's condemnation of "rhetorical swish" in the nineteenth, they are based on the Modernists' recognition of the rise of prose since the late Renaissance as an increasingly effective mode of linguistic presentation, and the concurrent "decline" of poetry as an increasingly obfuscated mode of presentation.

The remedy for dissociation of sensibility, obfuscation, "emotional slither," the depleted charge of poetic words in general is condensation. To use, for the moment, an example from a Modernist other than Pound: in Eliot's vivid reconstruction of the mind of the Metaphysical poet, images were "telescoped" so that, had the Metaphysical reappeared in the modern world, he would be able to respond at once to the smell of cooking, Spinoza's ideas, and the sound of a typewriter, and to unite these into a "new whole." Eliot purposely uses elements for his "new whole" which would usually be considered highly disparate; the only unity, in fact, that the olfactory, intellectual, and auditory experiences have is a contiguous one, a union in the reality of the poet's physical situation. And so, once again, the reader is confronted with a species of metonymy: the whole of a poem made up of the parts of cooking smells, one's reading, and typing sounds involves, as Lodge puts it, a "condensation of contexture," which contexture is here the entirety of the perceiver's surroundings. Deletion, which in turn involves selection and substitution, would apply to the many elements in the poet's environment which are not included in the whole. It is of passing interest, by the way, that Eliot does not pursue this obverse side of condensation, that he ignores the process of real deletion on which a "new whole" must be based.

Condensation, then, must depend on the deletion of syntactic and semantic elements in a metonymic chain, and on the consequent "bivalency" of the elements which remain. The Janus-faced nature of condensation traits in Pound's style is most easily approached through simple paronomasia (which, however, is far too common in poetic styles to be a marked trait), and more importantly through ambivalent references of pronouns. It is with an eye to this latter simple approach that I should like to forward some initial examples of condensation.

Pronouns and Condensation

I should like to return briefly to the topic of linguistic deletion since, as I indicated above and in Chapter 3, the process has affinities with both fragmentation and condensation. The reader will recall that Bolinger states deletions are done "under identity," and that "omitting something from a construction is generally a guarantee that the missing element is somewhere in the context." Pronouns are divided into two classes in English based on the type of context in which they occur; third-person pronouns employ a complex context which can range from a reference to an NP in the course of a preceding syntagm ("co-reference") to generalized or even metaphysical reference (a demonstrative referring to a bundle of ideas, or the "it" in "It's going to rain"). First- and second-person pronouns have an "existential" or "illocutionary" context in the real world; the pronoun "I" for example has the direct force of immediate identity. First-person pronouns can sometimes have a problematic status in *The Cantos,* and I will take these up in a later chapter. It is with third-person pronouns, however, that I am here concerned since they offer a simple paradigm of condensation.

It would be well to note that third-person pronouns usually undergo substitution relations and are thus a species of "metaphor." Freshman writers are ceaselessly cautioned against ambiguous pronoun reference on the basis of such "one to one" substitution. Most third-person pronouns, however, have a "gestural" significance, and thus they have a "demonstrative" quality (in fact, some linguists theorize that *all* third-person pronouns began as demonstratives). If I say to my auditor about a passing acquaintance, "He walks around in a daze," I am clearly not substituting "he" for a linguistic element, but for the actual person to whom the pronoun refers. Consequently, such reference is continuous and metonymic.

The advancing of the patterns of common speech, no matter how vague as a poetic program, has been one of the major tenets of Modernist poetry, and, indeed, it does seem as if writers like Pound use third-person pronouns in a manner much more like that employed in speech than in writing. Such is the case in the conflated anecdotes in Canto 19, the "Business" canto; this "pastiche," as the *Companion* rightly calls it, adopts the assumption between speaker and auditor of common reference in a real-world context. In each of the verse paragraphs which make up this canto, one or more pronouns arise which have ambivalent, complicated, or nonexistent reference. In the first verse paragraph, for example, the folk-hero who takes a crucial invention "up to Manhattan, / To the big company" which will "have to install" the mysterious device is never identified. The "he" here stands for all those small-time backyard inventors whose creations (like the carburetor which will make a gallon of gas stretch for two hundred miles) are suppressed by corporate giants whose profits are threatened. Verse paragraph two contains a number of "characters" only one of whom may be identified (and that only with the aid of the *Companion* or Edwards and Vasse); the initial "we" remains unspecified throughout what follows, the "I" refers to Pound (but to Pound-the-author-of-the-canto, or to the "historical" Pound?), the "he" which refers to the "stubby little man" can only be identified by another reference in the *ABC of Economics* to Arthur Griffiths, and the curious "pronomial" " 'Lemme-at-'em' " who is described as being "like a bull-dog in a mackintosh" is thoroughly enigmatic. The "jolly chaps" about whom "Vlettmann" (who is also unidentified) says that "they used to go by / Under my window . . . singing the *Hé Sloveny*" seem to be Czech nationalists, who may or may not reappear in the first line of the fifth verse paragraph: "Yes, Vlettmann, and the Russian boys didn't shoot 'em." The Steffens anecdote in this paragraph, which is itself unidentifiable, again, without recourse to material outside *The Cantos*, is made even more baffling by a confusing mixture of "he's" ("And he'd keep about three days ahead of the lobby," referring evidently to Carranza), and "they"s ("And then they jawed for two hours," referring probably to Carranza and Steffens). In verse paragraph eight (on page 87), two diplomats are identified by name as "Wurmsdorf" and "Ptierstoff" but the syntax of the anecdote effectively confuses the two:

1	"So there was my ole man sitting,
2	They were in arm-chairs, according to protocol,
3	And next him his nephew Mr. Wurmsdorf,
4	And old Ptierstoff, for purely family reasons,
5	Personal reasons, was held in great esteem
6	by his relatives,
7	And he had his despatches from St. Petersburg,
8	And Wurmsdorf had his from Vienna,
9	And he knew, and they knew, and each knew
10	That the other knew that the other knew he knew,
11	And Wurmsdorf was just reaching into his pocket,
12	That was to start things, and then my ole man
13	Said it:
14	Albert, and the rest of it.
15	Those days are gone by for ever."

The references in lines 4 through 8 are relatively clear, but to whom does the "ole man" refer (the *Companion* suggests that this is the uncle of Wurmsdorf), or, more importantly, the "my" which seems to indicate the storyteller himself? What of the concluding anecdote concerning the Indian prostitutes? This story follows immediately on the heels of the preceding anecdote, and like it is enclosed in quotation marks, and thus seems to be issue out of the mouth of the same person who describes the scene with the diplomats. But what is the connection between the two stories? On the other hand, the Wurmsdorf-Ptierstoff paragraph ends with a quoted re-mark by the "ole man," and yet the "ole man" does not seem to be the quoted speaker in the next verse paragraph. Meanwhile, every one of the proper names, with the exception of the familiar "Steff" for Lincoln Steffens, is either concocted by Pound, or, as in the case of "Jim" on page 87, is certainly not immediately clear.

My questions are not entirely rhetorical; many of them would come forward in the mind of the interested reader unequipped with a handbook to *The Cantos*. In Canto 19, our oft-beset but patient reader is not faced with a perplexing array of fragments and syntactic deletions with which he has hitherto dealt with such good faith, but with a series of stories which are fairly coherent syntactically; the problem, of course, is that the events and persons to which the stories so familiarly refer are, within the context of *The Cantos* alone, impossibly cryptic. And so are they meant to be by Pound. The mysterious pronouns here are only minor keys to a more important form of semantic condensation which accords to the canto's characters and actions a universality in the world of the text's discourse. Characters like the backyard inventor, the capitalist robber barons made powerless by their own convoluted holdings, and the wistful, ineffective diplomats are what Marxist critics would call "types." Of the type, Georg Lukács says it is "a peculiar synthesis which organically binds together the general and the particular both in characters and situations . . . rendering concrete the peaks and limits of men and epochs."[9] The Communist Lukacs' "peaks and limits of men and epochs" has a profound affinity here with Pound's desire to write an epic "including history"; Pound is after all aiming at a realism which eschews both the "lifeless average" (as Lukacs puts it) of the Naturalists, and the "subjective interior" of the Symbolists. The characters of *The Cantos* are at once historically authentic as individuals and psychologically authentic as types. The phrase "psychologically authentic" is inexact, but it is difficult to find a terminology which would fit Pound's conception of recurrent "mind states" which animate history. And Pound presents these mind states directly by allowing his characters throughout *The Cantos* to speak for themselves (Pound is not often enough given credit for his skill at recording dialogue and dialect); the "direct presentation" which bulked so large in Imagism and which was turned toward objects has in the latter part of the first thirty cantos become more and more concerned with persons.

Syntactic Aspects of Condensation

When I turn from the species of semantic condensation which enfolds the individuals who make up a type in the ambivalent pronoun or epithet and center my attention on various instances of purely syntactic condensation, I am once again on the familiar ground of the unfamiliar. In the interests of brevity, I should like first to advance three random examples of condensation before concluding this chapter with instances of condensation as it appears in a single canto. My "exhibits," then (the condensations have been italicized):

(1)   Great bulk, huge mass, thesaurus;
        Ecbatan, the clock ticks and fades out
        The bride awaiting the god's touch; Ecbatan,
        City of patterned streets;
                    (Canto 16, page 17, lines 1–4)
(2)   Then file and candles, e li mestiers ecoutes;
        Scene for the battle only, but still scene,
        Pennons and standards y cavals armatz
        Not mere succession of strokes, sightless narration
                    (Canto 7, page 24, lines 11–14)
(3)   Sound slender, quasi tinnula,
        Ligur' aoide: Si no'us vei, Domna don plus mi cal,
        Negus vezer mon bel pensar no val."
        Between the two almond trees flowering,
        The viel held close to his side;
        And another: s'adora".
        "Possum ego naturae
        non meminisse tuae!" Qui son Properzio ed Ovidio.
                    (Canto 20, page 89, lines 1–8)

I have already discussed the second and third passages and their uses of fragmentation in Chapter 3, the former in terms of embedded fragments, and the latter in regard to "cento" form. And, in fact, in each of the passages above the reader is confronted with some form of fragmentation with which I have dealt in the preceding chapter. Unfortunately, lacking the elaborate statistical coefficients which would corroborate the association, I can only suggest that fragmentation and condensation appear to occur together with high frequency in certain microcontexts. In the underlined microcontexts the reader will at once notice that condensation must be embedded between two structures, to each of which the condensation could refer. The effect of such Janus-faced signification, I shall argue, is that it often binds passages made otherwise disparate by fragmentation, although, given the high level of fragmentation in *A Draft of XXX Cantos*, condensations themselves are frequently fragments. Actually, as I pointed out in Chapter 3, linguistic markers for condensation, with the exception of the simple "pronoun-type," are absent; the reader notes a foregrounding only through semantic signals.

In the semantic field of quotation one, for example, most of the signifieds point to Ecbatan, "city of patterned streets." Line one's "bulk," "mass," and "thesaurus" surely share this field, and the "clock" of line two, although more obscurely related to the field, shares the feature "mortality" with the city on the basis of the hypogram "humans die, and thus their physical traces also fade," a very common matrix in poetry ("Ozymandias" immediately comes to mind). But what of the "bride" and "god" of line 3? Does the bride await as the "clock ticks?" Or is the "god" the deified city to whom the bride is to be "sacrificed"? The hypograms which allow the bivalence, like the "mortality" seme above, are common; brides are not infrequently kept waiting at the church, or temple, door for their spouses-to-be, be these gods or men. And the elevation of the city to the status of a god is not uncommon in antiquity (witness Rome). The *Companion's* explanation of the bride is ingenious: "the transition from the fertility rites of the earth cult to the cult of the sky and the heavenly bodies marks the beginnings of astronomy and the creation of the calendar, i.e., the measuring of time by observing the stars" (*Companion, 17*). Hence, in the terms of this interpretation, the bride is related (contrastively?) to the "clock" of line 2. She does not seem to be related to Ecbatan at all, or, if a relation exists, it is that the bride is a watershed between two ways of thinking about the universe in the physical and historical context of the city: this latter seems a strained proposition, but if we discount it, we are left with an unrelated shift of the field within these four lines. But the syntagm created by these lines is not unidirectional, and, thus, we do not have to choose between either one possible signified for the line, or no possible signifieds at all; in fact, the passage also points back to Danae who appears at the conclusion of the preceding canto. Moreover, these lines, and the verse paragraph in which they are embedded, act as a model for the remainder of the canto. The hypograms which inform Canto 5 make this clear; the "measureless seas and stars," the "three sorts of blue" which represent "shades" of time, the Catullan and Frazerian resonances of "Arunculeia," and even Varchi's exact historicism in recounting the assassination of Alessandro dei Medici all share the "barb of time" on which are stuck the cyclical, seasonal time of the bride, and the prolonged, historical time of the city.

Condensation in the second example is less problematic, but line 2 refers not only to the lines which bracket it, but to the final lines as well. In fact, it is the "file and candles" of line 1 which seem to give scholars trouble, and not the ambivalence of line 2. The *Companion* seems confused, and offers three possibilities: 1) the "file" refers to a line of people carrying "candles" in a religious procession 2) the "file" is a "large replica of a file" carried by craftsmen who, for some obscure reason, are also carrying candles 3) the "file" (after Makin) is the "traditional implement used by the Latin poets for polishing their verses, and the 'candles' [are] a means a lucubration for poets too poor to afford an oil lamp" (*Companion, 29*).[10] Line 1, then, includes a kind of mock-condensation which contrasts with true condensation in that the former is ambiguous rather than ambivalent. But to return to line 2: the foregrounded words here are, of course, "scene" and "battle." "Battle" shares an obvious semantic field with line 3, and "scene" may share signifieds with line 1, and certainly shares them with line 4. The line itself contains the relation between "battle" and "scene," and therefore unites the disparate fields of lines 1, 3, and 4; Pound intends us, I think, to read "scene" in both its meaning as "place of enactment" and as "place portrayed," thus allowing semantic associations with the "masters" and "masterly narration" implied by lines 1 and 4, as well as with the colorful "file" of armored horses in line 3.

Finally, in passage three it may be well to sort out the semantic elements which this unit comprises before I turn to the passage's condensations: line 1 seems to serve as the model for the lines following; line 2, in its Homeric "ligur' aoide" is in rough apposition to "sound slender," and the verses by Benart which follow in this line and the next one are in a kind of exemplary apposition to "ligur' aoide"; the singer holding the "viel" in lines 3 and 4 may be said to sing the "slender" song; and the quotes from Cavalcanti (line 6) and Propertius (lines 7 and 8) are further exhibits of the "ligur' aoide"; the passage concludes with the "presentation" of Ovid and Propertius. The juxtaposition of these privileged singers (chronologically, Homer, Propertius, Ovid, Benart, and Cavalcanti) is itself a kind of condensation, and one familiar to readers of Pound; each represents the Imagistic virtues of precision in observation and presentation. And, like the heroes "by their fountains" of Canto 16, these literary heroes are apotheosized statically in lines 4 and 5: the "movement" of the poets' words which surrounds these lines is in contrast to the stasis of the singer between the flowering trees. Consequently, these eight lines which open the canto, form the model for what follows; this is, after all, the "Lotus-Eaters" canto, and "stasis" is one of its reigning signs. The identification of the holder of the "viel" to which the "his" of line 5 refers is not specified. The pronoun, once again, might serve to designate any of the "makers" whom Pound presents in the passage. The "viel" to be sure is a Provençal instrument (or, at any rate, the Provençal *word* for this instrument), but since all of the poets are "singers" (as opposed to "writers"), the "viel" is a metonymy for them all.

Functions of Condensation in Canto 21

I have chosen examples of condensation from each page of this canto except the first:

(1)   "Doveva temerlo qualunque era in stato;"
      And *"that man sweated blood to put through that railway"*;
      "Could you", wrote Mr. Jefferson,
      "Find me a gardener . . ."

                                          (page 97)

(2)   Half a dozen years
                 (affatigandose per su piacer o non)
            And at the end of that time, to find them, if they
            Choose, a conveyance to their own country . . .
                                                        (page 97)
(3)   That signor Galeaz Sforza Visconti has wished me
            To stand sponsor to all of his children.
            Another war without glory, and another peace without
                                                              quiet.
            And the Sultan sent him an assassin, his brother;
                                                        (page 98)
(4)   And there was grass on the floor of the temple,
            Or where the floor of it might have been;
                 Gold fades in the gloom,
                 Under the blue-black roof, Placidia's,
            Of the exarchate; and we sit here
            By the arena, *les gradins.* . .
                                                        (page 98)
(5)   Floating flame in the air, gonads in organdy,
            Dry flamelet, a petal borne in the wind.
            Gignetei kalon.
            Impenetrable as the ignorance of old women.
                                                        (page 99)
(6)   Moon on the palm-leaf,
                          confusion;
            Confusion, source of renewals;
                                                        (page 100)

Once again, I have italicized the lines embodying condensation. Although I
have listed these passages in the order in which they appear in the canto, I
should like to discuss them in terms of the degrees of complexity they
reflect. Passages five and six, then, represent the simplest forms of condensation here, and I shall examine them first. Two and four (with one and
six) rely on intratextual reference, and are, moreover, in themselves more
complex than the last passages, while passage three seems thoroughly
enigmatic.

   The "gignetei kalon" of five, "beauty is born" (reminiscent of Yeats's
"terrible beauty"), is unlike the condensation structures I have discussed so
far in that it is pointed to, rather than being itself pointing. The thirteen
lines which precede it (which I have omitted for the sake, once again, of
brevity) "rise," as the *Companion* rightly puts it, "to a climax of passion out
of which 'a thing of beauty is born'" (*Companion*, 88). The line which
follows the structure can arguably be read in apposition to "beauty":
beauty, as *The Cantos* never tire of telling us, is a mystery (in all senses of
the word), and, as such, is "impenetrable"; the passage's fourth line, in
other words, is a rare example of simile in the early cantos. Passage six

harks back to the "basis of renewals" passage of the preceding canto (". . . jungle, / Basis of renewal, renewals . . . Wilderness of renewals, confusion / Basis of renewals, subsistence," pages 91 and 92). The use of "confusion" in that canto relies on the two senses of the word, "confusion" as "distraction," and "confusion" as "tumultuous mixture." In passage six, Pound uses the latter sense (with, however, echoes of the former). The "palm leaf," then, is part of the "jungle" which is the "source of renewals" in the third line, with the isolated "confusion" acting as a pivot between the two.

Of the condensations in the remaining four passages, three involve intratextual references; the reference to Pound's grandfather in (1) foreshadows the full anecdote in Canto 22 to which this characterization belongs, (2) recurs to the Malatesta cantos (Canto 8, page 29), and (4) comprises two intratextual references, one, "Gold fades . . .," to Cantos 11 and 17 (among others), and the second, "By the arena . . .," to Canto 12 (among others). The shift from intertextual to intratextual reference in *The Cantos* is interesting to observe, and I shall take it up shortly at the end of this chapter.

If condensation possesses the trait of being able to integrate itself "into either of two other discrete structures" (as Baker puts it), then passage one poses a dilemma: Pound's grandfather and his railroad seem to have nothing to do either with a quattrocento condottiere ("Doveva temerlo . . ."), or with Jefferson's whimsical desire for a french-horn-playing gardener. Yet, looking forward to Canto 21, the reader finds that Thaddeus Pound is offered as yet another example, like the Quaker Hamish in Canto 13, of the resourceful capitalist who creates real value through ingenuity and hard work, despite inertia and enmity from the powers-that-be. Jefferson's request for "domestic servants" who are also musicians is simply an example of his breadth of interests, his "Renaissance" quality, and the sporadic references to the Este family throughout demonstrate the problems that beset rational men in a treacherous polity. Hence, there are implied in the two bracketing lines an instance of a powerful man, Jefferson, who uses his power for enlightenment in a raw New World, and an instance of the idiocy of power in the Renaissance world; both of these instances bear on Thaddeus since he possesses the spirit of *bricolage* and broad-mindedness (he wishes to "educate" rather than "kill off" the "red warriors") which animates Jefferson, while trying to work under the constraints of the "American Curia" of robber barons.

The more cryptic "affatigandose per su . . ." of (2) relies on the reader's rereading the passage in Canto 8 where the line first occurs in regard to the hiring of a "maestro di pentore" by Malatesta:

> So that he may come to live the rest
> Of his life in my lands . . .
> And for this I mean to make due provision

> So that he can work as he likes,
> Or waste his time as he likes
> *(affatigandose per suo piacere o no*
> *non gli manchera la provixione mai)*
> never lacking
>
> provision.
> (page 29)

The intent of this passage is clear; the reader is to see Sigismundo, like Jefferson, as the man of affairs who, nonetheless, takes pains to use his fortune and influence to insure the well-being of the arts. The line which appears on page 97, then, is itself a signifier of the passage which occurs in Canto 8; as intratextuality increases in *The Cantos*, references undergo extreme deletion, to the extent that fragments serve to signify larger stretches of the text. Consequently, the condensation here involves not only the line's integration of the bracketing lines, but also the line's "digest" of an earlier, lengthier passage. The signified passage from Canto 8, then, points to "A certainty of employment for / Half a dozen years" in its reference to Sigismundo's willing allowance of freedom to the artist; and that passage points to "And at the end of that time, to find them, if they choose, a conveyance to their own country" through the same motive.

Passage four, the last of the passages having intratextual reference, although it seems the most enigmatic of the passages I have discussed so far, is actually one of the clearest. The difficulty here arises, yet again, from a combination of fragments, multiple intratextual references, and deletion. Moreover, the passage appears in a verse paragraph which begins with a continuation of the story of the Medici, and thus seems itself an abrupt departure from its context. Yet if the reader looks forward in this paragraph (which runs for roughly two pages, till the end of the canto), he will note that it is largely made up of other intratextual references, and that much of the paragraph is embodied in a mode of purely lyric Imagism. In fact, this canto turns out to be an amalgam; the first part, up to the passage in question, is given over to a meditation on history including references primarily to the Medici and secondarily to Malatesta and Jefferson; the canto's second part adopts a mystic stance and treats of Eleusinian mysteries (the "Gignetei kalon" passage) and the foundation of human endeavor, which nature provides and which is illustrated repeatedly by classical myth. The growing of the grass in what once was Placidia's temple, then, fuses the cyclic temporality of nature with the unidirectional temporality of history; the gold of Placidia's mausoleum may be, as the *Companion* puts it (74), a "Paradisal or 'otherwordly' image," signifying the Mysteries, but it also signifies the permanence of art-in-history. Passage four's condensation, then, points metonymically to the preceding two lines (the "gold in the gloom" literally lies within the "temple"), and points historically to the succeeding two lines (through "Placidia" as a representative of Byzantium and the "exarchate").

The final passage, (3), consequently, is a condensation in both models of this canto: it belongs clearly to the lines preceding it through its reference to the struggles of the Medici in quattrocento Italy; it is tied to what follows it through the contrastive relation between the cyclicity of nature and, here, of history as well, in the final long passage which I have just discussed.

In commenting above on the intratextuality of the condensation passages, I remarked on the shift from intertextual to intratextual reference as the first thirty cantos progress, and I should now like to conclude by suggesting a motive for this shift. It stands to reason that, as Pound builds up his own matrix through the accumulation of individual cantos, he ceases to need the allusive intertextuality of the early cantos. One very evident marker of this shift is the near-total intertextuality of Canto 1 and the near-total independence from other texts in Canto 30. Unfortunately, a quantitative analysis of this shift must await the identification of all references of both types in the first thirty cantos. But one final general comment needs to be made. The purpose of intratextuality within individual later cantos, like Canto 21, seems to be one of condensation. Here, I am using "condensation" in its widest possible sense in that the device transcends the microcontextual and linguistically local function I have discussed in this chapter. I might speak of the "condensation" of entire cantos as a species of semiotic code feature rather than as a style feature. The progression of this study, like the progression of *The Cantos* themselves, has moved gradually toward a wider semiotic matrix than that contained by microcontextual style traits like fragmentation and condensation. Henceforth, I shall have to speak of these stylistic elements as models for the wider semiotic range of the discourse of *The Cantos*. Consequently, in my next chapter, on coupling, I shall move to a semiotic principle which is, like metonymy, a function of the macrocontext as well as the microcontext, an informing principle which allows the disparate strands of microcontext and the enigmas of the macrocontext to engage and to create the form which means which is *The Cantos*.

5
COUPLING

I COME NOW to the last of the microcontextual devices which this study will examine. As I suggested at the conclusion of Chapter 4, "coupling" is, of the devices with which I shall have dealt, the one which is the most thoroughgoing in its cohesive effects on the style of *The Cantos*. Only fragmentation, in sheer quantity of appearances, is as universal in Pound's discourse, but fragmentation, by its very nature, cannot achieve the coherence, the epic unity of *The Cantos*, of which I spoke in the first chapter. In fact, I am now entering the realm of opinion, to an extent, since a significant body of hostile criticism sees no unity in *The Cantos*, and thus for such critics any device which would establish unity is necessarily a will-o'-the-wisp. A dilemma here, and one which I shall examine in greater detail in my final chapter, is the "unplanned" quality of *The Cantos*; it is a well-known fact that, as they were written, various portions of *The Cantos* were subject to Pound's changing artistic, political, and personal interests and that, consequently, *The Cantos* as a whole do not have a predetermined form. How, then, can this *soi-disant* "epic" be said to have *any* formal coherence if its author had no consistent overriding concept of that very form?[1] This is not to say that Pound partisans haven't devoted a good deal of thought to what William McNaughton calls "main form" in *The Cantos*.[2] Such main form often involves important thematic strains which are doubtless present in the poem. We are told by Pound that *The Cantos* are articulated on the model of the Schifanoia fresco, or that the work as a whole is modelled on the Inferno-Purgatorio-Paradiso progression of the *Commedia Divina*, or that *The Cantos*, like *Ulysses*, is a modern "nonorganic" *Odyssey*. Certainly, each of these instances of main form exists in *The Cantos*, as do others, but such *thematic* exegeses are not "form" in the semiotic sense which I am using throughout this study. Even the Hell cantos, for example, although they very loosely incorporate a "journey" into and out of an infernal region, can hardly be said to inform the structure of the first thirty cantos, to say nothing of *The Cantos* as a whole; too many "regions" in the work are left unaccounted for by a Dantean framework. Similar objections arise to the purported Odyssean structure of *The Cantos* since one would be hard put to place large stretches of texts embodying "exhibits" (the Malatesta cantos, the Adams cantos, and so forth) in a "voyaging-hero" structure. Myth, too, has an important purpose in *The Cantos* (especially certain myths like those having to do with Proserpina and Aphrodite), as it does in much Modernist literature, but *The Cantos* are obviously not the *Metamorphoses*. Again, Pound's epic is a poem *including* history, and is thus in some sense *above* (if not outside) history, or, at any rate, forms a dialectic between history and literature.

Yet, at the same time, fragmentation and condensation structures are equally unable to cause *The Cantos* to cohere into some sort of main form. If what I've called "thematic" form above errs in the direction of not being able to supply any cogent, verifiable set of features which articulate the whole work, my microcontextual structures fail in the direction of supplying only disparate linguistic traits which may suggest ways of overcoming reading difficulties, but which simply ignore the forest for the trees.

I should therefore like to advance the notion of coupling to account for the coherence that obtains among the various cantos themselves, as well as among the features, one of which, fragmentation, actually militates against coherence. I draw the term from S. R. Levin's *Linguistic Structures in Poetry*, a study which has achieved a largely favorable reception since its publication; in fact, the concept of coupling is in itself, of the devices discussed herein, the most widely accepted among scholars of poetics.[3] The reason for such fairly wide acceptance is apparent: the scope of Levin's study is not overly ambitious, and the means by which he substantiates his hypothesis are proven ones within the domain of linguistics. Levin seeks to "provide an explanation for" two common responses to poetry: the first is that "poetry is marked by a special kind of unity" which is achieved through "certain structures which are peculiar to the language of poetry"; the second response is illustrated by Valéry's remark that "poetry can be recognized by this remarkable fact, which could serve as its own definition: it tends to reproduce itself in its own form, it stimulates our minds to reconstruct it as it is."[4]

In searching for structures which are "sufficient" for an identification of a text as a poem, Levin argues that "neither meter nor rhyme" will fulfill the conditions necessary for such structures: "In poetry these two structures accompany a linguistic structure which is itself 'poetic.'" Such a linguistic structure

comprises the syntagmatic and paradigmatic functions of language. It is a structure in which semantically and/or phonically equivalent forms occur in equivalent syntagmatic positions, the forms so occurring thus constituting special types of paradigms. These semantic and phonic correspondences frequently extend throughout a poem, or through significant, multi-sentence portions of a poem. (*Structures*, 2, 4)

Levin initially identifies a paradigm as a form occurring within a distinct environment, traditionally the "word-base or -stem." Next, he widens the concept of environment so that it, and not word bases and stems, becomes the "point of departure" for establishing paradigms. Further, paradigms become "equivalence classes . . . whose members are equivalent in some respect to some feature or features, these features always to be understood as lying outside the forms in question—as constituting a *tertium comparationis*" (*Structures*, 2, 3). I shall use a trait of fragmentation as an example of how Levin's "equivalence classes" are built up: the reader may recall Pound's use of participials as supplanting underlying VPs in many fragments. For instance, in the succession of fragments in Canto 2, such structures occur as "Sea-fowl stretching wing-joints, / splashing in rock-hollows," giving the abstract structure NP-VPing-NP/NP (∅)-Ving-P-phrase. Consequently, in this "nominal" environment, where full VPs would be the automatized norm, the participials achieve an equivalence paradigm which, as Levin has explained, "extends throughout . . . significant, multi-sentence portions of a poem." Levin calls these paradigmatic classes "Type I or Position classes" whose "defining characteristic . . . is external; it lies in the way linguistic forms pattern in larger constructions, in the way they are related to other, contextual forms. Such forms are assigned to the same class because they may all occupy the same position in relation to other forms" (*Structures*, 3, 3). In the interests of simplicity, I shall refer to a Type I class as a "syntactic equivalence."

There is a second species of paradigm, a "Type II" paradigm, membership in which is defined by "features external to the class," such features being "extralinguistic" (*Structures*, 3, 6). The term "extralinguistic" rather misleadingly refers to semantic features (which, after all, are a legitimate object of linguistic study): I shall term Type II classes "semantic equivalences." Such extralinguistic features more or less lie in the same province as Riffaterre's matrices and models, and are, therefore, often intertextual in literature. Synonyms, of course, would provide semantic equivalences, as would antonyms. Semantic and syntactic equivalences may overlap; indeed, semantic motivation definitely plays a part in the construction of the syntagm, and, conversely, syntactic motivation to a certain extent motivates meaning. Condensations offer an illustration of combined semantic and syntactic equivalence in that the environment in which a condensation occurs comprises two discrete semantic/syntactic structures bracketing a third structure which can form a meaning link to either; any structure thus occurring in this environment and performing this function would form the paradigm "condensation."

Semantic equivalence is crucial to my discussion because its "exploitation" is "characteristic of poetry." Levin states that a "poem puts into combination, on the syntagmatic axis, elements which, on the basis of their natural [i.e., semantic] equivalences, constitute equivalence classes or para-digms" (*Structures*, 4, 1). This is merely to repeat Jakobson's celebrated dictum that "the poetic function projects the principle of equivalence from the axis of selection onto the axis of combination." Levin summarizes:

> This systematic exploitation takes the form of placing naturally equivalent linguistic elements in equivalent positions, or, put the other way, of using equivalent positions as settings for equivalent phonic and/or semantic elements. In this process there is a convergence of Type II and Type I equivalences, the former set in the latter. (*Structures*, 4, 1)

The convergence of equivalences Levin calls "coupling." A simple, but certainly not "privileged," example of coupling involves the oft-noted fact that two end-rhymed words sometimes foreground mutual synonymy or antonymy. A more complex ramification of coupling in poetry involves the effect that a paradigmatic coupling has on the remainder of the syntagm of which coupling is a part: "when the members of one couple occupying equivalent positions in a parallel construction are naturally equivalent, that fact will serve to foreground whatever phonic or semantic affinities exist" in the remainder of the construction (*Structures*, 4, 6). The following lines from Yeats's "Among School Children" are illustrative:

> The children learn to cipher and to sing,
> To study reading-books and history,
> To cut and sew, be neat in everything
> In the best modern way—[5]

The reader will note first of all the obvious, "traditional" couplings: the rhyme "sing/everything," and the alliteration "cipher/sing." This latter cou-pling, a phonic one, is further foregrounded by the syntactic/semantic equivalence of the two infinitives which is, of course, echoed by the parallel infinitives in lines 2 and 3. "Reading-books" and "history" in line 2 are equivalent in that both act as objects for "to study," and are additionally foregrounded through their identical rhythmic patterns ('u'). There are multiple semantic couplings throughout this brief passage: again, "cipher/sing" have obvious affinities, as do "reading-books/history," while "To study/To cut and sew" are coupled antonymously (and perhaps, ironically, as synonyms for the kind of "study" grammar schools promote). I might continue this analysis at some length, but the important points to be made concerning this example are the following: 1) coupling need not occur solely between two lines (as is the case with rhyme), but may arise within equivalent syntactic positions in one line; 2) coupling which primarily foregrounds one element (a phonic one, for instance) tends, secondarily, to foreground other elements (semantic ones); 3) coupling on the semantic level involves opposed as well as parallel features (especially, as here and in other twentieth-century poetry, for the purposes of irony); 4) coupling is not solely a microcontextual trait, as were fragmentation and condensation. This last is a crucial point because "any theory of poetics based on fusion of form and meaning, if it is to have any explanatory power at all, must not be limited to just a few linguistic forms; it must permit unification of large segments of a poem, and ultimately unification of the poem as a whole" (*Structures*, 4, 8).

Before I turn to the function of coupling in *The Cantos*, I should like to examine one minor problem connected with coupling in Modernist poetry, and to define the intimate association which exists between coupling and metonymy.

Levin's use of comparatively "short" (as well as traditional) texts presents an obstacle for the purposes of my study. Like Riffaterre, Levin aims at the establishment of structural devices in poetry rather than at explication of texts, and thus he confines himself to the examination of lyric poems (of less than thirty lines) for the purposes of illustration only. My aim, on the other hand, is chiefly that of defining the specific form of *A Draft of XXX Cantos*, a body of poetry of a length greater than any dreamt of in these two critics' philosophies. Nevertheless, as Levin's remarks above ("These correspondences frequently extend . . . through significant . . . portions of a poem") seem to suggest, coupling may be a device, if anything, even more appropriate for the development of a long poem than a short one, especially if such a long poem is microcontextually as fragmented as *The Cantos*.

Levin contends that an "important effect of coupling is to unite *in praesentia* terms that are otherwise united *in absentia*, and these forms that are united *in praesentia* are not simply members of the same syntactic paradigm; they are also members of the same Type II paradigm" (*Structures*, 4, 9). This means that actual, coupled terms (say, "to cipher/to sing") which belong to the same underlying semantic field ("school exercises," among others) not only function as syntactic "objects" of "to learn" (syntactic paradigm), but also as phonically and semantically related terms. Levin's "effect of coupling" actually echoes Jakobson's description of the processes of figuration; the difference here is that coupling unites the two terms of the figure within the syntagm. Moreover, to use again the Yeats example, "to cipher" is not a substitution for "to sing" since the two terms are not strictly synonymous; rather, they exist contiguously in the context "schoolroom," and are thus a metonymy. Furthermore, alliteration couples the two terms on the phonic level through a natural paradigm established by initial /s/; consequently, a new dimension is added to the figurative and semantic process—an aural dimension typical of (but not entirely restricted to) poetry.

Coupling and Fragmentation

In this section I shall examine, at the risk of redundancy, various instances of fragmentation types, and the novel role which coupling plays within fragmentation. In the following verse paragraph, with the exception of the repeated "The dogs leap . . ." and the concluding "The empty armor . . . ," the fragments are of the VP-deleted type:

1	The dogs leap on Actaeon,
2	"Hither, hither, Actaeon,"
3	Spotted stag of the wood;
4	Gold, gold, a sheaf of hair,
5	Thick like a wheat swath,
6	Blaze, blaze in the sun,
7	The dogs leap on Actaeon.
8	Stumbling, stumbling along in the wood,
9	Muttering, muttering Ovid:
10	"Pergusa . . . pool . . . pool . . . Gargaphia,
11	"Pool . . . pool of Salmacis."
12	The empty armour shakes as the cygnet moves

(Canto 4, pages 14–15)

For the rhetorically astute reader, the "syntactic anaphora" of lines 4 and 5, and 8 and 9 (and to an extent 11) will be foregrounded. The "gold/blaze" coupling demonstrates a syntactic paradigm if the reader is willing to view "gold," not as a modifier of "hair," but as a self-sufficient NP, and my discussion of the use of color terms in *The Cantos* in Chapter 2 should support this view. Obviously, semantic coupling is present between the two terms, and even phonic coupling can be argued on the basis of consonance (repeated /l/). "Muttering/stumbling" clearly involves a syntactic equivalence, and, for this reader at any rate, a semantic equivalence as well (both terms arguably share the seme "preoccupation"). "Pool . . . pool" and "Hither, hither" share the "duplex" feature of the couplings above, and the former, within its own immediate syntagm, is phonically and semantically coupled with "Pergusa" of the preceding line. Such foregrounded couplings abound in this passage: "Actaeon/Actaeon" (lines 1 and 2), "Pergusa/pool" and "pool/Gargaphia" (phonic and semantic convergence), and, over a large range, "The dogs leap/The empty armour shakes."

This last instance, in fact, brings me closer to my goal of demonstrating the function of coupling in uniting the disparate elements induced by fragmentation. These two full sentences which serve to bracket the passage at hand share rough syntactic identity (NP-VP-present), and a more obscure, but nonetheless undeniable, semantic identity; both, of course, involve metamorphoses, and thus share synonymy, and the stories from which the lines are drawn involve on the one hand capture and on the

other escape (and are therefore antonymous). The couplings of the fragmented NPs in lines 10 and 11, united under the intratextual feature "Ovid,"
exhibit the same sort of close interconnectedness; "pool" in line 10 acts as a
pivot for a kind of chiasmus, having the names of pools as end-terms, and
the same role is given to "Pool" of line 11 in joining "Gargaphia" to "Sal-
macis." Further, the imagined "wood" in which Actaeon sees Diana and
through which he attempts to escape (line 3) is coupled with the real (that
is, nonmythical) "wood" through which Ovid "stumbles and mutters" as
he composes the various "pool" stories (line 8).

Another example, this time a familiar one, from Canto 7:

> Another day, between walls of a sham Mycenian,
> "Toc" sphinxes, sham-Memphis columns,
> And beneath the jazz a cortex, a stiffness or stillness,
>   Shell of the older house.
> Brown-yellow wood, and the no colour plaster,
> Dry professorial talk . . .
>   now stilling the ill beat music,
> House expulsed by this house.
>
> (Canto 7, page 26)

I shan't tax my reader's patience any further with the iteration of obvious
phonic couplings (which, after all, can just as well be explained as standard
devices of prosody) except to say that phonic couplings here are not only
aural, but semantic as well; the coupling " 'Toc' sphinxes, sham-Memphis"
should illustrate this sufficiently. The rhetorical parallels of my preceding
example are absent here, and except for the common VP-deleted fragments, syntactic equivalence of *any* sort appears to be nonexistent. Semantic equivalences are copious in this passage, most sharing the field "sham,
empty." But the terms of such equivalences must also be included in similar
syntactic positions to effect coupling.

One avenue of syntactic approach to this passage is through the P-
phrases which begin in lines 1 and 3: "between walls . . ." and "beneath the
jazz . . ." Line 2 describes what is "beneath the jazz," and thus these lines
are in rough equivalence; the semantic feature "spurious" informs " 'Toc' "
and "sham" of line 2, and "shell" of line 4, and the "columns" of 2 and the
"house" of 4 share an obvious semantic field. Phonic equivalences in these
first four lines are copious, and include the following (among others):
"Sphinxes/cortex" (joined semantically as contained objects), "sham/shell"
("spurious" seme), and "stiffness/stillness" ("the cortex is a stiffness"/"the
cortex is a stillness"). Plausibly, an equivalence through absence is established here through the deletion of copulae after line 1 and after "the jazz"
in line 3; the deep structure of these syntagms, then, would be "between
walls are sphinxes and columns," and "beneath the jazz is a cortex." The

couplings in lines 5 through 8 are more complex than those in the initial four lines, and the more enigmatic intent of these lines compounds the difficulty. One coupling, line 5, is internal: phonically the two terms "Brown-yellow wood" and "no colour plaster" are united through repeated /l/, and semantically through the antonymy based on " ± color" and through the synonymy based on "building materials." A similar internal coupling occurs in line 7 where, once again, phonic equivalence is established through /l/; semantic equivalence occurs between "stilling" and "ill beat" through the antonymous "noise." This latter semantic coupling is carried over in line 8 where "expulsion" shares the same semantic field as "stilling the music."

Line 6, "Dry professorial talk . . .," cannot be accounted for in terms of coupling. In fact, line 6 is a condensation which may with equal justice be grouped with the objects "beneath the jazz," or with line 7 as that line's subject NP ("the talk stills the music"). If we read line 6 as a unit which ends lines 3 through 5, "Dry professorial talk" becomes the last term in a chain of catalogued NP fragments; if we read it in association with line 7, it becomes an NP "pivot" modified by the participial structure of 7. Since, however, the "ill beat music" is probably synonymous with the "jazz" of 3, and since the "talk" cannot both be beneath the "jazz" and "stilling" it, line 6 probably introduces a new syntagm. The self-sufficiency of line 6, finally, is compounded by the use of ellipses which signify deletion (cf. my discussion of "Papyrus" in Chapter 2). Before I turn to further instances of coupling, I should like to point out that the reason condensation may resist coupling is that the former is itself a unifying structure in *The Cantos*, and, because of its ambivalent semantic position, any couplings between a condensation and surrounding structures would be highly complicated (this is not to say, of course, that such "duplex" couplings do not exist).

I suggested above that Modernist verse perforce employs couplings in many ways different from couplings which arise in traditional verse. Two differences between a Modernist coupling and a traditional coupling involve the assumption of nondeleted syntax and accurate "positioning" through meter in most traditional poetry. Levin is able to mark interlinear syntactic equivalence in pre-twentieth-century poetry quite easily because some positions (that is, simply, prosodic feet) are given a priori. Further, more often than not, poets until the second half of the nineteenth century employ syntactic deletion either inadvertently or when deletion is automatized (as, for example, in the catalogue). Levin illustrates coupling early on, for instance, with four lines from Pope's *Epistle to James Craggs, Esq.*:

> A Soul as full of Worth as void of Pride,
> Which nothing seeks to show, or needs to hide,
> Which nor to guilt nor fear its Caution owes,
> And boasts warmth that from no passion flows;

This specimen is not exceptional; Levin devotes his most complete explication to Shakespeare's Sonnet 30, and he draws numerous examples from the more regular of Dickinson's short poems. The elaborate rhetorical schematization of Pope's couplets, the fact that these *are* couplets, the anaphora which joins the two couplets, and the "uniformity" (as Levin puts it) of the semantic field here all contribute to the ease with which couplings are established by the poet and detected by the reader. And, although these four lines do not themselves comprise a full syntactic structure (despite embedded VPs), they act as a modification for the full structure which follows. The reader may consider then how different, how irregular, seem Pound's eight lines from Canto 7. Pope uses his ten positions per line with predictable exactitude: "A Soul," occupying positions one and two, is followed by parallel constructions occupying, respectively, positions three through six, and seven through ten; the same sort of parallelism operates in line 2. Position ten, the end-rhymes, in lines 1 and 2 is occupied by terms which are phonically and semantically (through antonymy) equivalent. Pound's lines, on the other hand, are of course syllabically greatly unequal: the syllable-counts for Pound's eight lines are 14, 8, 14, 6, 11, 7, 8, and 6; since the initial positions in the only possibly equivalent lines (by virtue of equal syllables), lines 1 and 3, are syntactically and semantically at odds, and since, moreover, even the meter of these lines shifts repeatedly, it is impossible to determine interlinear couplings by position alone. Intralinear couplings are more apparent, and, in fact, Pound does seem to employ parallel syntactic structures for coupling nearly as much as, but in a different fashion from, Pope.

Coupling within Cantos

Within the microcontext of fragmentation structures, coupling and, to a lesser degree, condensation function as cohesive devices, and, equipped with a knowledge of the formal and semantic operations of fragmentation, condensation, and coupling, the reader may make his way through "local" difficulties in *The Cantos*. I shall now enlarge the scope of my examination to include the ways in which coupling in individual cantos functions to cause formal coherence.

I might begin this discussion by making a few brief remarks about Canto 45, the Usura canto, and Brooke-Rose's exhaustive description of that canto, referred to in Chapter 1. Although Canto 45 is outside the province of this study, it is so thorough an example of coupling on a "canto-wide" basis that it deserves notice. Nonetheless, this canto is probably not quantitatively typical of coupling in *The Cantos* as a whole; as Brooke-Rose's analysis demonstrates, the Usura canto is unusually cohesive on all levels, phonic, grammatical, rhetorical, and semantic. Moreover, some devices typical of most of the rest of *The Cantos*, like fragmentation, are nearly absent, and others, like nominalization, are present only "semantically" on the level of the deep structure. This is to say nothing, of course, of the exceptionally archaic diction of this canto, and its openly discursive intent.

Canto 45, although not typical of the majority of *The Cantos*, is not wholly exceptional, however. Two of the cantos in the first thirty, 14 and 30, are formally very similar; Canto 30, of course, bears the strongest resemblance to 45 through its use of a single informing matrix which might be made apparent as "Pity and Time work together to defeat humanity." Canto 14 is related to both 30 and 45 through the perjorative semantic intent of all three cantos, and, once again, through the homogeneity of the matrix.

Canto 14 comprises six verse paragraphs, and in the interests of brevity, I should first like to summarize the models and hypograms of each paragraph: 1) politicians, their characteristics, their audience in hell; 2) betrayers of language, their characteristics; 3) betrayers of language, catalogue of the "elements" of hell, "sadic mothers," the placards; 4) elements of hell, bigots, "agents provocateurs"; 5) elements of hell, vice crusaders; 6) elements of hell, a variety of its denizens (academics, slum owners and so on). In other words, these paragraphs deal with essentially two elements—the "topography" of hell and its inhabitants. And these elements are portrayed, as I pointed out in Chapter 3, in nominalized fragments. Consequently, since nominalized fragments monopolize this canto, positional equivalence will be easy to demonstrate; in the first paragraph, for example, (excluding the initial line from Dante), "[Lloyd Georg]e" and "[Wilso]n" stand in apposition to "politicians" of line 2, and these two are characterized in the five lines which follow by nearly identical structures (the underlying structure of which is possessive-NP-participial-P-phrase), the exception being line 5 which is the abbreviated participial-NP. Lines 9 and 10 are structurally and semantically interchangeable: participial-NP-P-phrase//"Addressing"/"audience" seme//"through-in"/"despicable place" seme. The first half of this paragraph is joined paratactically to the second at line 12 with the name of another politician ("Balfour"), who is characterized by the same concatenation of participials and NPs structurally, and by the same semantic field ("forbidden" body parts) as the first two politicians: and so through two further politicos and their attendant bodily horrors.

The "elements of hell," in verse paragraph five for example, enjoy even simpler coupling since a catalogue of NPs accompanied by characterizing participials and P-phrases is necessarily and even rigidly coupled.

Canto 30's first verse paragraph, like the entirety of Canto 14, presents so clear a case for coupling that I shan't indulge in a lengthy discussion of its constituent elements. Lines 1 through 3 are coupled by means of the doubled NPs in the first two lines ("Compleynt, compleynt"/"Artemis, Artemis"), and by means of the syntactic reversal that both clauses employ

("Compleynt I heard upon a day," and "Artemis agaynst Pity lifted her wail"). Lines 4 through 8 are coupled simply through anaphora and through semantic parallelism (by the model "unhealthy action of pity"). Lines 10 and 11, again, are anaphoric, and the remaining seven lines of this paragraph, although not positionally coupled through strict anaphora, are coupled by means of equally constraining end-rhymes and assonance (in fact, the paragraph as a whole is bound by fairly regular rhyming, including some internal rhymes like "season/reason" of lines 12 and 13). The orthography and lexicon of the paragraph mirror such "traditional" coupling: "agaynst," "causeth," "befouleth," "fayre," and so forth. Verse paragraph two embodies similar couplings and the same general lexicon.

The remaining four verse paragraphs of Canto 30, however, depart from the traditional couplings and archaic diction of one and two, and an analysis of this departure will serve to form a link between the obvious couplings in Canto 14 and in the opening of Canto 30, and the troublesome couplings of most of the remaining first thirty cantos. Verse paragraphs three and four are brief, and form a link between the matrix of the canto's first half and the slightly altered matrix of the second:

1	Time is the evil. Evil.
2	A day, and a day
3	Walked the young Pedro baffled,
4	a day and a day
5	After Ignez was murdered.
6	Came the Lords in Lisboa
7	a day, and a day
8	In homage. Seated there
9	dead eyes,
10	Dead hair under the crown,
11	The king still young there beside her.

(pages 147–48)

The most obvious coupling here, of course, is the refrain "A day, and a day" which intervenes between the lines of paragraph three and paragraph four to join the two paragraphs. A further linkage between the paragraphs is afforded by the VP-past in the initial position in lines 3 and 6, creating rough parallelism between these lines (VP-past-NP-modifier). In fact, there are numerous examples of internal syntactic and semantic equivalences in each of the verse paragraphs in this canto. Actually, once the reader becomes conscious of the modes of coupling within limited passages of a canto, the cohesion of individual verse paragraphs seems fairly indisputable; the problem, of course, is the relation, the coupling, between one verse paragraph and another. What, for example, does the initial matrix of paragraphs one and two have to do with the matrix of paragraphs three, four, and five? The initial matrix possesses the models "time-evil," and "history/

historical marriages." Clearly, one coupling involves the equivalence "pity" and "time" as "evils," but the "evil" seme appears to be the only shared semantic feature between the two.

In attempting to resolve the two apparently unrelated matrices, the reader must first recognize the nature of the two goddesses presented in paragraphs one and two: Artemis, as goddess of the hunt and in her character of punisher of Actaeon (Canto 4 and elsewhere), is an obvious enemy of "pity" (here evidently having the connotation "overly tender," "indiscriminately doting"); Aphrodite, quite literally Artemis's opposite number, is the defender of "pity" (having the connotation "compassionate sympathy"). Now, "pity" clearly takes the form, for Artemis, of prohibiting the "clean kill," so that "nothing is now clean slayne / But rotteth away." Skipping forward to paragraph three, the reader will note that this hypogram ("unclean decay") is repeated in the implied story of Pedro and Ignez; it is for Pedro, of course, that "time is the evil," so much so that he resurrects his dead queen in a pitiful attempt to abrogate time and its effects. Moreover, the movement of "levels of time" in this canto is from "mythic" to "historical," and thus pity, which is pernicious in a mythic setting, becomes time, which is equivalently pernicious in an historical setting. Consequently, the elliptical story of the marriage of Lucrezia Borgia (thoroughly descended into history as "Madame " YΛH") and Alfonso d'Este is semantically coupled with Aphrodite's pity and the love of Pedro and Ignez through a relationship of exact opposition; in fact, the Lucrezia-Alfonso story may arguably be the second term in a coupling involving an identical eschewing of "pity" (here with the connotation "sympathy") by Artemis, Alfonso ("has passed here with saying 'O' "), and Lucrezia.

The sixth verse paragraph of Canto 30, the final paragraph of the first thirty cantos, deals exclusively with the bringing of the type-designer Francesco da Bologna to Fano by the printer Soncino under the auspices of Cesare Borgia, and the two concluding lines indicate that, in the same year which saw the introduction of Francesco, the pope Alessandro Borgia (father of Cesare) died. The connection of this information with the subject of paragraph five is obviously provided by the Borgia family, but what does the Borgia family's patronage of a printer and his designer have to do with "pity" and "time" as "evils?" Moreover, this paragraph, like the one which precedes it, possesses none of the lexical and syntatic couplings which unite the first three verse paragraphs; in this regard I should like to mention in passing that cantos disposing of historical material, whether this matter be drawn intertextually from other documents or whether it be "composed" by Pound, do not display the frequency of coupling present in other, less "prosaic" passages (I shall deal with this problem in Chapter 8 on historicism in *The Cantos*). The confusion which surrounds this passage can to an extent be dissipated by concentrating on the familarly elusive and allusive pronouns in "Whence have we carved it in metal" and "and as for text we have taken it"; "it" in both lines refers to an edition of Petrarch issued by Soncino in 1503, the year after Lucrezia's marriage and the same year in which Pope Alexander dies. It is thus the attention to craft and its permanence on the one hand, and the death of the pope, the introduction of printing, and the publication of Petrarch (all signalling the end of the Rinascimento) on the other, with which this passage is concerned. The semantic coupling involving "time" between this passage and the remainder of the canto, then, is obvious; in fact, the lapsing of the Rinascimento is itself, for Pound, an "evil." But what of pity? The semantic relation of the canto's first verse paragraph to its last is not at all clear. Several couplings suggest themselves, although each is tenuous at best: the last paragraph treats of persons who are in Pound's bad books (Petrarch and the Borgias), and the reader is perhaps being instructed to have no pity on these; the introduction of printing allows useless authors to linger on, "rotting away," and consequently "none may seek purity,"; the usurpation by the Borgia of the "text" from a "codex once of the Lords Malatesta" may invoke an *ubi sunt* motif which calls upon both time and pity matrices.

None of these couplings is particularly convincing. Actually, the last verse paragraph of Canto 30 may not be coupled to the entirety of the canto at all; rather, this passage seems to be coupled in part with the canto to which it belongs and in part with the canto which follows it, Canto 31, dealing with the New World. Although, once again, as with my comments above on Canto 45, I have stepped outside the province of this study, it is impossible to discuss the macrocontextual structure of the first thirty cantos without occasional reference to the cantos which follow them. Obviously, the first thirty cantos are not self-sufficient; indeed, as I shall argue later, these cantos may provide a model, structurally and semantically, for much of the remainder of *The Cantos*. Moreover, coupling between cantos is so much a crucial element in causing *The Cantos* to cohere that "centrifugal" tensions are often created inside individual cantos which work against the force of internal, "centripetal" couplings (as in Canto 30), sometimes causing microcontextual fragmentation in those individual cantos.

I should like to remind my reader at this point that, as I noted above, a full explanation of how each individual canto within the first thirty coheres through coupling must await a thorough identification of the sources of these cantos; this is only to say that gaps must necessarily arise in our present readings of the first thirty cantos which cannot be overcome by the techniques of stylistic analysis alone. In the interests of clarification, I wish to advance a tentative grouping of those cantos whose internal unity is not seriously in question. Such a grouping is based on my discussion of formal devices in the preceding chapters, on general agreement among Pound scholars over sources and topoi in the first thirty cantos, and, chiefly, on the concepts of coupling outlined in this chapter; such "unified" cantos include 1 through 16 (with the exception of the "Byron" episode in 16), 18 and 19, 21 and 22, and 24 and 26. The reader will note that 17, 20, 23, 27, 28, and 29 (the problems with 30 being by now apparent) have been omitted from the group. Before I proceed to examine couplings between cantos, I should briefly like to examine the first three of these "anomalous" cantos, and to suggest a possible resolution of the dilemma posed by the conflict between my argument that the first thirty cantos are tightly bound through coupling and what seems to be the unresolvable disjunction of these cantos.

With the exception of Canto 17, the "disjunctive" cantos all lie within the last third of the first thirty, and, in fact, even 17 has a strong affinity with the final third since it is a "new beginning", signalled by the canto's initial "So that", which repeats the final "So that:" of Canto 1. As I argued above in Chapter 3, Canto 17 is characterized by various Imagist formal devices including, of course, highly foregrounded fragmentation. Actually, it is not until the third page of the canto (page 78) that difficulties in reading arise. The first two pages simply embody a reprise of the "ply over ply" hypogram employing familiar and easily decipherable fragmentation markers (VP-deletion, nominalization). I have discussed, again in Chapter 3, the enigmatic "pilot" passage (beginning "Guiding her with oar . . ."), and the shared properties within it of an initial absolute phrase followed by a disintegrating sentence. Whatever the internal difficulties of this passage, however, its coupling with the canto as a whole is clear; the metamorphosis of Venice from the sea repeats other "marine" transformations (the intratextual reference to Canto 2, for example) preceding it. It is the passage that follows the "pilot" passage, page 78, lines 22–35, which creates problems; how are Placidia's tomb ("In the gloom . . ."), the goddesses Athene, Zothar, Aletha, and Kore, and the enigmatic voyager (this last on page 79) related to each other and to the passages which surround them? Obviously, the goddesses have a fairly clear relationship as "privileged" deities of transformation in the universe of Pound's discourse, although the fields from which they are drawn are anomalous (Zothar and Aletha are goddesses from the Poundian pantheon). Moreover, the goddesses are presented within an Imagistic syntagm employing the stylistic devices of pages 76 and 77. The passage on page 79, lines 1–9, seems to be a conflation of the *Odyssey*, Book 10. The reader will recall that Book 10 encompasses the journey of Odysseus and his crew to Telepylos (home of the Laestrygonians) where the "path of day and night are close together" (which may accord with line 3, "Saw the sun for three days, the sun fulvid"), and that, following this disastrous visit, they travel on to Circe's island where Hermes (cf. line 7's "Splendour, as the splendour of Hermes") gives Odysseus a potion to ward off Circe's spell. If this canto does represent a new beginning within the first thirty cantos, then this reference to Odysseus (who has been absent since Canto 1) would be appropriate. Furthermore, lines 22 and 23, page 78 ("'In the gloom . . .'"), have similar intratextual associations, not strictly related to Canto 17.

In other words, Canto 17 presents a formal model of intratextual coupling between cantos. As with Canto 30 in the discussion above, Canto 17 must be read with an eye to the macrocontext of *The Cantos* as a whole (specifically, the *Draft of XXX Cantos*) if it is to be properly understood. Indeed, the other "anomalous" cantos, 20, 23, 27, 28, and 29, are similarly disjunctive within their respective microcontexts. The hypograms and models of Canto 20, for example—"sound slender," Lévy and "noigrandres," the ravings of Niccolo d'Este, Helen viewed by the old men of Troy, and the Lotophagoi—are comprised by one microcontextual model ("Sound slender"/Lévy), and three macrocontextual matrices (Niccolo, Helen/Eleanor/Woman as Destroyer, and the *Odyssey*).

To take one final example: the models and hypograms of Canto 23 are neoplatonic light/Malatesta, the nature of science, Heracles' journey to the West/the setting sun-Helios-Apollo, Provençe-the-wager-Mount Segur, Aeneas, and Phrygia. I shall not attempt to discover a common semantic field for this very disparate group of hypograms, although doubtless, with ingenuity, a semantic relationship might be advanced. Rather, I should like to draw the reader's attention to the fact that this canto shows a high degree of coupling despite its semantic diversity. This fact is especially remarkable considering the large number of intersplicings (even for Pound) of the various fields within the microcontext; these interjections are often confined to a single line, and are of various types. Verse paragraph three, for example, contains parts of three "versions" (one by Pound in English, two from Schweighaeuser's *Athenaeus* in, respectively, Greek and Latin) of a description of the sun's descent into the "low fords of ocean," and, by implication, Heracles' tenth labor.[6] These lines are interrupted by a line alluding to the preceding verse paragraph having to do with the nature of science, and by two lines wherein Pound offers his etymology of ἅλιος, and one line devoted to a similar philological effort ("alixantos, aliotrephes, eiskatebaine, down into"), and, finally, a comment on the "Dantean" accuracy of ἔβα δάφναισι κατάσκιον which Pound renders as "the selv'oscura." The same level of microcontextual disruption occurs in the following verse paragraph, although here the text is solely in English. Verse paragraph four, like verse paragraph six, is coupled quite simply through parataxis which orders the passage into four formal units; these units are internally coupled on the basis of syntactic equivalence through fragmentation and its consequent VP-deletion, and through the use of participials supporting NPs which are spatially coupled through P-phrases. Verse paragraph five is a repetition of the "ply over ply" hypogram, with several lines added in order to create a condensation wherein this hypogram points both to its earlier embodiment in Canto 4 and following and to its present insertion in the "sun descending" matrix. Verse paragraph seven, although representing, as I have noted, a shift in hypogram, is coupled, like four and six, through parataxis, VP-deletion, and spatial arrangement through P-phrases.

Cantos 17, 20, and 23 are parallel to Cantos 27 through 29 on the level of form; both groups exhibit within the individual cantos similar features of disparate semantic variety, microcontextual coupling, and the by now very familiar traits of fragmentation and condensation. When I began my discussion of these disjunctive cantos a few moments ago, I drew the reader's attention to the fact that such disjunction is, if not peculiar to Cantos 20 through 30, at least greatly foregrounded in them. I shall only comment on this tendency toward disjunction at present, noting that no matter how semantically diverse the microcontext may seem as the first thirty cantos progress, no novel matrices are introduced which have not appeared in earlier cantos, nor do new formal devices appear. For the time being, I shall suggest that the processes which cause *The Cantos* as a whole to cohere are established in the text early on, and the progressive "difficulties" of *The Cantos* are difficulties of degree only, the statement and resolution of such formal problems having been clearly outlined in *A Draft of XXX Cantos*.

Coupling between Cantos

The movement from the level of microcontext (which I have heretofore identified as the relation of the line to its verse paragraph or the verse paragraph to its canto) to the level of macrocontext (the relation of cantos to each other and the relation of each section of *The Cantos* to other sections) does not witness a necessary isotopy (see Glossary) between the two levels. It is not certain, for example, that the two types of coupling which exist in the microcontext will exist in the macrocontext; the discovery of positional equivalence between elements of the microcontext in two separate cantos would probably prove specious at best. This is not to say that syntactic equivalence cannot be achieved in a long poem: the *Commedia Divina* may embody sporadic or even frequent instances of such coupling, and, in fact, supporters of the "non-oral" compositions of the *Iliad* and the *Odyssey* would argue just such coupling as evidence of a written origin for these epics, just as supporters of oral origins see couplings as formulae. As I shall contend in the next chapter, however, *The Cantos* as an example of an extended, *free verse* epic are by definition barred from positional equivalence on the level of macrocontext for exactly the same reasons that rigid syntactic equivalence is infrequent on the level of the microcontext (that is, in terms of end-rhymes and so forth).

Nevertheless, as the reader may recall, true coupling in poetry must involve "convergence" of syntactic and semantic equivalences. Consequently, some species of positional "repetition" must occur in the first thirty cantos in order that macrocontextual coupling may take place. Such positions would not be the "natural" ones of the traditional poetic syntagm (the line or the stanza); rather, they would occupy spaces along the grammatical or rhetorical syntagm instead. What might such a grammatical-rhetorical syntagm for *The Cantos* look like? To answer this question, I shall first need to advance a tentative structure of matrices, with their derivative models, for *A Draft of Thirty Cantos*.

Since matrices are never actualized in the poetic text, and since it is the accurate description of actualized models which is crucial to textual analysis, my characterizations of the matrices underlying the first thirty cantos need not be absolutely fixed. Moreover, as will soon become apparent, the matrices I intend to advance are more or less supported by the proponents of main form whose ideas I discussed earlier in this chapter; in other words, what is often called "form," as I argued above, is really a traditional "theme." A "theme" in turn conveniently offers the basis for a matrix when such a theme is generally agreed upon by scholars to exist in a given work; whether such a theme provides an overriding "motive force" for the work (or whether the theme is equivalent to the work's "meaning") is unimportant for the discussion at hand. Although matrices are not made apparent on the level of the text except as models, I shall characterize various matrices by their initial or oft-repeated models when such characterizations are unambiguous. The matrices, then, of *A Draft of XXX Cantos*, in the order in which they appear, are as follows (matrices which appear only once in the first thirty cantos are for the time being omitted): "LORDS OF THE LYRE" (herafter, ANAXIFORMINGES or ANAX), WOMAN AS DE-STROYER (WAD), PROVENCE, LEVELS OF TIME, MYTHIC TRANSFOR-MATION, ELEUSIS, COITUS (hereafter, AURUNCULEIA or AURUN), KUNG, and NEKUIA. The reader will note that I have not attached evaluative designations to these matrices, and, in fact, as the matrices generate models, such models may be " ± benign" in the universe of the discourse. The models generated by these matrices are given below:

MATRIX	generates	*MODELS* (partial list)
ANAXIFORMINGES		Homer, Seafarer, Sordello, Aeschylus, Ovid, Pound.
WAD		Helen, Eleanor, Circe.
PROVENCE		Eleanor, Sordello, Cunizza, Bernart (and many others).
MYTHIC TRANSFORMATION		Sea and Land, Artemis and Actaeon, Dionysus, Aphrodite, Venice.
LEVELS OF TIME (historic)		Rinascimento, Malatesta, Murders, various families and their histories.

LEVELS OF TIME (personal)	"I" (Pound-in-history), Ghosts, Economics, Venice.
ELEUSIS	"Stone Posts," Neoplatonism.
COITUS	Aurunculeia, Aphrodite, Ione, Nicea, Circe.
KUNG	Kung.
NEKUIA	Hell, Purgatory, Paradiso Terrestre.

Let me stress that the importance of this listing for the present discussion does not lie in the establishment of a rigid and exhaustive catalogue of matrices. As I have pointed out previously, since all the sources for *A Draft of XXX Cantos* have not been discovered, such a listing would at any rate be impossible at present. The role of this table is simply to suggest a deep structure for the first thirty cantos analogous to the semes of a word or phrase; in semantics, the semes of a word have no true order (since they are never realized) and a complete listing of semes, given the shifting nature of language (which is parallel to the activity of an infinite series of readers of a text), is impossible. Furthermore, these matrices are evidently fore-grounded by critics through the attention they lend to the models as elements of "themes." Finally, the reader will surely notice both the du-plications that inevitably arise in such a listing, and the ambiguous hier-archy established between some matrices and models. "Helen," for example, is a model for 1) Homer's creation, made apparent in the old Trojan men's remarks on her, and 2) Woman as Destroyer; the distinction between the two models, in fact, would be hard to make. "Eleanor" has the same ambivalent status and such a status may be equivalent to microcon-textual condensation. The matrix I have rendered TRANSFORMATION may just as well have been rendered as a model for LEVELS OF TIME, as well as a distinct matrix (having its own models like "Sea and Land") apart from LEVELS OF TIME (so that "mythic transformation" would, again, repeat models from LEVELS OF TIME). And KUNG, finally, since it is an isotopic model of itself, may be seen as either a model for CHINANESS or a matrix for the later use in *The Cantos* of "Ching Ming."

The "overdetermination" of models from two or more matrices (is PROVENCE its own matrix, a model of "historical time," a model of TRANSFORMATION?) should not surprise anyone with experience of epics. In fact, although Riffaterre does not deal with such a contingency, it may well be that even shorter poems frequently exhibit such overdeter-mination. This condensation of two matrices in the production of one model is one of the basic means by which Pound binds together the macrocontext of the first thirty cantos.

It is now time to return to the problem of plotting a syntagm for *A Draft of XXX Cantos*. Allow me to summarize my remarks on matrices and models with an eye to creating that syntagm: the matricial structure of the first thirty cantos is analogous to the ordering of semes in a word; the "words" which are made apparent from the underlying matrices are overdetermined so that frequently they exhibit condensation; a hierarchy of matrices, or the exact relationship of matrices to models, is difficult to establish because matrices cannot by definition be made apparent. A further question: if condensation is mirrored in the macrocontext, is fragmentation similarly mirrored? The answer, of course, is positive: Cantos 13 ("Kung"), 23, and 30 seem to act as macrocontextual "fragments" wherein deletions seem to exist between the models in these cantos and the matrices and models of the cantos which precede and, in the case of 13, follow them in the first thirty.[7] The existence of macrotextual fragmentation is less important, however, than its infrequency; if fragmentation statistically dominates the microcontext, it is arguably insignificant on the level of the macrocontext. Such insignificance arises for a very good reason: as the text progresses from the smallest level of the microcontext (the line and its associated verse paragraph), to the broadest level of microcontext (the verse paragraph within the canto), and thence to the macrocontext (the first thirty cantos) and full macrocontext (*The Cantos* as a whole), coupling exerts a stronger and stronger influence on the poem's form.

The first thirty cantos, then, are coupled both syntagmatically and paradigmatically. Syntagmatic coupling is achieved linearly through syntactic and semantic equivalence between contiguous cantos, and paradigmatic equivalence arises throughout by means of couplings between models having a shared matrix. Consequently, a provisional syntagm for *A Draft of XXX Cantos* might be schematized as follows:

CANTOS	LINK
1 and 2	Matrix, ANAX; syntactic equivalence, speaker as epic poet, "I."
2 and 3	Matrix, TRANSFORMATION; syntactic equivalence, "I."
1, 2, 3, and 4	Matrices, ANAX, TRANSFORMATION; repetition of models (Artemis-Actaeon, Sea and Land, Troy).
4 and 5	Matrices, AURUN, LEVELS OF TIME; repetition of models (Ecbatan, Aurunculeia)
6 and 7	Matrix, WAD; repetition of models at beginnings of 6 and 7, and contrastively at end of 6 (Cunizza) and beginning of 7 (Eleanor).

7 and 8–11	Matrix, LEVELS OF TIME; repetition of Rinascimento model at end of 7 and throughout 8 through 11.
12 and 18 ff.	Matrix, LEVELS OF TIME; syntactic equivalence, "I" speaker; repetition of "Economics" model.
14–17 and 1	Matrix, NEKUIA; "progression of models" (Hell, etc.); Matrix, ANAX; Matrix, TRANSFORMATION; syntactic equivalence, "So that"; Odysseus.
18 and 19	Matrix, LEVELS OF TIME; syntactic equivalence, "Sabotage"; Economics.
18/19 and 20/21, 24	Matrix, LEVELS OF TIME; syntactic equivalence, "Borso,"; Economics, Rinascimento, Este models.
21 and 22	Marginally linked through Thaddeus Pound ("That man sweated blood . . .").
24 and 25	Matrix, LEVELS OF TIME; Rinascimento.
26 and 27	Matrix, LEVELS OF TIME; Venice.
27	Reprise of LEVELS OF TIME, mythic, historic, personal.
27, 28, 29	Syntactic and semantic equivalence through extreme fragmentation.
30	Matrix, AURUN, LEVELS OF TIME: end of Rinascimento.

The paradigms within this syntagm, of course, are determined by grouping the various matrices running vertically. Obviously, Cantos 4, 8, 12, 17, 27, and 30 are crucial units in the syntagm in that they are recursive (4, 17, 27), pivotal (8 and 17), or terminal (30, and to a lesser extent, 12).

6
PROSODY

CAVEAT LECTOR: in this chapter I shall not forward yet another description of free verse. If I may hark back to a point which I made in Chapter 1 concerning foregrounded stylistic devices, I should like to remind the reader that the basis for such foregrounding is the recognition in many readers and most critics that something in a poem "stands out." For readers of poetry in the last quarter of the twentieth century, it is very probable that free verse is neither more nor less foregrounded than, say, blank verse. Associating free with blank verse, however, implies a logical, typological assumption which may pass unnoticed: blank verse, after all, comprises only one very specific class of meter and line (unrhymed iambic pentameter). Free verse, on the other hand, comprises a number of classes; if we are to accept the designations of various prosodists, some forms of quantitative, concrete, open, "Projective," "Objective," "musical rhythmic," and mixed verse are all "free." If I add to this list the prosodies of individual poets like Goethe or Whitman (to name only two), I end up with a class which is so various that a common element, other than the nonexistence of a common element, is impossible to discover. In other words, "free verse" is not a concept like blank verse, rhymed couplets, or common measure, and the refusal to recognize this simple logical distinction leads to endless debates over the definition of free verse.

The class to which free verse belongs may be defined negatively, of course: free verse "is based not on the recurrence of stress accent in a regular, strictly measurable pattern," and it "treats the device of rhyme with a similar freedom and irregularity."[1] Obviously, such "exclusionary" definition does not state that free verse eschews meter and rhyme: it merely states that free verse is not "based" on them. Another way to define free verse is to class it with verse of a similar order of inclusion; hence, I might contrast free verse with "bound verse," verse which abides strictly by rules of recurrence in meter and/or rhyme. The problem with this contrastive definition, as most readers of poetry will immediately recognize, is that much verse which we normally would term "bound" (Shakespeare is a good example) will promptly become "free" since good poetry rarely follows *strict* (nondeviating) rules of recurrence. Another strategy of definition, followed especially by prosodists of Pound, is to place free verse in a tradition outside the prosodies of modern European languages; consequently, Pound's poetry is not accentual-syllabic but classically quantitative, not "Western" but "Oriental."

The whole problem of identifying the species of free verse which Pound in particular employs is compounded by his mastery and use of a wealth of verse forms throughout his career. Even verse forms for which he has a stated antipathy, like iambic pentameter, spring up from time to time in *The Cantos*. As Eliot says of him, it "is, in fact, just this adaptability of metre to mood, an adaptability due to an intensive study of metre, that constitutes an important element in Pound's technique."[2] Eliot's assessment of Pound's versification, as one might expect, remains in many ways the most perspicuous.

I shall shortly return to the problem of the definition and classification of free verse (at least as such verse appears in Pound), but I should first like to sketch the spectrum of opinions among critics as to what Pound is doing with his prosody in *The Cantos*.

On one end of the spectrum lie those analyses which argue that Pound's versification tends toward some little-used but nonetheless recognizable form of English prosody. According to Harvey Gross, for example, Pound employs a "favorite mixture of spondees and dactyls."[3] A more persuasive case for a traditionally recognizable form of prosody in Pound's free verse involves the imposition of classically quantitative measures on the verse form of *The Cantos*. James A. Powell's cogent argument for a quantitative principle is, in fact, nearly convincing, and I shall return to this argument at length below. Toward the middle of the prosodic spectrum are hypotheses which advance nontraditional scansions; most of these hypotheses emphasize "rhythmic" rather than "metronomic" principles. Sally M. Gall, for instance, follows Pound's own lead (forwarded in "Vers Libre and Arnold Dolmetsch") in adducing the use of a "modern melic tradition" as the impetus behind free verse. Gall contends that "anyone who reads [Pound's] poetry aloud with appropriate attention to musical values, who listens to his recordings, will realize how frequently there is an underlying regular rhythm." Gall is "convinced that much of Pound's verse is metrical in the musical sense: it has a temporal order that can be expressed by a time signature."[4] Moving yet farther from traditional concepts of scansion, John Kuan-Terry is typical of those prosodists who advance a "syntactic" or "phrasal" rhythm for *The Cantos*: "The syntactical structure of Pound's phrases can provide [a] rhythmic definition or 'roughly fixed element' . . . The movement of the cadences can also be guided by metrical, accentual, syllabic schemes or measures, and by consonantal and assonantal devices."[5] Finally, a common response of readers familiar with Japanese and Chinese poetry is to assign Pound's versification to an "Oriental tradition." Wai-Lim Yip, for example, sees "The River Song" as one of the stylistic percursors of *The Cantos;* the poem is important because of "the step Pound took in the manipulation of line units in translation."[6]

I might extend this listing of prosodic hypotheses over several more pages, but this sampling is sufficient, I believe, to demonstrate the disparity of opinions regarding the proper way to scan Pound's verse. Each of these hypotheses is, moreover, representative of a single basic flaw: each fails to account, to paraphrase Chomsky, for all the lines of *The Cantos* and only the lines of *The Cantos.* Assigning traditional prosodic structures to *The Cantos* is of course a valid procedure, but necessary admission of an extremely wide range of possible meters into *The Cantos* tends to defeat the aims of formal description. The problem with the "musical rhythmic" school of prosody, furthermore, is not with the valuable analogies between music and poetry which it affords, but with the use of analogy in itself as a descriptive procedure. Certainly, most readers of Pound recognize that he writes according to the "musical phrase" and not to the dictates of the "metronome." But one wonders if all good poets in all periods have not written "musically." Assigning quarter-notes, half-notes, and time signatures to various portions of *The Cantos* does not solve the problems of formal description for much the same reason that quantitative scansions do not solve those problems (and, again, I shall take up this issue below). Like the "metrical variety" hypothesis of Gross, Kuan-Terry's "syntactic" appraisal is guilty of allowing far too much breadth into prosodic description; Kuan-Terry ends up defining free verse as verse which follows not only syntactic cadences, but any other cadences as well. And, finally, the "Orientalist" approach to Pound's prosody really involves questions of translation rather than the actual prosodic structures of the entire poem (albeit such problems of translation are sometimes useful in deciphering Pound's form).

Eliot, in "Ezra Pound: His Metric and Poetry," outlines in miniature several of the approaches discussed above. He notes a strong "tendency toward quantitative measure" in Pound's poetry, and he contends that Pound's canzoni were "like the Elizabethan lyric . . . written for music." He even comments briefly on Pound's introduction of Oriental verse forms into English poetry. But it is Eliot's notion of the "freedom" in free verse which is important for this discussion.

> The freedom of Pound's verse is rather a state of tension due to constant opposition between free and strict. There are not, as a matter of fact, two kinds of verse, the strict and the free; there is only a mastery which comes of being so well trained that form is an instinct and can be adapted to the particular purpose at hand.[7]

Contemporary literary semiotics would infer an "isomorphic" element in Eliot's explanation of Pound's verse practices; this is merely to say that mastery of form in Modernist poetry involves the absolute equivalence of form and meaning: not in itself a particularly novel insight (even in 1919 when Eliot's essay was first published). Such isomorphism, like free verse itself, presents great difficulties of definition. Even though poetic theorists from T. E. Hulme to Charles Olson have proclaimed the necessity for an intimacy of form and content, it is not clear how modern responses to isomorphism differ from responses of great poets in the past: can one really argue, for example, that Keats and Shelley do not often succeed in casting their formal structures so as to echo the sense which those structures embody? Isomorphism between prosodic structure and content, then (and the reader should note that I am speaking here solely of well-regarded poetry of any period) is one criterion for a successful poem. Consequently, the distinction between pre-twentieth-century isomorphism and Modernist isomorphism must be statistical; the Modernists simply possess a greater variety of prosodic resources than their predecessors. In what, then, does that variety consist?

In order to answer this question, I should like first to invent an imaginary prosody which would account (albeit absurdly) for Pound's scansion in any given line of *The Cantos*. My curious invention will not have the property, however, of being *consistent;* in other words, although I may account for any particular line in a canto, I cannot necessarily account for the line's relation to any of the canto's other lines. The problem of the relation of consistency to a definition of verse form is one to which I shall shortly return when I take up the question of quantitative prosodies. At any rate, my imaginary system of scansion would operate on a very simple rule which might be written imperatively as follows: scan any individual line on the basis of whatever prosody seems most appropriate to it without regard to the scansion of any preceding line (actually, this general principle seems to be the one many prosodists follow anyway). Because I shall soon return to it in discussing Powell's quantitative prosody below, I have chosen the following passage from Canto 7 as a test case:

1 Life to make mock of motion:

2 For the husks, before me, move,

3 The words rattle: shells given out by shells.

4 The live man, out of lands and prisons,

5 Shakes the dry pods,

6 Probes for old wills and friendships, and the big

locust-casques

7   /   x x   /   x   /   x
        Bend to the tawdry table,

8   /   (/)   x   /   x   /   (/)   /   x / x
        Lift up their spoons to mouths, put forks in cutlets,

9   x   /   /   x   x   /   x / x
        And make sound like the sound of voices.

(page 27)

Powell offers an initial "traditional" scansion of these lines (this appears here), but concludes that "in anything approaching the sense of 'iambic pentameter', we find no common denominator, no feet, no metra, and hence, no metre."[8] My scansion device, like Powell's, can quite happily set about specifying the stresses in these lines; the device produces a scansion much like Powell's except that it recognizes a possible stress on "make" in line 1, a secondary stress at most on "man" in line 4, and ambiguous

      /   x   x   /

stresses on "Lift up" in line 8 ("Lift up" or "Lift up?"). Indeed, it would be surprising if our scansions, even though based on the same principles, were identical; such diversity is the inevitable lot of prosodists. How, then, would the scansion device characterize the passage? Line 1 does seem to abide by Gross's "falling rhythm" since it appears to be made up of two dactyls and a trochee; the rhythm of lines 4, 7, and 9 seems also to be generally "falling." Lines 2 and 8, conversely, seem to be informed by a rising rhythm: line 2 comprises an anapest followed by two iambs, and line 8 a nearly "regular" series of iambs. Lines 3, 5, and 6 remain, about the scansion of which Powell and I agree. Line 3 has ten syllables if one ignores the caesura after the colon, line 5 possesses four syllables, and line 6 has thirteen. The scansion device, by the way, notes and then discards the fact that the passage does not seem to forward a "norm" for the number of syllables in each line unless one cares to argue that the initial seven syllables of lines 1 and 2, and of line 7 is some sort of norm. At any rate, the syllable counts of lines 3, 5, and 6 will give us no clue as to what one should expect of the scansions of those lines. The scansion might offer, for instance, a generally rising scansion for line 3; thus, foot one would be an iamb, foot two a trochaic reversal, and a caesura *would* appear after the colon, making the rest of the line a more or less recognizable iambic.

In the last analysis, however, the scansion device tells us nothing; as Powell puts it, "once we have thus specified the rhythms, we are lost." Powell's avenue of escape from this quandary is to scan *The Cantos* quantitatively. He states that early on Pound "began to evolve from a synthesis of Greek quantitative prosody and English accentual potency a new rhythmic base for English verse . . . this adaptation of Greek prosodic techniques and rhythmic forms remained basic, primary, and central to his rhythmic artifice" (Powell, 1979: 34). Powell's argument is very persuasive, and the numerous examples of quantitative scansion he offers seem convincing. Yet upon closer examination these scansions provoke a number of questions. Powell's quantitative scansion of the passage from Canto 7, for instance, assigns the same stresses to the lines as does the "traditional" scansion. This is in itself not remarkable in view of the fact that attempts at the use of quantity as a metrical principle in English verse frequently come up with quantitative stresses at the same positions at which accentual stresses would occur.

Leaving aside for the moment the question of whether quantity, in the sense it is used in classical prosody, can even exist in English poetry, I should like to explore the nature of this coincidence. Generally, prosodists and linguists agree that Classical Greek possessed fixed quantities for its vowels; Powell himself says that in Greek "a syllable *is* long or short: it cannot be somewhere in between." Actually, the "fixity" of vocalic quantities is a moot question since our evidence of such fixity is itself Greek literature. English, on the other hand, does not have fixed vowel quantities. One factor in lengthening the quantities of vowels in English involves the quality of consonants which succeed vowels; in classical prosody it is the "association" of a consonant with the vowel which precedes it which may determine the length of that vowel. In other words, speaking simply, if a double consonant follows a short vowel, or if a short vowel is followed by a consonant not belonging to its syllable, the syllable in which that vowel appears is quantitatively long. Long vowels and diphthongs, of course, always produce long syllables. In contrast, I should invite the reader's consideration of the following series each word of which, strictly speaking, employs the same vowel: /pea/, /peat/, /peed/, /peas/. The phoneme /i/ appears in each word, and yet each appearance is slightly longer than the one which precedes it. This lengthening occurs because in /pea/ the phoneme has no following consonant to "augment" it. In /peat/ the unvoiced stop which follows /i/ lends to it a slightly longer length, and in /peed/ the voiced stop contributes to greater length still. Finally, in /peas/ the semi-vowel /s/ (which is also a continuant) creates a markedly longer vowel than in any of the preceding words.[9] Added to the effect the sounds of consonants have on preceding vowels is the fact that *stress itself* can create quantity in English. In the first line of the passage from Canto 7, for example, Powell assigns length to "mock" and not to "make." He is probably right in doing so even though quantitative metrics would not admit this scansion: "mock" contains a short vowel /a/ followed by a single consonant and is therefore a short syllable; "make," on the other hand, contains the long vowel /e/ and is thus a long syllable. Yet most readers would hear "mock" as longer than "make," not because of any internal phonology, but because of suprasegmental stresses which are usually applied to infinitive phrases, especially in the presence of extreme consonance. "Make mock," in other words, would only be stressed /x in

English if the two morphemes constituted a compound noun (a "makemock" is one who constantly derides others); the reader will note a similar situation in line 9 in "make sound." In fact, throughout Powell's scansions, the same problems arise; "before" in line 2, for example, can only be quantitatively scanned if we assign to the word the value /bəfor/ and not /bifor/.

Returning to the coincidence of Powell's accentual scansion with his quantitative scansion, I should like to advance the argument that he, like most English-speakers, quite rightly uses accentual stress as one of the criteria for quantity. It should by now be obvious that any attempt to assign quantitative meters to English verse is tautologous; length often occurs because of stress which creates length.

Be all this as it may, what of the classical feet which Powell construes (whether on the basis of accent or quantity) in this passage? Lines 1, 4, 6, and 7, Powell points out, contain aristophaneans (/xx/x/x, where the final syllable in ending a line is an anceps). Lines 3 and 8 each contain a dodrans (/xx/x/). This leaves the following lines and parts of lines unaccounted for: the entirety of line 2, which I assume Powell scans "traditionally" as an anapest and two iambs; "The words rattle" of line 3; "The live" of line 4; the entirety of line 5 ("shakes the dry pods,"which I am equally unwilling to try to scan; the last half of line 6, "and the big locust-casques" (an anapest followed by a dactyl or cretic?); the last half of line 8, "put fork in cutlets" (iamb and amphibrach); the "And make" of line 9. These unscanned portions amount to twenty-nine out of the passage's total of seventy-seven syllables: thirty-eight percent of the passage, in other words, is prosodically unaccounted for.

I concede, however, that such gaps are unimportant for Powell's essential argument. What is important is that "these related rhythmic shapes focus musical tensions, pattern the passage's rhythmic energies, as a plucked string patterns air." Powell goes on to admit that although

> Pound gains a tremendous melodic versatility. . . . we must also realize to what extent he loses the ability to produce a clearly defined rhythmic expectation in the reader and thus to what degree he loses the chance to play his actual rhythms against that expectation. No "predetermined pattern" governs these lines; no matter how thoroughly we analyze their accentual patterns, we will never be in a position to *predict* the rhythmic shape of a given line, will never find a pre-ordained *metrical* pattern. (Powell, 1979: 12)

This is only to say, as readers of Pound have suspected all along, that free verse does not possess meter, which last may be defined as regular (that is, predictable) rhythm. I shall state the obvious and say that free verse, as all the above prosodists agree, has rhythm; yet speech too has rhythm. Thus I may say that free verse possesses a rhythm which lies somewhere on the spectrum between the poles of strict meter and the suprasegmental rhythms of speech. In fact, the reader will note that I have come full circle: in opening this chapter, I argued that a definition of free verse must take into account the types of classes to which various verse forms belong, and that free verse, as opposed, say, to blank verse, belongs to a very wide class of definition indeed.

The imposition of quantitative measures on Pound's free verse is appealing for reasons which may or may not be obvious. A primary attraction is the orderly way in which quantitative scansion deals with the disparity of syllables in free verse lines. Above, I cited the wide variation of syllable counts in the passage from Canto 7, and, of course, the number of accentual-syllabic feet in the passage will vary accordingly. When I determine the weights of these lines, however, by means of quantitative scansion, I discover much less disparity: each line, with the exceptions of 6 and 8, "weighs" from five to seven long stresses. In fact, Powell cites Pound's avowed practice of "composition using lines of approximately the same weight in more or less continuous series" as support for his contention that *The Cantos* are grounded in a "rhythmic artifice based on lines of equal weight" (Powell, 1979: 31). This is a peculiar contention on the part of both Powell and Pound: a cursory glance through the pages of *The Cantos* will confirm that there can be no possible quantitative norm for many, many passages.

A further attraction of the quantitative scansion of free verse is that such scansion lends support, through the "music" of vowel "harmony," to Pound's oft-proclaimed composition on the basis of the "musical phrase" instead of on the basis of the "metronome." Powell, Gall, and other critics who hear a sonority among vowels in Pound's lines, who mark new and intricate rhythms in *The Cantos,* are not mistaken, but whether such rhythms may be described through quantitative scansion is, as I hope I have demonstrated, doubtful. I shall even concede here that Pound often employs, probably consciously, those very quantitative measures which Powell discovers in *The Cantos,* but such measures have no greater importance than Pound's use of traditional feet, prose clausulae, or no determinable rhythm at all. Again, we are thrown back on that part of the definition of free verse which allows of, or even insists on, great rhythmic variety.

Speech and Poetry, Syntax and Meter

It is probably by now apparent that none of the descriptions of free verse which I have reviewed is thoroughly incorrect. Each prosodist merely detects some one feature of free verse which, for him or her, is foregrounded. Kuan-Terry's "phrasal" rhythms, for example, find support in the early, Imagist attempt to approximate the rhythms of speech. In fact, like the coincidence of accentual and quantitative stress, the coincidence between Kuan-Terry's phrasal units and Powell's quantitative feet comes about for a good reason; like the perceived isomorphism between stress and quantity, the isomorphism between quantitative unit and phrase arises out of a formal organizing principle wherein phonology, morphology, and suprasegmental stress converge. In most pre-twentieth-century metrical poetry, another factor is added: regular recurrence of stress in the macrocontext, and regular (although not regulated) recurrence of morphology and phonology in the microcontext. Macrocontextual recurrence simply involves meter, and often rhyme and stanza form, and microcontextual recurrence involves elements like assonance, consonance, and semantic synonymy and antonymy, all such recurrences coming under the head of forms of coupling. In free verse, I would argue, there is at least one factor which is susceptible of macrocontextual recurrence: the physical disposition of gaps and graphemes on the page. In keeping with the tenor of the rest of this study, I shall not advocate as an additional feature of recurrence the commonly accepted notion that in free verse rhythm corresponds to thought. In fact, I have dealt with this subject above in my comments on isomorphism between form and content in traditional and Modernist poetry. The reader will recall that it is nearly impossible to prove that free verse poets effect any greater convergence of form and thought than good poets of any period or tradition.

Actually, the most immediately perceptible feature of free verse is its "unevenness" on the page; such visual irregularity may even have been the most foregrounded element for many readers when free verse began to appear. In *The Cantos*, at any rate, the visual effect of the page reaches a degree of extreme foregrounding, even for contemporary readers well-used to free verse; here we find one-word lines, blocks of prose, peculiar uses of punctuation, switches of alphabet, and a rich variety of non-graphemic signs like ampersands, icons, ideograms, and hieroglyphs.

I should like to advance the idea that irregularity of line length and a highly conscious use of punctuation in the free verse of *The Cantos* are prompted by the quantitative-phrasal isomorphism I referred to above. That is, Pound often uses the unit of the line to designate a phonological, morphological, and suprasegmental whole. If, for example, I carefully consider Powell's quantitative feet, I discover an interesting syntactic phenomenon. In Canto 7, Powell designates the following portions of lines as aristophaneans and dodrans (I have included the punctuation in each quotation for reasons which will become obvious): (1) "Life to make mock of motion:" (2) ":shells given out by shells." (3) "man, out of lands and prisons," (4) "Probes for old wills and friendships," (5) "Bend to the tawdry table," (6) "Life up their spoons to mouths," (7) "sound like the sounds of voices." We have here an effect like that of end-stopped lines; when the semantic-syntactic unit ends, the prosodic unit ends. The effect is reinforced in every case by "bracketing" punctuation. (1) clearly acts as the model for the verse paragraph which follows (over half of which Powell omits), and the colon which ends that line serves both to end-stop it and to signal an expansion of the model ("living/dead," "reality/appearance"). (2) is coupled to (1) through a reversal; the "shells" expand on the meaning of "The words rattle" in the first half of the line. (4) concludes a series of characterizations of the "live man," and, unlike the other two "appositive" units ("Out of lands" and "shake the dry pods") is set at the beginning of a new line. The action of the hollow "locust-casques" is similarly given its own line, "Bend to the tawdry table" in (5), as is the next characterization of the "casques," "Lift up their spoons" in (6). And, finally, (7) also stands as a syntactic and suprasegmental unit. Of these seven quantitative feet, then, only (5) is "broken," and yet even it is arguably self-sufficient (especially in the context of fragmentation).

I would thus advance the argument that Pound's free verse (and it remains to be seen whether this verse is typical of free verse as a whole) frequently employs a species of "end-stopping," if an end-stopped line is defined as one in which meaning "undergoes a pause at the end of a line."[10] In lines in which enjambement of sense takes place, it appears that line length, whether measured quantitatively or syllabically, is much more regular. Canto 7 presents good examples of both usages. In the first verse paragraph (page 24), each line is self-contained, and the single line set off after that paragraph is by definition self-contained. The "couplet" from "Un Coeur Simple" which next occurs is paradoxically (since it is a prose sentence in the intertext) one of the most "metrical" units in this canto. The next verse paragraph begins with several self-contained lines (the first five), and then continues with a series of enjambed lines. In the initial twelve lines on page 25, enjambement seems to correspond to a rough hendecasyllabic norm; the variations on this norm are supported by Pound's comments on the varying hendecasyllabic line in Dante.[11] The three lines beginning "Ione, dead the long year" return to a self-sufficient mode, and in the passage which occupies the second half of the page, the use of catalogue fragmentation reinforces this self-sufficiency. Fragmentation and end-stopping continue throughout page 26. The last two verse paragraphs on this page, beginning respectively "Another day, between walls of a sham Mycenian," and "Square even shoulders and the satin skin," are ones I have already discussed in detail in regard to fragmentation. The first complete verse paragraph on page 27, "And the life goes on," also employs fragmentation and end-stopping (except for the last two lines), and thus we are brought full circle back to "Life to make mock. . . ."

The role of punctuation in poetry is not well understood. Textual studies seem only to confirm that some poets are conscious and careful in their use of punctuation, and that others are not. Charles Olson, in his well-known remarks in "Projective Verse," argues that Pound and his successors make a novel effort to employ punctuation and the nonalphabetic signs of the typewriter keyboard as "reading signals," and statements Pound has made seem to confirm this usage.[12] Frequently, it does seem as if Pound is quite careful of his disposition of punctuation so as to mark pauses or stresses. And there does seem to be a coherent role for some punctuation marks, chiefly semicolons and ellipses, in *The Cantos*. Semicolons seem to introduce appositions or analogies, and in this role are markers of rhetoric rather than of prosody. In Canto 7, for example, lines 5 and 6, page 24, are separated by a semicolon: "Ear, ear for the sea-surge; / rattle of old men's voices." In the microcontext of "poor old Homer," who appears in line 3, both the "sea-surge" and the "rattle" are sounds Homer has an "ear for." A gap precedes "rattle of . . ." and this absence, if it is "read" as a pause, reinforces the apposition which this line creates. Ellipses, as I argued in Chapter 2, sometimes have the properties of ideograms in that they signify iconically. We find three uses of ellipses, again in Canto 7, on page 26, lines 12 and 13, "Speaking a shell of speech. . . / Propped between chairs and tables. . ." and line 21, "Dry professorial talk. . . ." "Attenuation" might very plausibly be the signified of these ellipses since the lines in which they occur comprise the model for the "locust-shells" hypogram, one seme of which is "emptiness." These ellipses might also, however, signal a lengthening of quantity, not merely of the words which conclude the lines, but of the whole phonological-syntactic-semantic complex of the lines. I would suggest that, because there is no means by which "diminuendo" can be marked in verse, these ellipses seem to signal an attenuated "dying off" at the end of the lines.

"Gapping," or indentation of a line from the left margin at a point which does not indicate the commencement of a new verse paragraph, appears to be a frequent feature of free verse, but, as is the case with punctuation, its uses seem obscure. The following passage from Canto 17, page 77 seems typical:

1	Zagreus, feeding his panthers,
2	the turf clear as on hills under light.
3	And under the almond-trees, gods,
4	with them, *choros nympharum*. Gods,
5	Hermes and Athene,
6	As shaft of compass,
7	Between them, trembled—
8	To the left is the place of fauns,
9	*sylva nympharum;*
10	The low wood, moor-scrub,
11	the doe, the young spotted deer,
12	leap up through the broom-plants,
13	as dry leaf amid yellow.

The reader will perhaps note here the mixture of end-stopped (1, 2, 3, 8, 9, 10, 13) and partially enjambed lines (4 and 5, 6 and 7, and 11 and 12), and the use of the semicolon in line 9 to introduce the appositive, "The low wood . . . ." More interesting, however, are the three types of indentation: lines 11 and 12, nearest the margin, lines 2 and 4, set thirteen spaces from the margin, and lines 6, 9, and 13, set twenty-one spaces from the margin. Other than their respective indentations, there seems to be nothing internally joining these groups together. Neither accentual-syllabic nor quantitative scansion gives the reader a motive for the gapping in this passage. Like the lines from Canto 7, these possess portions which can be accounted for under one system of scansion or another, and other portions which cannot; lines 3 and 4, for instance, comprise Powell's typical aristophanean and dodrans, respectively, while line 8 "rises" with two anapests and an iamb, and line 10 (like the "shakes the dry pods" of Canto 7) probably includes one spondee, and perhaps even two. I should like to suggest then that, in this passage at least, gapping responds to a combination of semantic and phrasal, rather than prosodic, forces.

There are five syntagms in this microcontext: "Zagreus . . . under light" (lines 1 and 2), "And under . . . *nympharum*" (lines 3 and 4), "Gods . . . trembled—," (lines 8 and 9), and "The low wood . . . yellow" (lines 10 through 13). Each syntagm, except for the third, begins in a line which is set full to the left margin; the third syntagm, beginning "Gods" in line 4, is not an anomaly since "Hermes and Athene" may be said to act as the true subject NP of this syntagm. Lines which augment or modify structures in the initial part of the syntagm occur in indented lines. Line 7, which does not commence a syntagm, is plausibly separated from line 6 to reduce the too great regularity which would result from the conjunction of two structures which have identical accentual scansions (although line 7 might just as well have been indented to the right of line 6). Those lines which are indented closest to the left (11 and 12) seem semantically more self-sufficient than the other indented lines, and, in fact, the doe and faun of line 11 appear to be the underlying subject NPs of the syntagm which begins with the "low wood." The two lines indented at "midpoint" (2 and 4) also seem relatively self-sufficient, and, moreover, each possesses more weight, both syllabically and quantitatively, than the other lines. The lines indented farthest to the right (6, 9, and 13) are semantically curious. Although line 9 stands in apposition to "place of fauns" and its indentation may thus be viewed as the "demotion" of a syntactic and prosodic "parenthesis," lines 6 and 13 seem to create their own semantic pivots. Indeed, both "As shaft of compass," and "as dry leaf amid yellow", through their use of the analogous "as", appear to set up comparisons, and yet the terms of the comparison are enigmatic. On the other hand, the "as" of line 6 may introduce some sort of adverbial clause of time, but since "Hermes and Athene" possesses no VP, it would be difficult to state what such a clause might modify. Of course, this ambiguous structure is itself familiar; line 5 is a VP-deleted fragment, and line 6 acts as a condensation. Line 13, although more closely approximating an analogy, also embodies a condensation; the doe and faun may appear to be the color of a "dry leaf amid yellow" of the broom, or the "dry leaf amid yellow" may be a metonymy for the entire plant or a patch of plants.

The gapping of lines to indicate semantic, phonological, and phrasal units, then, responds to a variety of factors, only one of which (and perhaps the least of which) is some form of meter. The phenomenon of gapping in free verse, moreover, suggests clues to a future description of this verse form. The organization of lines in *The Cantos*, their spatial layout on the page and their internal semantic and syntactic structures, reflects a grounding in a complex of factors, some of which are implicit in the description of the overall verse form of *The Cantos*.

Formal Devices and Free Verse

In describing the uses to which formal devices are put in *The Cantos*, I have already offered a partial description of Pound's verse form. I should like to stress, however, that such formal features mold, motivate, and limit verse form, but are not themselves the basic constituents of it. If Modernist verse is written, as William Carlos Williams and Charles Olson claim, in an "open field," that field is conditioned by identifiable semiotic forces.

I characterize such forces as "semiotic" because one major signifier of verse form in some Modernist poetry concerns spatial arrangement. In Pound, Cummings, and Williams, for example, typesetting, type fonts, pictograms, and gaps play an important role in cluing the reader as to auditory or "intellectual" rhythms. I shall not go so far as to argue that the Modernists deploy graphemes to the same ends and for the same reasons as do the "spatialist" and "concrete" poets (whose aims seem to be in part the "deconstruction" of linguistic and semantic forms), but I should like to note that the conscious and continuous foregrounding of an irregular graphemic level of poetic discourse is peculiar to the twentieth century.[13] Such disruption of automatized reading procedures necessarily undercuts the ability to perceive meter and other auditory devices in poetry. I shall not, however, pursue this subject because extreme graphemic alteration, and the kindred use of ideograms, is a formal feature which, although it appears in the remainder of *The Cantos*, does not appear prominently in *A Draft of XXX Cantos*.

My discussion above of the passage from Canto 17 should suggest the role which fragmentation plays in directing prosodic variation in free verse. As the dominant microcontextual device in the first thirty cantos, fragmentation is bound to order such prosodic factors as line length, length and character of feet, and phrasal units. The recognition by Kuan-Terry and others of a phrasal factor in Pound's free verse may be prompted by an earlier, and not entirely conscious, response to extreme fragmentation of the syntagm. It could well be that deletion of VPs, and to a lesser extent NPs, in either the catalogue or the disintegrating sentence makes the metrical "filling out" of a verse line pointless. Enjambement, too, is rendered statistically less important because the use of deletion can always ensure the compacting of syntagm into one line. Positively, fragmentation seems to cause the basic syntactic unit of the free verse line to be the phrase as opposed to the clause. As I noted above, English phrases are subject to suprasegmental forces which are more or less inalterable. In Pound's much-used P-phrase, for example, prepositions are rarely stressed, inevitably causing accentuation of the phrase's NP: a cursory consideration of the stresses in the series of P-phrases in Canto 2 should suffice to demonstrate this:

> / x x x / (/)
> quiet in the buff sands . . .
>
> x x / x x x / (/)
> In the wave-runs by the half-dune;
>
> / / x / x x / x x x / x
> Glass-glint of wave in the tide-rips against sunlight . . .
>
> x x / x / x x / x x
> in the smell of hay under olive-trees

> (page 10)

Since English P-phrases commonly consist of two unstressed syllables (the preposition plus article), anapests ("In the buff," "In the wave") and other associations of unstressed syllables will abound in many fragments. In fact, where P-phrases are numerous, as in the lines above, traditional scansion will be impossible because these lines will comprise too frequent a succession of unstressed syllables: "Wave-runs by the half dunes," and "hay under the olive-trees" present two or three problems in scansion, one of which is the dilemma created by the "overweighting" of NPs at the end of a string of unstressed syllables.

The nominalization which is one result of fragmentation in *The Cantos* poses another problem. The compound nouns typical of nominalization cause Pound's lines in cantos like the one excerpted above to possess a large number of trochees. "Wave-runs," "half-dune," "Glass-glint," "tide-rips," and "sunlight" (and, in an altered fashion, "buff sands" and "olive-trees") require careful placement within the syntagm if a falling rhythm is not to dominate the line. Furthermore, where consonance adds to the effect of the compound noun ("Glass-glint") or where compounding is uncertain ("buff sands"), spondees tend to arise.

Finally, the frequent appearance of participials in fragmentation will have rhythmic consequences similar to those caused by P-phrases. In the highly fragmented Canto 14, for example, the reader will recall that participials entirely supplant VPs. On page 61 the following structures occur: "Standing bare bum," "Bush hanging for beard," "Addressing the multitudes in the ooze," and "pushing over the collar's edge," to note only a few. Since in a two-syllable participial the first syllable will be stressed (the penultimate, of course, is stressed in participials over two syllables), such stress will inevitably affect the rhythm of the line. The second example, "Bush hanging for beard," offers an instance of the sort of confusion in scansion which participials cause: "Bush" may either be stressed, in which case a pause of greater or lesser duration ensues, or unstressed, in which case the "natural" rhythm of the line seems askew. When participials are combined with P-phrases, as in "pushing over the collar's edge," the result can be a series of unstressed syllables which cause parts of the line to lose rhythm.

The effect of condensation, the reader will recall, is partly semantic, although the ambivalence characteristic of this device can sometimes carry over into the prosodic structure in which it appears. I cited the following two instances of condensation from Canto 21 in Chapter 4:

> x   x   /   x x /   / x   x / x x   /   x
> That signor Galeaz Sforza Visconti has wished me
> x x   /   x x / x x   / x
> To stand sponsor to all of his children.
> / (/) x /   x x / x   x x (/) x /   x x
> Another war without glory, and another peace without
>   / x
>   quiet.
> x x   / x   / x   x x / x   x / x
> And the Sultan sent him an assassin, his brother;

and

> /   x x   /   x
> Moon on the palm leaf,
>   x / x
>   confusion;
> x / x   /   x x / x
> Confusion, source of renewals;

In the first example, the very regular structure of the line representing the condensation contrasts it rhetorically and prosodically with the two surrounding structures while at the same time it exhibits features of those structures. The strict syntactic parallelism between the two NPs which make up the condensation, of course, seem to dictate an equal prosodic parallelism, the pivotal stresses occurring with "war," "glory," "peace," and "quiet." The second syllable of "another" is probably stressed so that the line becomes generally rising, although ambiguity of stress within the line (on "without" and "quiet") may provoke occasional "falling" reversals. The first two lines of this example, conversely, seem to comprise initial rising stresses followed by falling stresses (in the first line, for instance, the accentual scansion seems to be xx/xx/-/xx/xx/x); whereas in the example's last line the scansion is arguably rising until the last word, "brother." Thus, a rhythmic condensation may here echo a semantic condensation.

In the second example, a similar process is at work. The first line is strictly falling and the third line, again with the exception of the last word, rises. Consequently, the second line's "amphibrach," the condensation, seems to mediate between the two rhythms.

The relationship between coupling and rhythmic structures is, I hope, clear enough; the reader will recall my discussion in the preceding chapter of positional equivalence, and the influence of equivalence, regularity, and convergence on prosody should be obvious. Suffice it to say that microcontextual coupling is so closely allied to rhythm in poetry that the two features are often indistinguishable. The abovementioned line from Canto 21, "Another war without glory, and another peace without quiet," is exemplary of such an alliance. As I pointed out in Chapter 5, the repetition of a certain structure, like fragmentation, will often automatically give rise to coupling, and my discussion of fragmentation immediately above should suggest that such repetition, for similar reasons, will often give rise to distinctive rhythms in the microcontext.

It should thus be apparent that each of the features with which I have dealt—fragmentation, condensation, coupling, and free verse—is not structurally isolable. At the risk of repetition, I shall once again stress that unity of phonic, syntactic, rhetorical, and semantic structures is an inarguable quality of admirable poetry in any period. But, as with the assignment of coupling structures in twentieth-century poetry, the designation of prosodic structures is made very difficult by a thoroughgoing formal irregularity which is, by definition, a crucial element in Modernist verse. The problems raised by attempting to discover the "rules" of prosody in free verse, however, should point to an important fact about free verse in general: although structural and semantic norms are not as foregrounded in twentieth-century poetry as they are in traditional verse, norms do exist. Such norms, however, are established in a limited microcontext and do not apply throughout a given text. As competent poets of all periods have recognized, predictability is not equivalent to regularity; departure from a norm is central to a reader's enjoyment of a poem. As Pound reminds us, "Most arts attain their effects by using a fixed element and a variable."[14] Whether such departure be rhetorical (the "surprise" of an unexpected comparison), syntactic (the abolition of normal word order), or prosodic (the substitution of feet), its presence is as important as unity to the successful reading of poetry.

7

MACROCONTEXTS: SPEAKERS

Note that cohesive ties are what might be called microstructural devices: they operate very locally, linking neighbor sentences by means of constituents in the observable surface structure of the text. Theorists of text have also hypothesized deep structure or macrostructural components of texts: these would include traditional literary categories such as plot and theme. Structuralism in the tradition of Propp has given some lead in the study of macrostructural components, but needless to say they have not yet been formalized. However, I would regard the study of textual deep structure as very much on the agenda of an enlarged linguistics.[1]

With a slight alteration in terminology (microstructural and macrostructural devices are of course my microcontextual and macrocontextual devices), Roger Fowler's comments here may serve as an epigraph to the remaining three chapters of this study. Although I briefly touched on aspects of the macrocontext in discussing coupling, I shall now devote my remaining efforts to, as Fowler puts it, a "study of textual deep structure."

In the interests of the clarity of what follows, it is important that the linguistic relationship between surface and deep structures in discourse be well understood. Chomsky's own formulation of that relation is as follows:

The syntactic component consists of a base that generates deep structures and a transformational part that maps them into surface structures. The deep structure of a sentence is submitted to the semantic component for semantic interpretation, and its surface structure enters the phonological component and undergoes phonetic interpretation. The final effect of a grammar, then, is to relate a semantic interpretation of a phonetic representation—that is, to state how a sentence is interpreted. This relation is mediated by the syntactic component of the grammar, which constitutes its sole "creative" part.[2]

Chomsky's definition clarifies three aspects of the concept of deep structure: these structures are not separable from the utterances which are their phonic expression; the deep structure is in turn interpreted by a "semantic component"; lastly, although this is not immediately apparent in this particular set of Chomsky's remarks, the deep structure is undiscoverable without recourse to the surface structure of an utterance. If conceptual abstractions underlie utterances, the surface utterance, print on a page or the sound of words, is no less abstract, and neither structure achieves concreteness except in association with the other. In a poem, for example, the isomorphism which I remarked on in reference to prosody is exemplary of the inseparable reality, the impact, of rhythm and meaning.

I have delayed my examination of the relation between surface and deep structures not because such a relation does not hold in the microcontext, but because the macrocontext of *The Cantos* shares the same level of abstraction as does the deep structure of a sentence or group of sentences. In a microcontextual device like fragmentation, for example, I would argue that interpretation is very largely a result of the mediation of the "syntactic component of the grammar," which itself enters into a relation with the deep structure. In the macrocontext, however, the markedness of the microcontextual device is very nearly absent: one reason I cannot easily mark a macrocontextual device is that such markers are by definition widely intratextual, and another is that macrocontextual markers, unlike microcontextual markers, follow no necessary order.

Linguists may recognize in my distinction between macro- and micro-context an analogous distinction between phrase structure rules and transformations. And, in fact, I might well have described fragmentation and condensation as various kinds of phrase structures similar to that which describes an NP as

$$
NP \quad \left\{ \begin{array}{l} \text{Name} \\ \text{Personal Pronoun} \\ \text{Indefinite} \\ \text{Pronoun} \\ \text{Det } + \text{ N } + \text{ No.} \end{array} \right.
$$

so that fragmentation would be described as

$$
FRAG \quad \left\{ \begin{array}{l} \text{NP } + \text{ VP } \emptyset \\ \text{NP } + \text{ VPing} \\ \text{NP } \emptyset + \text{ VP} \end{array} \right.
$$

and so forth. It should be abundantly clear that, in contrast, no possible phrase structure rule can be written for intratextual coupling. The production of models from matrices, however, *is* susceptible of being described as analogous to a transformation from a deep structure to an apparent structure. But since the relation of models to matrices is merely analogous to syntactic transformations, and since the subject of generative transformations is complex and much disputed, I shall not belabor the analogy.[3]

I should like to pursue another avenue which is opened by the enlarge-
ment of scope which my introduction of macrocontexts affords, and this
involves the relation of macrocontextual devices to rhetoric. It is by no
means clear, despite the efforts of proponents of *la rhétorique restreinte*,
whether rhetoric pertains more to the level of macrocontext or the level of
microcontext. Metonymy, as I have used it in this study for instance,
possesses features of both levels: a metonymy in *The Cantos* may take the
traditional form of a trope as in the use of the word "yellow" to designate
the broom plant in Canto 17, page 77, line 25, or it may take the form of an
"operating principle" as in the Imagist passages which I examined in
Chapter 2. Certainly, many traditional rhetoricians, as well as moderns like
Group μ, do not recognize this macrocontextual role for metonymy, and, as
Chapter 2 indicated, even the microcontextual markers of metonymy are in
dispute. On the other hand, if I extend the field of rhetoric to include all
those features of discourse which taken together cause an effective response in a listener or reader, then I may well contend that a thoroughgoing metonymy or metaphor or synecdoche orders invention, disposition,
and the other elements of rhetoric. Actually, adoption of strategies of
macrocontextual rhetorical analysis has been more or less accepted in prose
stylistics; witness the inclusion of such works as Booth's *The Rhetoric of
Fiction* into the contemporary canon of literary theory. It is not surprising
that a macrocontextual rhetoric has achieved recognition in prose analysis
because, for what I suspect are not thoroughly examined reasons, prose
style is viewed generally as a concatenation of "contextual" effects whereas
poetic style is seen as evocative of "local" effects. This dichotomy between
the wider stylistic context of prose and the narrow stylistic context of
poetry was, if not initiated by the New Critics, at least fostered by them
(see, for example, Ransom's well-known remarks on local texture). Moreover, the division may seem "natural" owing to the merely greater length of
most prose texts compared to most poetry texts. At any rate, the sheer
length of *The Cantos*, their use of stretches of prose, and their "discursive"
quality should dispel any notion of the need to treat them locally; rather, as
with modern studies of narrative, a more extensive rhetorical apparatus,
including "global" macrocontextual figures like metonymy and coupling, is
necessary.

Person, Mask, Effacement

The important stages in the modern development of a theory of impersonality in literature are well-known: it is a genealogy which begins with
Stendhal and Flaubert, continues through Henry James and finds its salient
twentieth-century expressions in the Dedalean narrator paring his nails,
the young Pound donning his masks, and the querulous Eliot acidly stating

that "only those who have personality and emotion know what it means to want to escape from those things." It is in "Tradition and the Individual Talent," of course, that we find the most extreme expression of poetic impersonality. Most readers are familiar with the celebrated phrases of that essay: "the more perfect the artist, the more completely separate in him will be the man who suffers and the mind which creates"; "the poet, has not a 'personality' to express, but a particular medium"; "Poetry is not a turning loose of emotion, but an escape from emotion; it is not the expression of a personality but an escape from personality." I shall not engage in a deconstruction of this essay, but the reader may recall Eliot's tacit insistence, in an essay devoted to the eschewal of emotion as a poetic impetus, on the equivalence between personality and emotion. Indeed, the essay argues, poets must escape personality because personality *is* emotion. Even the Eliotic reader does not experience emotion in any usual sense because the "effect of a work of art upon the person who enjoys it is an experience different in kind from any experience not of art."[4]

Pound's view of the effacement of the poet's personality differs significantly from that of Eliot, although the two poets adopt much the same perspective regarding the relation of personality to history. Herbert Schneidau comments about *The Cantos* that "they give me no feeling of knowing 'Pound the man' while reading; if autobiography, it is that of a reagent in history who tests what he comes in contact with" (Schneidau, 1969: 67). And Jacob Korg notes that

> The poetic fact pre-exists, not only in the poet's intuition, but also in earlier literature, so that the question of recording an individual experience shades off into that of responding to a tradition, the accumulation of many psychological experiences. (Korg, 1979: 87)

On the other hand, Schneidau points out, by "1914 Pound made it clear . . . that he had not really been much interested in character anyhow, and that his *personae* were really 'masks of the self,' seeming verities in the 'search for oneself' " (Schneidau, 1969: 166). Schneidau concedes that such a search does not involve "self-revelation or self-projection in the ultra-Romantic sense."

Actually, Pound seems not to accord to emotion a privileged status as either *bête noire* or poetic mainspring. Pound's adoption of a persona is in many respects the adoption of a linguistic mask, a mask which, to be sure, embodies emotion, but which involves emotion in a cultural complex of which it is just one facet. It may be of note that the "subjects" which Pound chooses for translation are significant of a tradition (Anglo-Saxon, Provençal, classical Chinese) and not reflective of an individual. Even the exceptions—Cavalcanti, Propertius, Villon—are evocative of entire periods which Pound values. Moreover, set beside his translations are many, many "occasional" poems which achieve the amalgam of "personality" and "tradition" which, I suspect, is the hallmark of universality in any poem: this dual aspect of Pound's poetic interests is nicely demonstrated by the nearly concurrent publication of *Lustra*, essentially a "personal" collection, and *Cathay*, essentially an "impersonal" one.

In fact, like Pound's prosodic practices, his use of personae is founded in variety. Any attempt to assess his employment of masks on the basis of his performance in a given poem, say "Homage to Sextus Propertius," is doomed to failure for exactly the same reasons that the attempt to describe his prosody on the basis of Propertian rhythms fails. Further, the problem which confronts the analyst of speakers in *The Cantos* is closely parallel to the dilemma facing the prosodist; voices, like rhythms, are constantly shifting. On the other hand, prosodic analysis is at least accessible to the kind of exiguous analysis which my scansion device provided; lines may be sorted out individually as to whether they seem to be informed by quantitative, accentual-syllabic or other prosodic systems. Often, although not always, a persona possesses no microcontextual markers, and thus, like condensation, its identification is a question of establishing shaky semantic macrocontexts. This is to say that for several reasons, which I shall presently examine, personae in *The Cantos* are a feature of the macrocontext.

I have attempted throughout this study to demonstrate that the much-noted discontinuity of Modernist texts is illusory. The prosodic regularity which most readers associate with pre-twentieth-century verse, for instance, is largely conventionalized; it is a function of metrical recurrence. But, as the previous chapter indicated, other forms of recurrence are possible in prosody. Similarly, condensation structures are only perceived as disjunctive in traditional reading procedures (and even these procedures allow for some degree of condensation) which by and large disallow ambivalence in poetic structures; when, in contrast, the reader is attuned to the functions of ambivalence in condensation, the device augments, rather than disjoins, the microcontext. And, finally, in the most commonly cited form of disjunction, fragmentation, the effect of disunity is only apparent; once the reader has automatized the rather clear-cut device of deletion in *A Draft of XXX Cantos*, fragmentation structures present no greater difficulties than traditional "full" structures. The macrocontext, too, achieves a unity which is established through intratextual coupling by means of matrices, models, and various types of equivalence. So too with the supposedly "fractured" point of view in *The Cantos*: personae are influenced by each of the other micro- and macrocontextual factors, and the foregrounding of a confusing variety of voices arises from factors which can be to a large degree systematized.

Discontinuity in a Modernist work like *The Cantos* is sometimes attributed to the very high level of covert or overt allusions which seems to appear in twentieth-century literature. In fact, Stanley Sultan in a recent study sees allusion as the central device of Modernist literature; indeed, he refers to the allusive practices of Pound, Eliot, and Joyce as "The Method" of Modernism. The relationship among allusion, point of view, and discontinuity is fairly apparent: in the inserted quotations of *The Waste Land* and *The Cantos*, for example, whether these be marked or not, a speaker other than Eliot or Pound is definitely "present." And when such quotations are inserted into passages seemingly at random, the semantic and syntactic shift alone is sufficient to give rise to a feeling of bafflement in the reader. Sultan actually assigns to shifts in point of view the role of the main culprit in the seeming disjointedness of Modernist literature:

> However, this discontinuity is not independently present. It is symbiotic with both the "method" and the manipulation of point-of-view, and is largely generated by the latter. Furthermore, in it they meet and accommodate each other. The significant truth about . . . Modernism [involves an] intricate relationship among the principal determinants of the modernist formal characteristics of each work, especially the unavoidable complementary role that the disruption of linear progression plays in the manipulation of point-of-view.[5]

Sultan expends a good deal of ingenuity in attempting to make coherent the "multiplicity of narrators and dramatic speakers who are not identified" in *The Waste Land*, concluding that there are "three classes of speaker" in the poem and that "two are rendered dramatically in his narrative by the third" (Sultan, 1977: 71).

Intertextuality in *The Cantos* (Sultan's "method") is at once clearer and more complex than Sultan's analysis of Modernist uses of allusion would suggest—clearer because Pound frequently foregrounds his intertexts (the Malatesta cantos and the Adams cantos are obvious examples of this practice), more complex because shifts in persona respond to shifts in features of the microcontext and shifts in matrices.

Personae and the Microcontext

Speaker designation is obviously not a simple matter of identifying and categorizing pronouns in a discourse, with, of course, the central and occasional exception of the use of "I." The "I-Speaker" of course is a primary marker of the lyric mode in poetry, but identification of the "I" who is speaking in a given twentieth-century poem can be as troubled as was the discovery of reference in a condensation structure. Both identifications hinge on an ambivalence: in a condensation structure syntactic or semantic markers for reference are absent, confused, or polysemic; in the "I," whether explicit or implicit, of Modernist poetry a similar ambivalence arises for similar reasons. In poets like Pound, Eliot, Stevens, Olson, and Berryman, elements which might confirm identity are often effaced or deliberately confused. Contemporary poems like *The Dream Songs*, for example, employ speakers like Mr. Bones who are alternately the addressee of the poet-addresser and themselves addressers of the audience (and the confusion is further compounded when in this latter role the speaker refers to himself in the third person). Fortunately, such obfuscation is absent in Pound.

Pound's models, as I have argued all along, need not be drawn from literary or nonliterary intertexts because one major process in *The Cantos* is the establishing of intratextual matrices. Hence, if I am to seek models which will aid in discovering the identity of speakers, I shall look back to the intratext of the early cantos. It obviously stands to reason that the first cantos, wherein intratexts have not had time to be established, will not possess such models, and here I shall be confronted with a situation more like that of identification of speakers in some earlier poetry. In Canto 1, for instance, the first speaker is marked prosodically as a speaker *like* the speaker of "The Seafarer," and intertextually as Odysseus-Homer by way of Andreas Divus. At the end of this canto, Pound emerges in a role which will continue to direct shifts from persona to persona throughout *A Draft of XXX Cantos*. A hierarchy of voices in the first thirty cantos might be dominated by a persona assuming a primary status under which all other personae are subsumed. Semantic markers (foremost among these is often the LEVELS OF HISTORY matrix) and the use of "I" would serve initially to indicate the presence of the dominating persona. Significantly, Canto 1 possesses no initial dominant voice because the first syntagm is an example of NP-depleted fragmentation (inspired perhaps by the conventional "in medias res" of epics). Moreover, at this early stage, it is not entirely clear that the "I" which concludes the canto is the dominant one. The semantic content of this speaker's remarks, however, is "metatextual"; that is, foregrounding of intertextuality, here commentary on Divus and Dartona, marks the "intrusion" of a "commanding" point of view (although not necessarily that of Pound the historical author). Actually, the reader goes about the construction of a dominant voice inductively through the accumulation of semantic traits: at the end of Canto 1, for example, the persona accrues to himself a trait which may be long-windedly construed as "learned commentary on obscure texts from a relatively recent historical perspective."

I should stress here that the identification of any persona in *The Cantos* hinges on the identification of a relatively dominant voice. Part of the reason for this has to do with historical relativity; the movements along the linear scale of history, for example, which are so central an element of the first thirty cantos, can only take place in reference to a temporal situation constituted by a central voice. Further, not only does a dominant persona "organize" other, subsidiary personae, but also it contrastively defines the traits those subsidiary personae possess. Condensation, then, operates macrocontextually in the speaker's "I" to create ambivalence (although not ambiguity) in a point of view "powerful" enough to organize a text which is macrocontextually, as well as microcontextually, fragmented.

Another facet of Poundian personae is introduced by the voice at the beginning of Canto 2. This speaker is not identical with the speaker who immediately precedes him; for one thing, the speaking situation here is different, in that Canto 2's opening speaker addresses himself to Robert Browning rather than to the preceding speaker's "interested reader" at the conclusion of Canto 1. In fact, the speaker in Canto 2 can be differentiated by other linguistic factors as well; the register he uses ("Hang it all"), his foregrounded fragmentation ("But Sordello, and my Sordello?"), and his abrupt shifts in hypograms (from Sordello to So-shu) discriminate this speaker from the persona of Canto 1. Equally important is the former speaker's easy movement from direct address and inward question to Imagist compounds and fragmentation structures in the lines which follow. The shift to the Ovid intertext on page 7, too, confirms this speaker's more "immediate" relation with the other speakers (here, Acoetes) he dominates. And the persona who orders Canto 2 continues to speak in Canto 3 where the matrix PERSONAL LEVEL OF HISTORY is immediately foregrounded. However, I shall return below to the relation between persona identification and matrices.

In Canto 4 the speaker assumes a flickering presence; he appears in the "Hear me" of the apostrophe which begins the canto, in "as at Gourdon that time" of page 15, line 21, and in the canto's concluding concluding two lines, "And we sit here . . . / there in the arena. . . ." And yet this speaker gives rise to another persona who is not easily dissociated from either of the first two. It is in this third subsidiary speaker that Eliot's Modernist impersonality may be enacted because, unlike the quotation of an intertext in Canto 1, the use of intertexts in Canto 4 (the stories of Cabestan, Procne and Philomela, Actaeon, *Takasago*) are "filtered" through the "catalyst" of the speaker's mind, the result being a voice wherein metatextual and personal commentary are absent. And in the canto's final verse paragraph, I would argue, the reader is confronted with an epitome of all three personae:

> Père Henri Jacques would speak with the Sennin, on Rokku,
> Mount Rokku between the rock and the cedars,
> Polhonac,
> As Gyges on Thracian platter set the feast,
> Cabestan, Tereus,
>   It is Cabestan's heart in the dish,
> Vidal, or Ecbatan, upon the gilded tower in Ecbatan

Lay the god's bride, lay ever, waiting the golden rain.
By Garonne. "Saave!"
The Garonne is thick like paint,
Procession,—"Et sa'ave, sa'ave, sa'ave Regina!"—
Moves like a worm, in the crowd.
Adige, thin film of images,
Across the Adige, by Stefano, Madonna in hortulo,
As Cavalcanti had seen her.
            The Cerntaur's heel plants in the earth loam.
And we sit here . . .
            there in the arena . . .

                                                            (page 16)

The first persona who tells of Père Henri Jacques fades into the extreme fragmentation of "Polhonac" which is, as the *Companion* puts it, a "subject rhyme" with "Gyges on Thracian platter" (a condensation of Polhonac, Cabestan, and Tereus)—all of which is dominated, if not spoken, by the first persona, as are plausibly the next two lines concerning Vidal, Ecbatan, and Danae. At "By Garonne" a second speaker enters, to be joined perhaps by the first with "As Cavalcanti had seen her." The passage concludes with the "historical" Pound persona's "arena" lines.

The point I should like to make concerning this verse paragraph is that the appearance of the respective speakers is governed by the same principles as are the uses of condensation, fragmentation, coupling, and shifting rhythms. The entire passage, in fact, has as its base structure a recurrently disintegrating sentence begun by the syntagm concerning Père Henri, extended by means of the line beginning "Vidal, or Ecbatan," and compounded by the reference to the procession, the Adige, and the "Madonna in hortulo" and Cavalcanti. The gapping at line 6 seems to present a pivotal condensation in a passage containing a series of embedded condensations ("By Garonne" a condensation of PROVENÇE and LEVELS OF HISTORY matrices, for example), wherein it points through recurrence to "Cabestan, Tereus" which precedes it, and through coupling to "Vidal" which introduces the line which follows. Rhythmically, each syntactic or semantic shift roughly corresponds to a syllabic or quantitative shortening of the line. "Polhonac" introduces the shift to the "cannibalism" model, the gapped and quantitatively "light" "It is Cabestan's heart in the dish" introduces the shift to the Ecbatan model, and "By Garonne" introduces the shift to the procession model.

In the interests of formal description, the attribution of specific structural elements to each of the voices in *A Draft of XXX Cantos* is a goal devoutly to be wished, but the foregrounded features of Pound's style are too thoroughgoing to act as definite "markers" of a single voice. A similar situation arose when, in attempting to determine a correlation between end-stopping and fragmentation, I was compelled to note only very limited tendencies as regards prosody and structural devices. The fact remains, however, that readers of *The Cantos* do seem to distinguish between various speakers in the poem. As I remarked above, there are at least two distinguishable personae attributable to the poet himself in *The Cantos,* as well as a very probable third persona, and, in various mixtures of these basic speakers, probably more.

Canto 14 offers a good illustration of the dilemmas associated with speaker identification. In the preceding canto, an impersonal persona dominates the acts and epigrams of Kung, there being, however, no "I" by which to identify this persona with certainty. Consequently, the "Io venni" which commences Canto 14 may assume a point of view which is superior to that of the persona in Canto 13 and which thereby "brackets" the canto. But the introduction of the "Io" is to a degree confused; obviously, the direct (and, moreover, quite well-known) quotation from Dante seems to deflect the reader's identification of the "Io" with a Poundian speaker. On the other hand, one persona has in all of its previous appearances made a point of its easy commerce with other poets; witness that persona's associations with Ovid, for example, in Canto 2. The speaker who opens Canto 14 is marked by an "epic poet" hypogram appropriate to the persona of Canto 2. I might argue, then, that whatever syntactic or prosodic features characterize this canto can be attached to the speaker of Canto 14. And I might support this notion by the fact that this initial "Io" syntactially dominates both Canto 14 and the next canto, where it again appears on page 65, line 21; the semicolon which ends "Io venni in luogo d'ogni luce muto" and the VP-deletion of this canto (which by definition disallows any other subject NPs) cause this dominance. Yet the matrix of the Hell cantos, and I shall soon argue this point more thoroughly, seems partly inappropriate for the persona of Canto 2.

But the difficulties with persona identification in Cantos 14 and 15 pale beside the problems which arise in Canto 16. The persona's issuance from hell which begins the canto is clear enough, and the prosodic regularity which arises with his cleansing and Eleusinian descent offers no reason to assume that the point of view will soon shift (such regularity being a function of coupling formed by alternating catalogue and participial fragmentation, and of a prosody influenced by a high level of compounds and P-phrases—the passage is typically Imagist). But then the dream intrudes. The foreign-language "j'entendis des voix" of line 7, page 70, like the "Io venni" of Canto 14, seems to imply that the speaker is the voice of Canto 2. Yet the italicized, bracketed, and scholiastic "[*Plarr's narration*]" three lines down must be attributed to the "scholarly" persona of Canto 1. Freudians might argue with some justice that the latter persona represents a conscious or preconscious voice which intrudes on the dreaming voice of the former persona; be that as it may, no other identifiable intrusion of this scholarly voice occurs, and thus the reader must assume that "Plarr's narration" ends with the series of ellipses after "And he stank" in line 18. An enigmatic anecdote about "Brother Percy," the "old Admiral," and Lord Byron follows: does the "our" in "our Brother" refer to the dreaming voice, or is this story the dreamt retelling of another's experience? As with the source and significance of the anecdote itself, there is no way of knowing.

In any of the cantos treating of clearly historical material—as distinguished, say, from cantos dealing with the mythic world or with the intertexts of other poets like Ovid and Homer—the identification of personae can be troublesome in a manner different from that which I have just discussed. If, for example, Canto 21 is ordered, with the better part of Canto 20, by Pound's reminiscence concerning Lèvy on pages 89 and 90, the interjected question ("Where are we?") in Canto 21's first line is perplexing; the line appears to be addressed to the reader by a persona who is himself confused by the management of several voices. Such confusion is not surprising. The initial "Keep the peace, Borso!" is clear enough, being an intratextual coupling with the preceding canto. But the status of Giovanni dei Medici's remarks thereafter is unclear. The reader may assume that the quotations here are partly Giovanni's, which Pound drew from Giovanni's "red leather note book," and that some of the commentary on Giovanni is Machiavelli's ("Col credito suo . . . / Napoli e Venezia di danari. . ."). Yet the perplexed speaker who initially loses his place seems to reappear in line 21 dismissing his collapsing series of voices ("Or another time . . . oh well, pass it."); in fact, the deletions from the Machiavelli intertext make these lines the dominant persona's as well; it as if he reads Machiavelli absentmindedly to his readers, passing, as absorbed readers tend to do, from audible speech to silent perusal and back to speech. Indeed, in nearly all of the "historical cantos" where more or less foregrounded quotation takes place, the reader is unsure whether the historical personage who speaks does so in his "own voice" through direct quotations or in a plausible speech invented by Pound. Obviously, in this latter situation, the reader is confronted with a point of view very different from that of other personae who appear in *A Draft of XXX Cantos*: the very use of actual quotation interlarded with "unmarked" or invented quotation insures this difference. Quotation marks, of course, are uncertain guides to the authenticity of an historical speaking voice; on page 97, an unmarked quote, "E difficile . . . Senza aver lo stato" (lines 7–9) is juxtaposed with a marked one, "'E non avendo . . . era in stato'," (lines 10 and 11), and yet both are equally "authentic." And on page 98 a long quotation from Lorenzo comprised by the first complete verse paragraph on that page is unmarked, and this is followed by a line on which I have already commented at some length: "Another war without glory, and another peace without quiet." This line is apparently not quotation, and yet its epigrammatic quality seems to signify its origin in Lorenzo's writings; again, there are absolutely no formal markers to indicate the shift. Finally, in the long verse paragraph which runs to the end of the canto, the persona who ended Canto 1 seems to return to summarize the later fortunes of Lorenzo, and this persona is in turn interrupted by the historical Pound at line 24 (and perhaps two lines before) with "we sit here / By the arena," very nearly the motto of this speaker.

I should like to stress that, although one persona may dominate other personae in the first thirty cantos, the relations between each appearance of a dominant persona are complicated and not easily describable. I might suggest that the fundamental dilemma posed by the uncertain shifts among personae concerns narrative authority. For one thing, many speakers seem to introduce quotation (whether marked or not); unless the reader is aware of the source of a speaker's statement, she may very well be unsure of a given passage's origin in Pound or in an intertext. The issue is further complicated by Pound's use of his own experiences, as in the war anecdotes of Canto 16, and in the remarks on Thaddeus Pound which open Canto 22. The whole of this latter canto is taken up with Pound's narrative of various incidents, chiefly one concerning Mohamed and the elders in the synagogue. I should note in passing moreover, that the presence of the icon of the "Off Limits" sign in this canto presents a nearly insoluble problem in speaker identification; what *is* the status, as regards point of view, of a more or less visual image in discourse? The question, as far as *The Cantos* are concerned, is not a specialized one, since the later use of ideograms presents much the same problem.

But to return to the problem of authority: Canto 26 offers as broad a medley of historical speakers as the reader will find in the first thirty cantos, but, although some persona always directs these voices, it is doubtful whether any one speaker has any greater authority in the discourse than any other. On page 121 in the first verse paragraph of Canto 26, for example, two competing speakers seem to appear. The historical Pound seems to take precedence for three reasons: the paratactic "And," which introduces the canto and couples it with the "Venetian" model of Canto 25, is joined to a direct reference to Pound's life, "I came here in my young youth"; the Pound persona, therefore, has a direct, lived relation to the central model of this canto; the appearance of this persona has simple syntagmatic precedence. And yet by far the greater part of this canto is occupied with quotation and commentary on quotation. After quoting a decree of the Venetian council, a speaker glosses a reference to a book therein, "the book being Valurio's 'Re Militari,' " and, throughout this and the next two verse paragraphs, this persona introduces matter ("To Nicolo Segundino, the next year"), summarizes his texts ("'Faithful sons [we are] of the church' / [for two pages]") and provides factual links ("Came Messire Hannibal from Cesena"). When quotation marks are abandoned in the next verse paragraph (the second one on page 122), the reader must assume that the scholarly persona has thoroughly taken over, impatiently and fussily translating as he goes along: "And his wife that would touch food but with forks, / Sed aureis furculis, that is / with small golden prongs." I might argue with some confidence, then, that this voice has textual authority over this canto, but for the fact that the "interlinear" extrapolation of Mozart's original letter to the archbishop of Salzburg (according to the *Companion*, "quite politely worded") does not seem to represent the acme of disinterested scholarship: "To the supreme pig, the archbishop of Salzburg: / Lasting filth and perdition. Since your exalted pustulence is too stingy / To give me a decent income. . . ." Actually, the reader must have recourse to Pound's own feelings about the vicissitudes of patronage in order to attribute a reasonable identity to this speaker.

The point I wish to make about the authority of a given persona is this: if multiplicity of point of view is one of the hallmarks of Modernism, as many critics like Sultan argue, it would seem to stand to reason either that the Modernist text is highly disjunctive, even fractured (as Sultan, again, contends) or that it achieves some sort of coherence despite its apparent disjunctions. Reader reactions are difficult to gauge on this subject; clearly many competent readers do perceive thorough and irresolvable fragmentation in many Modernist texts, although whether this perception is the outcome of multiplicity of point of view is a vexed question. As I trust this study has shown, the perception of fragmentation in Modernism is the result of a complex of causes, and, moreover, complete fragmentation, at least on the microcontextual level, is illusory.

Furthermore, in a text with many speakers, it is very difficult to single out one speaker as more authorititative than another.[6] I can, as I have demonstrated above, construct a fairly concrete definition of authority in a speaker; such authority involves the ordering of other speakers by means of foregrounded commentary on the speeches of other personae, or by means of simple signifiers of "second order" discourse like quotation marks. But when I attempt to establish a hierarchy between "dominant" personae (those who bracket other personae), my efforts turn out to be futile. This is because, in trying to discover the chief among equals, I am forced to construct "personalities" for my dominant personae, as I have done to an extent above. Now, since "personalities" in the discourse can have no structural characteristics, I cannot with any certainty designate markers for personae, and thus I have failed to give a semiotic description of point of view. Indeed, multiplicity of point of view in the Modernist text may rely on complex conventions which are not now very well understood. It is true that markers have been found for narrative strategies like direct, indirect, and free indirect discourse, but what of texts (and I suspect this is by no means rare in Modernism) which embody two or more free indirect points of view? This last question bears on the heart of the issue at hand: point of view, as it is now defined by literary theorists, is an inevitably psychological concept, and, as such, it is not susceptible of description by contemporary semiotic procedures (although post-Freudians like Jacques Lacan may point the way to a solution of this impasse).

Consequently, I should like briefly to consider in the remainder of this chapter a compromise position on the issue of multiplicity of point of view in *The Cantos;* this position will necessarily have recourse to macrocontextual semantics—that is to say, to a foundation in the matrices of the first thirty cantos.

Personae and the Macrocontext

One very popular way among students of Modernism to account for multiplicity of point of view is to assign a single narrator to the discourse who possesses a large number of different facets, each of which appears in turn. Undoubtedly, part of the stimulus for this view comes from Modernists themselves who are to a greater or lesser extent indebted to the insights of twentieth-century psychology; the division of the narrator's point of view, for example, may be created either on the basis of the tripartite Freudian ordering of consciousness, or on the basis of a species of "split personality." My remarks above on personae imply just such a "fracturing" of a single personality; it would be disingenuous to argue that any of the personae is anyone other than Ezra Pound, and, if nothing else, the concept of the "persona," the mask, confirms Pound's "identity" with his speakers.

Yet even after I have conceded the existence of one many-faceted persona, I have still not solved the problem of how I am to describe each of those facets: a structural description of one multilevelled persona may even be more difficult than the description of several "personalities." Albert Cook argues that in the rhythms of *The Cantos* the reader will discover a clue to shifts in personae:

> The rhythmic virtuosity is not displayed for its own sake. It could only have been invented, in fact, to perform the poetic task of providing a musical ground for the shifts and convergencies in the *personae*-persons, the masks and faces, of the poem. The person of the *Cantos* is both multiple and moving; the motion of the face and its masks, instead of governing the shifts from short poem to short poem, has become the organizing principle of a very long one.[7]

This "organizing principle" is a variation, according to Cook, on Pound's use of the ideogram; in fact, Cook continues, the employment of personae and ideograms gives rise to the basic articulation of *The Cantos:*

> Each individual canto is made up of blocks of statement, and each block tends to centre in a visual perception (ideogram) or an event from someone's life *(persona),* or occasionally in something that possesses the dual character of ideogram and *persona.* Ideogram exists, then, 'paratactically', on an absolute level with *persona,* so that one cannot be signifier and the other signified. Beyond the smaller blocks within cantos, each canto itself constitutes a larger block, usually a *persona,* which is set off against other blocks: the Odysseus-block of Canto I sets off a Sordello-block in Canto II; the two set off a Cid-block; all set off a Dionysus-block, etc. (Cook, 1969: 359)

Although Cook states that, to understand the functioning of the "basic principle" of *The Cantos,* a "close examination of its linguistic technique is required," unfortunately his examination is not particularly "close" and only remotely "linguistic": what, for instance, does the mechanism of one canto's "setting off" another involve? Nonetheless, much in his remarks is valid. Ideogram and persona do not stand in the relation of signifier to signified because both are essentially functions of the macrocontext, neither having clear markers. Moreover, Cook's views on "main form," disjunction, and shifts in personality are succinct and cogent:

> To see the *Cantos* as conversational improvisations . . . on the one hand, or on the other hand as some newer 'rose-in-the-steel-dust' version of classical repetition with variation . . . is to ignore the interaction of the speaking self with what the self has thought over. The poet of the *Cantos* represents a person too moving in his multiplicities to allow either for random fragmentation or for any sort of structured organization. (Cook, 1969: 355)

After these insights, Cook goes on, not very successfully, to align personae and rhythms. Yet a common theme runs through all of his remarks above: the personae in *The Cantos* are ordered macrocontextually on the basis of recurrent concerns and these concerns are what I have termed the matrices of *The Cantos.*

But to return full circle to my initial remarks in this chapter on the topic of deep and surface structures and their relation to macrocontexts in general and personae in *The Cantos* in particular: I noted there that the "reality" of discourse, like that of grammar as a whole, is achieved solely through the relation of "a semantic interpretation to a phonetic representation," as Chomsky states it, and that this mediation comes about through a "syntactic component." Now, microcontextual structures as I have used them in this study are direct functions of the syntactic component which is, as Chomsky once again puts it, the "sole 'creative' part" of a linguistic structure. The reader should note that this creativity involves linguistic factors and has nothing to do with intellectual, philosophical or spiritual creativity.

At any rate, since I can formally describe microcontextual structures, it stands to reason that I can thus describe linguistic creativity in a discourse like *The Cantos*. And because syntactic creativity is a mediator which offers the linguistic analyst an avenue by which to enter the region of semantic interpretation, I may use the description of the microcontext to forward a "model" of the macrocontext. The reader will pardon my use of the word "model" here (which comes into conflict with Riffaterre's employment of "model"): I am constrained to the usage because the concept of the model in the sense used by science is the nearest I may come to the manner in which it is necessary to describe semantic systems. Like subatomic systems, like early evolutionary mechanisms, or like infant perception, the semantic foundation of language, although it is itself "invisible" and abstract, provokes very "visible" and concrete effects. The problem of the reality of the semantic, and thus literary macrocontextual, systems is one that has concerned modern linguistics since the inception of Chomsky's theories twenty-five years ago. In fact, one of Chomsky's earliest queries, one of the problems which stimulated the ideas which later became coherent in transformational generative grammar, involved the way in which speakers distinguish between two identical syntactic structures like the well-known "He is easy to please" and "He is eager to please." Traditional linguistics could not account, on the basis of surface structure alone, for the fact that although these statements seem structurally identical, any average English-speaker automatically interprets them as semantically diverse. Chomsky's solution to the dilemma, of course, was to posit a common deep structure wherein the "true" semantic nature of these statements was generated in the mind of the speaker and was interpreted in the mind of the listener.

In a like manner, literary semiotics must assume an underlying macrocontextual structure which informs microcontextual structures; this is partly because the formal properties of the microcontext do not by themselves explain the way in which such structures are interpreted by the reader. There are many reasons this assumption is crucial; one of these is that the debate over the distinction between ordinary and literary discourse will probably only be resolved through a study of models of macrocontexts. For my immediate purposes, however, the assumption of a macrocontext in the first thirty cantos, which can be approached but not fully described, is decisive. I wish to stress that neither am I discussing "themes" under a species of pseudo-scientism tricked out with terms like "macrocontext," nor am I dismissing the existence of themes. Rather, I am making what seems to me a clear distinction between "thematic meaning" and "macrocontextual structure." The differences between the two concepts are as follows.

Let us consider the argument of another thorny and stylistically difficult English epic, *Paradise Lost:* Milton says that his theme is to "assert Eternal

Providence / And justify the ways of God to men." "Theme" here for Milton is equivalent to "persuasive intent," and the intention to persuade a reader to think or feel a certain way about a certain subject is one of the oldest and most honorable offices of literature. If I augment this concept of theme to include such factors as the deployment of motifs ("a type of recurrent incident, device, or formula" as Abrams's *A Glossary of Literary Terms* has it), the "fresh stimulation of tied images" of meaning in the reader's mind (I. A. Richards), and the sublimation of cathexes or the literary embodiment of Archetypes (Freud and Jung), I have a fairly thorough definition of "theme" as it is used by literary critics. But neither the intent to persuade, nor the recurrence of motifs, nor affective stimulation, nor psychological process is, as I hope I have demonstrated here, a factor in the macrocontext. Nonetheless, I am only stating the obvious when I note that *The Cantos*, too, clearly embody themes in these senses: *The Cantos* attempt to persuade, to repeat motifs (which are, by the way, species of hypograms), to stimulate images, and, of course, to move the reader emotionally.

But when I turn to a macrocontextual structure like point of view, the dichotomy between theme and macrocontext is clear. Certainly, a persona, like a given theme, may run through the entirety of a discourse, and both a theme and a persona may be elusive when we come to try to define them, but here the similarities end. Fundamentally, a macrocontextual structure differs from a theme in that, although identification of that structure relies on semantic clues, its formal presence is clear-cut. The use of a given persona may acquire meaning, but such meaning has affinities closer to the sense in which music has meaning than to the sense in which a statement like "Hang it all, Robert Browning, / there can be but the one 'Sordello' " has meaning. Simply speaking, a macrocontextual structure is not paraphrasable in the sense that a theme is paraphrasable. Matrices, which are so integral an element of the macrocontext, are similarly nonparaphrasable; although I have repeatedly affixed labels to the matrices of *The Cantos*, this is the appropriate time to point out that, as Riffaterre clearly states, matrices are never realized in the text except through models. But, just as critics are forced to use figurative language to describe figurative language (as Barthes perspicaciously notes), so am I constrained to use linguistic means to describe the elements which lie below linguistic structures. Finally, the presence of a macrocontextual structure like the persona is indisputable. Themes are open to debate. We may (and do) contest Milton's own statement of the theme of *Paradise Lost*. But can we seriously question the presence of that living voice which orders, rants, sings, and records in *The Cantos?*

8
MACROCONTEXTS: THE HISTORICAL DIMENSION

THE PARADIGMS OF Modernism—*The Waste Land, Ulysses,* and *The Cantos*—
defeat one crucial assumption concerning the types of formal experiment
these paradigms offer: if, as I have argued throughout, form in Modernist
literature assumes a degree of significance it had not hitherto had, if *The
Cantos* in particular signify through identifiable linguistic elements of the
poem's structure, how is the critic to account for the clearly stated programmatic basis which authors like Eliot and Pound offer for their major works?
Specifically, can semiotic description afford to dismiss the Anglican and
traditionalist intent of *Ash Wednesday* or the historical and economic "revisionism" of *The Cantos?* The dichotomy posed between intention and form
arose in the critical aftermath of the appearance of several important Modernist works. I shall summarize what is only a well-known state of affairs in
the analysis of works like *The Waste Land, Ulysses,* and *The Cantos:* each of
the works seems to seek formal self-sufficiency, to refer to itself as text, as
global discourse; this attempt at self-sufficiency is the outcome of factors
like radical structural defamiliarization, disruption of traditional reading
procedures, and foregrounded intratextuality. Even the high degree of
allusiveness in Modernist literature, which seems to militate against the
self-sufficiency of the text, assumes the character of a kind of cooption of
other texts, a predation on tradition.

Accompanying the notion of the text's self-sufficiency is the modern
critics' inherited reluctance (inherited from the New Critics as the "intentional fallacy") to ascribe "intention" to the text. Herein lies the dilemma for
the critic; as a matter of critical procedure and in accordance with the ways
in which these texts "ask" to be read, the analysis of the Modernist text
must ignore authorial intention. Yet certainly with a Modernist like Pound,
and to a lesser extent with Eliot and others, the intentions of the text are
stated not only in a number of the author's other texts, but also in the text
itself. No Pound scholar is in any doubt about the general cast of Pound's
opinions concerning economics, Renaissance history, literary tradition,
and many other subjects; and it is a simple fact that that scholar's certainty

is a product not only of "extracurricular" reading by and about Pound, but of distinct statements in *The Cantos* themselves. Portions of *The Cantos* are indubitably didactic in the traditional, uncomplicated sense of the term.

How then can a semiotic viewpoint account for Pound's avowed intent to introduce a fairly definite and unambiguous content into a poem which, I have argued, largely achieves its signification through formal devices? My answer is disingenuous: groups of cantos having an "undiluted" historical matrix (the Malatesta cantos, the Adams cantos, the Chinese cantos) are best viewed macrocontextually. This is of course not to say that the major macrocontextual formal devices which I have adumbrated here are some-how absent in groups like Cantos 8 through 11, and, before I proceed to discuss the problems associated with the macrocontext in these groups, it would perhaps be best to designate the formal properties of the Malatesta cantos.

In a valuable essay to which I shall return, Michael F. Harper remarks of Pius II's indictment of Sigismundo in Canto 10 that it possesses, as one might suppose, a "documentary" style:

> The rhetorical strategy of the document is exactly this: the list, the series. Sometimes its terms are single words, sometimes whole clauses or sentences, but always the style seems to be trying to establish guilt by repetition and rhetorical elaboration. Pound compresses a great deal; or rather he "highlights," singling out what he considers essential and assembling his poem from these materials.[1]

If I deleted small portions of this description (the remark about "establishing guilt," for instance) and expanded it to include the Malatesta cantos as a whole, I would have a fairly coherent definition of catalogue fragmentation and condensation in these cantos, and, predictably, the style of the Malatesta sequence, like that of the remainder of the first thirty cantos, exhibits a high degree of fragmentation and condensation. Although VP- and NP-deleted fragmentation occurs often on the level of the microcontext (the reader may consider, for example, the deleted letter which opens Canto 8), I am here concerned with that species of fragmentation which takes the form, as Harper puts it, of the "list, the series," which signifies through "repetition." Harper is chiefly interested in the series constituted by the "charges" brought against Sigismundo by Pius II and in the historicity of the rhetoric of those charges, and I shall return to this subject shortly. For the moment, however, I should like to point out that what I have termed the "catalogue" is the essential structure of the Malatesta cantos. Roughly three-quarters of Cantos 8 through 11 is based on intertexts, and each separate intertext, I would argue, constitutes an "item" in a serial catalogue, to the intent of which, once again, I shall return. Each item, considered as a syntagm, although sometimes possessing either initial or final deletion (as in Sigismundo's "second" letter on page 29) is a self-sufficient signifying structure. Canto 9, the so-called "Post-Bag" canto, which I discussed in Chapter 4 in terms of its uses of spatiality and condensation, although in part organized on the basis of the adventitious relation of letters in Sigismundo's captured post-bag, comprises a number of these self-sufficient syntagms, grouped serially through parataxis. The various syntagms are not solely related metonymically through chance, however; like the units of the opening verse paragraph, in which the various images have spatial and metonymic relations, the elements of the canto as a whole are related metonymically. The third verse paragraph, following the succession of events in paragraphs one and two, is joined to them, obviously, through an expansion on line 24, page 35, "And he began building the TEMPIO," as the post-bag contents themselves are joined to preceding verse paragraphs by line 17, verse paragraph five, page 37. The letters themselves, as one might expect, are joined by their concern, again, with the Tempio and with the domestic economy of the Malatesta household. The letters exhibit a typical combination of fragmentation and condensation; the deleted ending of the first letter (on page 37, from Matteo Nuti) is joined continuously in actual space with the overseer's letter which immediately follows as it is joined to the latter through the letter-writers' common concern with the " 'valts of the cherch.' " Another deleted ending, this time of a postscript to the overseer's letter, occurs in the line which follows on page 38 (" 'Sagramoro . . .' "), and the superscript of a third letter dealing with the materials needed for the Tempio, which are then listed catalogue-fashion, follows. The end of this letter is also lopped off, and the letter-writers turn to the subject of individuals in Sigismundo's household; the first of these letters is followed by two lines properly belonging to the postscript beginning " 'Sagramoro . . .' " above, and these two lines establish a condensation structure pointing to the equivalent claims on Sigismundo of his family and of the Tempio. Two further fragments follow which are, again like the Sagramoro lines, inserted between "family" letters, and these letters, again like the first insertion, are highly fragmented. The long final letter on page 40, which seems a condensation of the Tempio model in the preceding letters, is end-bracketed by the first lines in page 41, "That's what they found in the post-bag / And some more of it to the effect that / he 'lived and ruled'." The last verse paragraph of this canto offers a structural reprise of the devices of Cantos 8 and 9; fragments from various intertexts—Pius II, a chronicler of Rimini, Landor—are employed in a condensation structure which both sets forth the attributes of Isotta and points to Isotta's importance to the Tempio—which last is joined metonymically (by contrast) to the sarcophagi of San Vitale.

I might summarize this complicated analysis by merely stating that Canto 9, like the other Malatesta cantos, presents a surface level whose formal features are the same (with one exception) as those of the other cantos I have examined. The sole exception, a novel formal device, is the use of "prose-form" in these cantos; in order to sidestep the inevitable debate over what constitutes "prose-form" in poetry, I shall simply define "prose-form" as a typographical form characterized by equal length of a set of lines with fixed boundaries. The setting of prose intertexts, largely letters and chronicles, in "poetry-form" is introduced in these cantos, although it is not peculiar to them. It is very difficult to determine the prosodic standards which dictate whether a letter in the Malatesta cantos is to be reproduced in its original format, or whether it is to be set in verse lines; when a letter *is* set in verse, however, line length seems to be ordered on the basis of phrasal structure, although enough anomalies exist that such a basis cannot be said to be the sole informing criterion. I shall note in passing one final feature on the surface level which is notable because of its rarity in pre-twentieth-century literature: iconicity. Pound's reproduction of documents as they exist in fact (the signal example, of course, is the letter to Giovanni dei Medici, which opens Canto 8, wherein Sigismundo's seal has obliterated part of the text) is a small but important step in the enlarging of poetry's scope in the direction of "open form."

Perhaps the most important macrocontextual feature of the Malatesta cantos, and the one which is most highly foregrounded for the careful student of *A Draft of XXX Cantos*, is the homogeneity of the matrix here. Not until later cantos, after the first thirty, will such long stretches of text be given over to an undiluted matrix; indeed, possibly the most highly foregrounded aspect of the Malatesta cantos is precisely this "centering" on a subject without the rapid and frequent shifts in matrix and model which characterize the remainder of the first thirty cantos, and for which the reader has been prepared by Cantos 1 through 7. I suspect, then—to return to the question of intention—that this foregrounded concern with Malatesta and his milieu, virtually without a typically Poundian excursus into other matrices, is at the foundation of most readers' interest in the historicity of these cantos, and to this subject I shall now turn.

Intention and Historicity

There is much in the critical debate over Pound's merits and failings as an historian which will remind readers of similar questions having to do with Pound's abilities as a translator, prosodist, economist, and manipulator of masks. And my comments earlier in this study—chiefly in regard to translation and prosody—have some bearing on the role of history in *The Cantos*. There can be little doubt concerning Pound's intention to introduce "history" into *The Cantos*. But history, and I shall for the time being use the word "history" in its widest and most popular sense, is properly the "subject," or "motif," or "theme" of a poem, and may or may not lend the sort of bias to a work from which the reader may infer intent. Certainly, *The*

Cantos do possess such bias, and Pound's other writings make more or less clear what the content of that bias may be. About all this Poundians are generally in agreement.

I should like at this stage, however, to shift the perspective from critics' views of Pound's historicity to what might plausibly be said to be the reader's reaction to the stretch of material presented by Cantos 8 through 11. The reader, like the critics, will be interested in Pound's intent here, although her questions might not be those of the critics: one set of queries concerns Sigismundo himself. Is he to be viewed as an archetype of the age? Is his life merely a convenient platform from which to view Quattro-centro life? Is Pound sympathetic to his political and esthetic and economic views? Is he simply a colorful character? All these questions, of course, have to do with Pound's intentions, and, like the more obscure intentions of poets less exegetical about their own works, these are in the end fundamentally undiscoverable. Sigismundo Malatesta is without doubt a colorful character, but then so are the other heroes of *The Cantos*, from Odysseus to Pound himself. Malatesta seems not to have had coherent political and economic views except, like the majority of the condottieri of his age, a view to the main chance. His esthetic views are crystallized in the Tempio, which Pound himself felt was a "monumental failure." Obviously, Malatesta's life offers a very good perspective through which to view Quattro-cento society, but the lives of the Este family and of the Medici (to name only two groups who appear prominently in *A Draft*) are equally attractive on this score. And, although he is an appropriate archetype of his age, he is no more so, once again, than many of the Este and Medici. I shall not forward the simplistic argument that Pound chose Malatesta as the subject of Cantos 8 through 11 on the basis of the condottiere's personality alone, but, on the other hand, such a basis for selection is not to be entirely dismissed: "Sigismundo cut his notch. He registered a state of mind, of sensibility, of all-roundedness and awareness."[2]

The question of why Pound chose the life of Sigismundo as the matrix for four cantos, then, is to a degree insoluble, dealing as it does with precisely the sort of intentional fallacy which the New Critics proscribed. Yet the question is not frivolous, because it provokes more serious ones involving the above-noted problems with Pound's historicity. The degree of Pound's historical accuracy, or for that matter the accuracy of any historian, will be a function of his motives, his intentions in presenting this figure and no other in his text. Pound himself has commented in this regard that "no one has claimed that the Malatesta cantos are obscure. They are openly volitionist, establishing . . . the effect of the factive personality, Sigismundo, an entire man."[3] Actually, the types of information which are presented in the Malatesta cantos, viewed objectively, are so various that attempts to assign one kind of purely historiographic intent to these cantos are inevitably defeated by the presence of other information which seems to have nothing to do with that intent. The introduction of Sigismundo's remarks on patronage and the arts, the reproduction of correspondence concerning the Tempio, seems to outline a peculiarly Quattrocento view of classicism and esthetics, but the vivid portrayal of Sigismundo's enemies in Canto 10 appears solely aimed at historical revisionism.

The presence or absence of historicity, the degree of historicity if present, is not the first problem a reader may have with the Malatesta cantos. A more pressing concern, for the reader interested in the poetics of *The Cantos*, involves the admission of certain kinds of intertexts from the "historical record"—the notes, letters, journals, and so forth, of Sigismundo Malatesta and his contemporaries. No doubt Pound exercised a great deal of care in assembling these materials, and such painstaking labor may in itself suggest something about his intentions:

> All this research and talk of verification [in Pound's] letters implies an overriding concern with historical accuracy; work of this extent and depth would hardly have been necessary or even appropriate if Pound had wanted merely an example to "flesh out" his ideas. . . . Pound's characterization grew out of much research and close attention to language and deserves to be considered with just as much care in its turn. (Harper, 1981: 90)

As Harper here cogently argues, one must grant to Pound scholarly diligence and precision in regard to his sources. But to what end are those sources deployed in what is after all a poem? Harper answers that the "portrayal" of Malatesta

> is implicated by (and itself implicates) a whole system of beliefs and assumptions that it is the business of *The Cantos* to articulate and that a secure judgment of the poem would have to take into account. . . . I would urge a preliminary claim for the value of *The Cantos* based not on agreement or disagreement with any particular reading of history that Pound presents but rather on the very nature of the poem he wrought, on his denial of the conventional separation between "poetry" and "history." (Harper, 1981: 100)

These remarks are fairly representative of a balanced critical judgment of the Malatesta cantos, and I certainly would deny nothing in them. Some familiar problems, however, arise: that the "beliefs and assumptions that it is the business of *The Cantos* to articulate," whatever these may be for a given critic, should make Sigismundo Malatesta the sole subject in the first thirty cantos for a relatively full-scale biography seems implausible; the choice seems gratuitous.

Harper's claim for an assessment of *The Cantos* "based not on agreement or disagreement with any particular reading of history" is more to the point (even though Harper himself takes great pains to show the "accuracy" of Pound's "evidence"). Harper implies that part of the value of *The Cantos* relies on Pound's "denial of the conventional separation between" poetry and history.

In what way does something that is not history enter the poem, and how does material which *is* history show itself? For it is not "history" which enters the Malatesta cantos, but texts. History, after all, is a created entity, not a "natural" one, or, if natural, it is so great a sum of events as to be uncapturable. Now, Pound does much in *The Cantos* to reflect this multi-fariousness of human chronology through the sheer number of persons and events which *The Cantos* recall, and much to show the "dialectical" impact of events on one man's life, his own. In fact, it may perhaps be that Sigismundo Malatesta, far from being an "exhibit" of an historical moment, is a paradigm, a psychological "type." History, both Marx and Derrida inform us, advances through differences; movement is decipherable, like the phonemes of spoken language, only through oppositions. Yet Pound, like Yeats, with his gyres and Joyce with his Vico, stresses cyclicity, repetition. Whether a model of history which is ever-advancing is an inheritance of the West's Christian millenarianism, of the capitalist virtue of economic "progress," or of Marxist dialectics, the unidirectional theory of history seems unappealing to many Modernists (even those, like Eliot, who subscribe to it subscribe in unorthodox ways).[4]

But to return to the materials of history: it seems difficult for us (by "us" I mean informed citizens of the late twentieth century) to separate the primary textual sources *in* history from history itself. Harper is correct: Pound does not recognize a split between history and poetry because both deal with signifiers of signifiers, with "records" inevitably isolated from objective phenomena in time. Calliope and Clio, as the Ancients were well aware, are sisters too enigmatic, or too coy, to divulge which is the eldest. Pound was fond of demonstrating the *concret Allgemeine* of the Renaissance's universal influence by pointing to Valla's exposure of the forgery of the Donation of Constantine, and the appeal to him of this bit of textual detective work reveals much about the interest for him of the various materials concerning Malatesta which have come down to us. I do not feel that Pound's enthusiasm, his near-connoiseurship, for the text-as-artifact can be overrated; his essay on Cavalcanti and the work which clearly underlies *The Spirit of Romance* (to say nothing of the Malatesta cantos themselves) attest to this fascination with text-as-object. Further corroboration for such enthusiasm is given us within *The Cantos* themselves by Pound's use of iconicity, to which I referred above.

It does then matter whether the intertexts of the Malatesta cantos are "accurate," but such accuracy is not the accuracy of historiography as historians are accustomed to view it. Harper comments that "the Malatesta sequence is a critical *reading* of some of the chief primary sources for any understanding of Sigismundo," and that Pound's reading leads to the writing of the sequence—historiography in the literal sense (Harper, 1981: 99). But the accuracy of Pound's *use* of the materials is not employed for revisionist ends: it is, by the way, only the *use* of the texts which can be accurate (as any historian knows); we can never confirm the accuracy of a text except through another text, and so on ad infinitum. I will grant that the resuscitation of Sigismundo's reputation is a subsidiary aim of the Malatesta cantos, but Pound's chief concern is with accurately portraying textual inaccuracy. He is interested in the distortions of texts (like the Donation) and their influence on life; just as Pound abhorred the devaluations of currency and language, and their subsequent "inflation," as moral evils, so he excoriated the sort of "textual inflation" we witness in Pius II's commination of Sigismundo in Canto 10.

Furthermore, there is much in the "revised" version of Sigismundo's character which is for Pound, as I noted above, paradigmatic: he is, like Odysseus, "poliorcetes" and "polumetis;" in his love for Isotta he is an inheritor of the Provençal tradition; like the Cid he is a desperate joiner of divided territories; and like many of his own contemporaries whom Pound admires he is an "amateur" of art and philosophy; in Canto 16 he is named as one of the "heroes" and "founders."

But, once again, it is really the "discourse" of Malatesta's life with which Pound is intrigued. He finds himself confronted with a received tradition and a secret history, and the ur-texts which make up these two strands are overlayered with the prejudices of later chroniclers. Pound is without doubt concerned with distilling truth from this mélange, but he is even more interested in the genesis of the mélange itself; in the Malatesta cantos it is the signifiers of the records themselves, and not the signified of Malatesta's life, which are important. Harper confirms this: "Pound does not just present his results, he invites us to repeat the process by which he arrived at them: to study and weigh the styles—and hence, Pound believed, the essences, les hommes mêmes—of Malatesta and his chief accuser" (Harper, 1981: 99). Unfortunately, the debate over the accuracy of Pound's "results" obscures this invitation to "repeat the process by which he arrived at them." Harper himself is a victim of the obscurantism he warns against; his discussion of Pound's presentation of Pius's "bear's-greased latinity" is perspicacious and thorough, clearly revealing Harper's recognition that the style of Pius's documents itself is what is meant to be foregrounded in Canto 10. When, however, Harper characterizes the "ideogrammic" presentation of the various documents of the Malatesta cantos, their contrastive and reflecting juxtaposition, as Pound's "historical method at its best," he seems to lose the very tendency of his own argument: as any careful student of *The Cantos* (and Harper is certainly this) should be aware, the juxtaposition of documents in *The Cantos* is one of the poem's major macro-contextual devices. I shall not utterly dismiss the importance of the content of these documents, but, on the other hand, the valid historicity of the historical documents, like the valid translation of literary documents or the valid reading of ideograms, is not crucial to the understanding of the poem: as Harper himself makes clear, it is the repetition of the process of "documentation" which is important. I should like now to pursue the nature of this process, and to do so I shall need to examine the document-as-signifier.

Convention and the Intertext

One widely recognized assumption of poststructuralist criticism involves the pervasive role which convention plays in the production of literary texts: this last phrase itself, *"production of literary texts,"* suggests the importance of that role in the eyes of literary semioticians. A literary work, according to many contemporary critics of various persuasions, is a cultural artifact which is produced and consumed; like any other cultural artifact, like, for example, a piece of pottery or an item of fashionable clothing, the literary work is so enmeshed in a system of cultural codes that disentangling the work's "original" elements is a difficult chore indeed. As literary historians have been long aware, "originality" as an aspect in the composition of literature is a relatively recent notion; moreover, deconstructionist theory, whatever its opacities, has performed the valuable service of calling into question the very concept of "origins." This study, however (and the reader may here breathe a sigh of relief), cannot pursue the very complex argument which seeks to deconstruct the "metaphysical" fallacy of "The Origin," nor, in fact, is it the office of a formal description of a work's poetics to do so (a fact many theory-enchanted critics ignore). I need look to no more abstruse a work than *The Road to Xanadu* to demonstrate poetry's reliance on intertexts and hypograms. Roughly speaking, however, the use of intertexts since the Romantic period (and the advent of the "cult" of originality) has been, if not covert, at least not highly foregrounded (I am, of course, leaving out of account here the foregrounding of fictional intertexts in works like *The Ring and The Book*). *The Cantos*, in contrast, as I am certain most readers will concede, make a clear effort to foreground their intertexts, even to the extent of offering citations (see, for instance, the *dual* reference to Pius's *Commentaries* and to Yriarte on page 44, Canto 10). I have suggested throughout this study, however, that intertexts abound in *The Cantos* and that, at a very early stage in the first thirty cantos, Pound is manufacturing yet more intertexts by means of his own *intra*texts.

A twofold dilemma is thus presented to the reader: is the convention which states that all or most of a poem be the "original work" of the poet supplanted by a more recent convention which recognizes the pervasiveness of convention and allows the poet, in light of this pervasiveness, to introduce a "prewritten" content into a literary work (just as that poet might introduce a previously established formal convention—like the villanelle, for instance—into his work)? Secondly, if this prewritten intertext is a legitimate component of the poem, what effect does its introduction have on the notion of persona, of poetic authority?

I take up again the subject of the last chapter because I have now, in discussing a portion of the first thirty cantos which deals nearly exclusively with intertexts, reached a more abstract, or perhaps a more general, perspective through which to view the question of personal authority in a poem. In the last chapter I adopted the device of a "divided" central speaker who possesses ultimate authority over the discourse, and I went on to concede that it would be factitious to argue a true separation between this speaker and Ezra Pound. I *shall* be able, however, to make the distinction between the speakers of the Malatesta cantos and Pound. Further, I shall call into question the senses in which readers normally assume that a poet is *in* his poem. Both of these projects rest on the concept of individuality in literature. Lawrence Manley, in an essay which intelligently surveys conceptual aspects of convention, summarizes structuralist and post-structuralist views of the individual in culture:

> The elevation of social codes and systems to the level of universals suggests that within these codes the present and consciousness are "toujours-déjà-donnée." The absorption of consciousness into codes therefore entails the abolition of the distinction between self and world and hence implies a radical critique of the Cartesian *cogito*. The self "comes to appear more and more as a construct, the result of systems of convention" [here Manley is quoting Jonathan Culler]. Thus, Lévi-Strauss observes, the goal of the human sciences "is not to constitute but to dissolve man."[5]

That a Self, a cogito, exists within the work (structuralism states) is a convention, but poststructuralism goes on to add that the work cannot be seen as the simple effect of an originary cause. Manley continues:

> No one convention . . . will be self-determinate or independent of relation with others of the same order, or intersection with different orders of convention . . . or of the unstable and productive play unleashed on all of these wherever the convention is deployed. At any given point, some of the multi-lateral relations will be less well defined or important than others; but the very possibility of their interanimation depends upon some nonoriginary but relatively fixed and determinate formation from which the play of difference departs. (Manley, 1981: 46)

This "relatively fixed and determinate formation" is, I would argue in the present instance, the macrocontext of *A Draft of Thirty Cantos*. Does not the macrocontext, however, (the sensible reader will ask) originate in Ezra Pound? The answer to this question, like *The Cantos* themselves, must be ambivalent; in the very real and simple sense that the first thirty cantos comprise a number of passages which are intertexts, the answer will be "no"; in the sense that certain matrices, most notably LEVELS OF HISTORY (PERSONAL), are impossible without reference to the individual existence of Pound, the answer will be "yes." This ambivalence departs, however, when I turn from the signified of the work, whether of intertexts or "personal" matrices, and look to the signifier, the "writing" (or *écriture* if you will) of *The Cantos*. The origins of the discourse have little direct bearing on the production of the text; in the realm of text production only conventions have force. Consequently, to speak of the persona's authority over the text, as I did in the last chapter, is merely to create a "model" (in the sense of the word, again, which I employed in Chapter 7).

It is extremely difficult to dissociate textual conventions from reading conventions, and indeed many critics contend there is no real distinction to be made between the two. Very early on in this study I pointed up the paradox which surrounds the reading of a Modernist work, arguing that a poem like *The Cantos* can only be reread. Pound himself has outlined the difficulties confronting the Modernist wishing to create a structure of "counterpoint."[6] It follows that any hierarchy of speakers dominated by one persona has no validity in a "unidirectional" linear reading of the text. It is as if the first reading of the poem is necessarily "dramatic" in a quite uncomplicated sense: each speaker, while he is speaking, holds the stage—the affect experienced by the listener/reader is unconcerned with the "author" in whom the speech "originates." This analogy with *The Cantos* fails, of course, because, in order to make it legitimate, I should have to postulate a dramatic situation in which the actor speaks lines which are neither his nor the playwright's, and which are, moreover, somehow foregrounded (curiously, some contemporary drama has attempted to do just this—as, for example, in *Rosencrantz and Guildenstern Are Dead*).

Since speakers in *The Cantos* only acquire authority after the text has been produced, and since the production of the text is indistinguishable from the establishing of the macrocontext, it stands to reason that the relations between speakers are achieved solely through the macrocontext. In the system of the macrocontext there can be no "privileging" of elements, and thus the question I asked above (does the macrocontext originate in Ezra Pound?) is rendered moot. The speakers of the Malatesta cantos are only allomorphic signifiers of the signified which is the macrocontext.

Many readers will find it difficult to accept that the "bear's-greased latinity" of Pius's commination, the boyish gravity of Sallustio's letter to his father, or Genari's businesslike "memo" are all merely expressions of the same deep structure; they will insist that, if this *is* the case, then this same structure must lie within or be Ezra Pound. And yet I have argued that the macrocontext is not the vehicle for Pound's individuality. The avenue of escape from this labyrinth of personae, conventions, and subjectivity lies, as the reader of this study may well expect, in the formal system of the Malatesta cantos: that system is clearly dialectical.

As I implied earlier in this chapter, the concept of history, as thinkers from Hegel to Derrida have recognized, relies on difference. Manley approvingly quotes Derrida on this topic:

> If the word "history" did not carry with it the theme of a final repression of difference, we could say differences alone could be "historical" through and through from the start. . . . we shall designate by the term *différance* the movement by which language, or any code, any system of reference in general, becomes "historically" constituted as a fabric of differences.[7]

But we do not really need Derrida to inform us of a principle commonly accepted in the "human sciences," although Derrida might object (probably with justice) that "hidden ethical/political agendas" undermine the broader theories of these sciences. At any rate, if I consider a very simple example of a dialectic, that involving the distinction between two phonemes, I discover that opposition, difference, has little to do with the "contrariness" of two physical entities and a greal deal to do with the definition of either one of these two entities. I know that /bin/ signifies a container and not a tiny sharpened piece of of steel solely because an "extra" phonemic feature, that of being voiced, distinguishes /b/ from /p/. In the same fashion, I distinguish /bin/ from /fin/ because in the former signifier both lips are used to form the initial sound (as opposed to the use of lips and teeth), and so on. These distinctions are based on physical events which are established in binary groups in the real world; I can only know the meaning of a sound, in other words, through the dialectical system of which it is a part. The oppositions of the Malatesta cantos, like the oppositions of history itself, are far more complex, but they operate on the same fundamental principle. This means that events do not "grow out" of other events, there is no simple genesis of historical cause and effect. Frederic Jameson in *Marxism and Form* offers a lucid example of the dialectic in recent history: the development of the atomic bomb by the United States stimulated, of course, the Soviets to create their own atomic payload; Soviet technology, however, was not as "delicate" as that of the Americans, and this caused the Soviets to develop larger payloads with larger rockets to launch those payloads; the result of Soviet experiments with larger rockets and larger nuclear payloads was their ability to launch sputniks. I might add a further dialectical "move" to this series: the launching of the sputnik caused American educators to strengthen and augment science and mathematics programs in American schools, and this, in turn, created a displacement of certain other aspects of education, which had various effects on society, and so on. The point of this illustration is simple: although historians commonly view the Cold War as a series of moves and countermoves resulting in arms build-ups and nuclear proliferation (which, of course, in part it was and is), in reality the historical situation is far more complex, involving events impinging upon all areas of both American and Soviet society—thus is history created.

If I then turn my attention to the various speakers of the Malatesta cantos, I shall observe a dialectical pattern which unites the various viewpoints and which obviates quarrels over which "opinion" of Malatesta's life is the historically "accurate" one. That Pound was sincerely interested in setting down Sigismundo's "factive" personality there is no doubt, but that he intended his readers to derive from the Malatesta cantos an unambiguous "revised" version of Malatesta's reputation is less certain. With great justice Harper remarks that "Pound does not just present his results, he invites us to repeat the process by which he arrived at them." I am not sure that Pound "presents results" of any definitive kind, except to say that Sigismundo "lived and ruled"; it is, as Harper stresses, the process which is foregrounded.

This process—whether we wish to call it a dialectic or whether we term it the ideogrammic method—occupies, as I am of course arguing, the role of central signification in the Malatesta cantos. Certainly, Malatesta himself is paradigmatic of certain values with which the reader of *The Cantos* is quite familiar:

> In a Europe not YET rotted by usury, but outside the then system, and pretty much against the power that was, and in any case without great material resources, Sigismundo cut his notch. He registered a state of mind, of sensibility, of all-roundedness and awareness.[8]

"All that a single mind could," Pound goes on to point out, "Malatesta managed *against* the current of power." The emphasis on "against" here is well taken: the Quattrocento, for Pound, was itself a paradigm, a period wherein could be found elements which embodied the "cultural 'high' " represented by Sigismundo, and elements which presaged the "rot" of usury, the cultural devaluation signalled by the verbal corruption of Pius's style.

I said early in this chapter that the Malatesta cantos are didactic, and now I would supplement that remark by saying that what Cantos 8 through 11 teach is not principally the culturally salutary value of the life of Sigismundo Malatesta. Rather, readers of the Malatesta cantos may be expected to learn the value of search and comparison: search for the essential materials of history, and comparison of those materials with an eye not only toward their individual contents, but also toward the meaning evoked in the content of one document by the content of another. This process of search and comparison infuses *The Cantos* as a whole, of course, and is not limited to historiography, but encompasses intertexts from literature and myth, and from Pound's own individual experience. In fact, if I widen the scope of the dialectic operating in the Malatesta cantos, I may see that historical passages are variations on lyric passages, which are variations on personal reminiscence, which are (coming full circle) variations on history. By "variation" here I mean that formal and semantic elements exist in each type of passage which complement or supplement elements in each of the other types of passages. I have already noted above that the fragmentation and condensation structures developed in Cantos 1 through 7 are utilized in a slightly different form—in the use of prose quotation, for instance—in Cantos 8 through 11, and that devices which characterize lyric, Imagistic passages are formally akin to the devices of more "didactic" cantos like the Malatesta sequence. Moreover, although the cantos which bracket Cantos 8 through 11 are placed adventitiously (a point which I shall argue at greater length in the next and last chapter) and are not ordered on an "organic" basis, Cantos 7 and 12, are, nevertheless, paradigmatic of the two major macrocontextual fields which are opposed to the didactic, historical intent of the Malatesta cantos; Canto 7, as I have pointed out repeatedly in this study, is a microcontextual paradigm of Imagist style and is macrocontextually an embodiment of WAD, AURUN, and MYTHIC TRANSFORMATION; Canto 12, on the level of the microcontext, possesses a high degree of condensation, and its matrix LEVELS OF HISTORY (PERSONAL) provides a "polar" supplement to the matrices of Canto 7. Thus, the bracketing cantos reflect the microcontextual structure of the Malatesta sequence while, at the same time, they offer a macrocontextual antithesis to the LEVELS OF HISTORY (HISTORIC) matrix of the Malatesta cantos.

I should like to conclude this chapter by briefly stressing the broader implications of the process of historiography which, I have argued, informs the Malatesta cantos. Charles Altieri, in a discussion of traditional Romantic symbols as opposed to ironic Modernist symbols, comments on the familiar dichotomy which Lévi-Strauss posits between "mythic" and modern societies:

> While mythic societies adapt particulars to pre-existing structures of meaning and thus reinforce them, modern societies posit structures "only to establish a difference as a difference" and on these differences the discipline of history and the dilemmas of historicism have their foundation. Historicism is, I think, Lévi-Strauss' own deepest metaphor for metonymic thinking, because it breeds relativism instead of mythic repetition and a sense of a unified world. The primary psychological aspect of relativism is a continual sense of the incompleteness of one's own discourse; each statement and, indeed, each world view is at best a

fragment of a deeper whole that can be recognized only as a nagging absence or shadow.[9]

Altieri further argues that the typical Modernist symbol is itself metonymic and is therefore a departure from the metaphoric symbols of the preceding literary period—a view, of course, which this study shares. If the reader will recall that metonymy involves a relation of contiguity, whether ideational or objective, she may realize that one implication of the above quote is that the traditional, and still quite current, notion of historical change as a succession of "substitutions" of one period for another is actually typical of "mythic" thinking. Poststructuralism, however, chiefly owing to the influence of Marxism perhaps, forwards the metonymic model of history which Altieri attributes to Lévi-Strauss, but which is not original with the French anthropologist. In fact, as I believe I have shown, Pound forwards a distinctly metonymic, dialectical view of history in the Malatesta cantos. That Pound *does* hold such a view runs counter to the received opinion of many Pound scholars that *The Cantos* express precisely simple repetitions of history. My argument in this chapter, of course, rejects this opinion; the various documents which make up the Malatesta cantos bear out Altieri's contention concerning metonymic relativism that the "primary psychological aspect of relativism is a continual sense of the incompleteness of one's own discourse." It might further be said of the Malatesta cantos that "each statement and, indeed, each world view is at best a fragment of a deeper whole"—which whole, in the terms of the present study, is the macrocontext of *A Draft of XXX Cantos*. Once again, then, it is not accuracy of documentary evidence which the reader finds enacted in the Malatesta cantos, but a precision of method: Pound the poet, the "best maker" of verbal form, is well aware of the duplicities and uncertainties of documents, of the sort of incompleteness iconically mirrored in Canto 8's opening letter. On the other hand, Pound the deliberate student of history is highly conscious of the salutary and corrective influence documents have on one another. Returning to a linguistic stance, I should say that, as usual, Pound is unconcerned with the valid or invalid reference of his documents—their signifieds in the objective world; rather, he is interested in demonstrating to his reader that discourse gains validity only in reference to other discourse, and that only through a dialectic of discourses can one approximate either historic or esthetic truth.

9
READING, REFERENCE, AND CHANCE

ONE AIM OF this study has been to answer the question "How does the reader of the Modernist text overcome inevitable difficulties in reading?" Obviously, the question itself is based on the significant presupposition that Modernist texts are difficult to understand, at least on first reading. Many students of twentieth-century literature will counter that most of the important works of this century offer no greater or no more obstacles to understanding than many of the works of the immediate past. Is *Sons and Lovers* more difficult than, say, *Middlemarch*? Is *The Testament of Beauty* more difficult than *Sordello*? Of course, the answers to such questions hinge on each reader's perception of "difficulties" in reading. It should be abundantly clear here in the final stages of this study that I am not concerned with difficulties of *interpretation*; consequently, responses to the queries above which involve correctly assessing the characters of Paul Morel or Edward Casaubon, or accurately paraphrasing the philosophical intent of Bridges or Browning are not germane in this context. I am concerned with a problem in esthetic perception at once simple and, like many simple things, at the same time productive of complexity: how does the reader comprehend enough of the Modernist text *to begin* making interpretative judgments of the kind I have just suggested? Barring actual linguistic difficulties such as archaic language or a strange dialect, there is no body of works in English literature which presents as great an obstacle to the mere interpretation of phrases and sentences as the seminal works of Modernism.

I readily concede, as my choice of Lawrence and Bridges as representative twentieth-century writers indicates, that much literature written between 1900 and 1940 is stylistically lucid. Yet much literature of this period, especially poetry, is not.

In poetry written in the period from 1900 to 1940, a "transparent" style, wherein word-order deviations are few or well within the Tradition, where syntax is at least "recoverable," where the shift from line to line or from stanza to stanza is marginally logical, or where the semantics of a word is not intended to baffle or frustrate the reader, is very often absent. In fact, I am willing to go further: no well-regarded Modernist poet possesses a thoroughgoingly transparent style as I have just defined it. Some Modernists (Yeats and Pound are excellent examples) can actually be observed becoming Modernists through their abandonment of formal transparency. Clearly, the impulse among Modernist poets to frustrate reader expectation, to create difficulties in the simple decipherment of lines, is intentional. Undoubtedly, this state of affairs is the root cause of the so-called increasing "Mandarinism" of modern poetry (although, curiously, readers of poetry do not appear to be falling off in terms of sheer numbers; in fact they may be increasing).

Nonetheless, as I have indicated here from time to time, several counterforces are at work which appear to militate against utter formal opacity. One such force is the tendency, arguably initiated by Pound himself, to employ "speech as it is spoken" in poetry. Another is the existence of a number of "programmatic" exegeses, which nearly all Modernists present extratextually; the list runs from Yeats's *A Vision* through the many essays of Pound and Eliot and Williams to recent examples like Charles Olson's "Projective Verse." Whether such prose "explications" do not themselves occlude understanding is another question, and one which I shall not attempt to answer. Moreover, all readers of good will agree, I should hope, that all poets of good will are not intent on forever veiling their poems in intransigently disruptive syntax and impossibly recondite allusions. That the Modernist poem, then, *is* difficult to read is a fact which must be confronted in order that the poet's work may be understood. The first stage in such a confrontation, as this study has of course assumed, is the understanding of the formal procedures enacted in the Modernist poem. I have chosen the early cantos of Ezra Pound for the object of the study because this body issues from the hand of the poet who, for many reasons (the importance and exemplariness of his own innovations, his great influence on other poets), may be regarded as the arch-Modernist; moreover, *The Cantos* themselves must inevitably be placed among the great long poems of the post-Renaissance period. And, finally, *The Cantos* are considered by many scholars to be a watershed between the practices of Modernism and the as yet partially defined practices of post-Modernism.

One such practice which *is* fairly evident involves the calling into question of the poet's authority. In a perceptive study which in its fundamental assumptions is very similar to the one at hand, Alan Durant confronts the dilemma of the speaker in *The Cantos*; the authority of the speaker often lapses, Durant claims: it is "disturbed in certain moments when the instrumentality of language functions with a complexity in excess of the writer's presumed powers." The result of this disturbance is the engendering of a "possible multiplication of meanings which has made Pound's poetry an object of such difficulty for a criticism concerned to trace particular and definable meanings in the various texts."[1] Consequently,

> The poem's intelligibility has now to be rethought. It can no longer be reliant upon a relation of discourse to author—the relation which holds the text to its author's affirmed and unquestioned unity—but instead depends upon interrelations of the discourses themselves, and upon the various positions relative to language these discourses inscribe for the reader. (Durant, 1981: 41)

Finally, "such a reading process restores contradiction as an element of the text, and so inaugurates forms of reading no longer presuming the coherence provided by the category of an author whom language subserves" (Durant, 1981: 41). I have commented several times on Joseph Frank's observation that Modernist texts can only be "reread," and such rereading is part of the "process" to which Durant refers. The speaker at any given time in *The Cantos* is only another formal element of the discourse, and the reader, cast adrift from the intentional authority of the author, must seek meaning in the relations within and between the cantos themselves. These relations are primarily linguistic and have little commerce with the "definable meanings" of much traditional poetry. Again, I shall stress that I am here concerned with the reader's difficulty in deciphering the form of Modernist poetry, and with the process of signification stimulated by that decipherment. I do not contend that interpretation of the text by other than semiotic means is impossible: I am only arguing that an understanding of formal structures in *The Cantos* must precede other modes of interpretation and that, in fact, such formal analysis is the foundation of interpretation in very many Modernist poems.

This study has also advanced the view that *The Cantos*, and other Modernist texts, signify through novel means which have much to do with the referentiality or nonreferentiality of language itself. To this subject I shall turn next.

Abstraction of Reference

I should like to begin my discussion of this difficult topic with a dictum: in a poetic structure, each signifier is a signifier of the system of that structure. This is neither a particularly original observation, nor one peculiar to the twentieth century. But what are the ramifications of this assumption? One implication occupies the role of near law in stylistics: synonymity (whatever its possibility in ordinary language) is impossible in poetry.[2] Another implication—and one far more crucial to a formal description of Modernist poetry—is that referentiality in poetry is undermined *a priori* by the very nature of poetic language. If the function of the signifier is to make visible or audible a signified, and if in a poem that signified is the inseparable poem-as-a-whole, then the "one-to-one" correspondence normally expected of signifiers is deferred. This "différance" (and Derrida's term is very useful in this context) always tends toward the conditions established by the formal tensions of the poems as opposed to the "propositional" or "predicative" or objective field to which language normally tends. Do words in *The Cantos* then lack common denotative meanings? No, but such meanings are secondary, and it is this reordering of linguistic priorities which is one of the obstacles to reading the Modernist text erects. If my reader has borne with my argument this far, then he will have no need of copious examples of the situation I have just described. Suffice it to say: when syntagms are continually "broken" both semantically and syntactically, when certain words become vortices or ideograms, and when the speaker becomes his own message, then it is obvious that the normal referential usages of language have been cast aside.

The "unified field" theory of poetry has been something of a critical canon at least since Coleridge. The reader may consider, for example, Frank Kermode's comments on this topic written over twenty-five years ago:

> The one thing nearly everybody seems to be agreed upon is that the work of art has to be considered as a whole and that considerations of "thought" must be subordinated to a critical effort to see the whole as one image; the total work is not *about* anything—"a poem should not mean but *be*"—which is simply a vernacular way of saying what modern critics mean when they speak of it as "autotelic."[3]

It is not within the scope of this study to examine the etiology of Kermode's famous "Romantic Image"; the reader may select his own particular explanation, from the many now current, of why modern poets have come to view their poems as self-referential, as "autotelic." The important point is that most students of modern poetry argue that self-referentiality is the norm in twentieth-century verse. The relation of Imagism to self-referentiality is not obscure: the distinction between the unitary image which Kermode states is the goal of poets since Romanticism and the Image of Imagist doctrine is, for my present purposes, negligible. Curiously, Pound never really makes clear whether an Image is equivalent to the poem-as-a-whole, whether it is an element of a poem, or whether it occupies both roles; it seems arguable, however, that the last is the case. In fact, as I hope I have shown in Chapter 4, the Image is by its nature constituted of superimposed perceptions, and these perceptions may be elicited by the limited framework of a microcontext, or by the entirety of the macrocontext which is the poem (or individual canto). The discursive, linear quality of language thus tends to be greatly diminished in Modernist poetry. Frequently, individual lines are more comprehensible than the passages in which they are set; readers are perhaps more prepared to make attempts to discover meanings in a limited syntagm than to try to couple meanings which arise in adjacent lines and which seem semantically diverse.

But there is another sense in which many lines in *The Cantos* are incomprehensible. As I have often noted, the textual universe of *The Cantos* is various and farflung, and the outer-space analogy is apt. The poem which is *The Cantos* is much like a central star or planet around which revolve extratextual satellites; these are not only the constituents of intertexts or hypograms, but also the various exegeses offered first by Pound and later by several commentators whom I have often had cause to thank in these pages. Undoubtedly, the exegetical writings will multiply, but I wonder if Pound intends this situation. It seems more likely that he wishes each reader to do his own digging, to seek out the intertexts for lines and passages for himself. Thus, part of the process of reading *The Cantos* would ideally involve the same sort of process Charles Olson envisioned for *Moby-Dick*: the reader reads a sentence or paragraph in the novel dealing with an aspect of, say, ship's carpentry, and he turns from the novel to a handbook on ship's carpentry; when he has digested this information, he returns to the novel, and so on. The Modernist text, then (and it should come as no surprise that *Moby-Dick* is in many respects a Modernist novel), has a very powerful tendency to become not merely an "imaginative" world, but an entire solar system in which the reader would live for days or months or (like Joyce's ideal reader affected by an ideal insomnia) years. Consequently, if abrupt shifts in semantic field and extreme fragmentation have not baffled the reader of *The Cantos*, a line's recondite allusion very likely will.

I have argued, however, that *The Cantos* are self-referential, and Pound's use of intertext and allusions from a wealth of authors seems to undermine that argument. If a passage is a Poundian translation from Ovid or a reconstructed experience from Pound's life, how can that passage refer only to itself? I am at this stage at risk of constructing a "super-reader" who would be capable of recognizing intertexts in *The Cantos* at first sight. It is highly doubtful, as Pound's letters attest, that any first reader of *The Cantos* has ever possessed such a capability. This is not even a question of erudition because a reader who would be acquainted with exactly the intertexts (of whatever kind) of *The Cantos* would have had to live Pound's life. In fact, I shall shortly turn to the aleatory and adventitious quality of *The Cantos*, but for the moment I should like to point out that *The Cantos*, in Pound's eyes at least, are self-illuminating. Like the foreign words and ideograms in the poem, intertexts in *The Cantos* are meant to be explicated by other parts of the discourse; sometimes these explicatory sections are adjacent to the puzzling reference, sometimes they are widely separated from it. The Malatesta cantos are exemplary in this regard because they largely comprise intertexts and because they deal with a relatively obscure Quattrocento condottiere who, if he is known at all to the first reader of *The Cantos*, is truly highlighted, defined, only by Cantos 8 through 11 themselves.

Throughout this investigation of Modernist form, I have been tempted to use explanatory analogies adopted from arts other than literature, but I have tried to avoid these as inevitably misleading. Music, for example, supplies an excellent—too excellent—model for a nonreferential form which nevertheless means mightily. Cubism, to take another instance, suggests a number of correspondences with the spatial form of Modernist literature. In treating of abstraction, I am of course again lured into parallels between modern visual and modern literary art. I feel, however, that Jacob Korg's following remarks on abstraction in modern literature do not compare apples and oranges, and are thus valuable for the topic at hand:

> In general, the experimentalists developed the abstract potentialities of language without absolutely opposing its normal referential function. They seem to have agreed, at least insofar as language is concerned, with Kandinsky's view that the abstract retains "the timbre of the organic" rather than with Mondrian's idea that any allusion to natural forms interferes with a work's capacity to capture pure reality. (Korg, 1979: 165)

Korg also notes, in keeping with my remarks immediately above on the "cross-referencing" of signifiers in *The Cantos*, that "the specific term must find its interpretation laterally rather than in depth, and its relation to the rest of the structure is less likely to be an identification with something than the assumption of a position within a design" (Korg, 1979: 134).

If the reader will grant, then, that Pound at least tends to undermine (if not destroy) referential meaning, that he erects his own "definitions" of signifiers through the "design" of *The Cantos*, I may turn to the true core of the problem: in what exactly does *abstraction* of reference, as opposed to "ordinary" reference, consist? Indeed, it may with justice be objected that, when I say that a signifier in *The Cantos* signifies a signified elsewhere in *The Cantos*, I am not really positing a form of linguistic referentiality very much different from the shiftings of garden-variety connotation in literature and in common speech. If a syntagm in a poem is to refer "abstractly," it cannot merely be nondenotative, nonobjective, and nonsituational: much ordinary verbal expression uses words in unusual ways to refer to subjective events which may have no relation of any kind to the speaker and his audience. Moreover, I am here attempting to distinguish the forms of referentiality which Pound and certain other Modernist poets use from the forms used by their predecessors, and it is common knowledge that literary theorists have for centuries tried to resolve the dilemma posed by the "true" reference of poetry. Nevertheless, the attitude of poets toward their "subjects," and thus toward their readers, seems to change greatly at some point in the nineteenth century, and this attitude assumes concrete expression in twentieth-century verse.

I should like to consider briefly some of the pieces of intellectual equipment which poets have traditionally expected of their readers. To begin with the simplest set of assumptions: a reader must have some experience of the "manners of men" and the actions of nature. Such experience is the essential component of the field of reference in most traditional literature. Additionally, a reader must possess an elaborate system of conventional behaviors which have to do with reading poems; this system, it is generally agreed, is very little understood, although its exploration is one of the most exciting undertakings in modern literary theory. An example, at any rate, of one of these conventional behaviors is the poet's assumption that most of his allusions will be understood by his reader. Readers reading Pope in the eighteenth century (and it must be understood throughout that by "read-ers" I mean readers with literary competence) would be well acquainted with certain classical texts and would thus be expected to recognize refer-ences to those texts. Even formal devices, like the hexameter line, may of course be allusive references. "When swift Camilla scours the plain" in Pope, her appearance is obviously not referential in the way ordinary language is referential; Pope here is indulging in what would now be called "metatextuality"—he is calling attention to his own text, his reference is to itself. My point is commonplace: poets have always relied on their readers to do more than merely respond to ordinary language; poets expect readers to possess a certain body of fairly specialized knowledge and to be pre-pared for the poem to refer to itself in any number of ways. It is, of course, the job of undergraduate literature courses to instill the sort of knowledge in student readers which will fulfill poets' expectations.

But the reader of Pope could have expected to meet with classical allu-sions, moral reflections, and certain formal traits in his poet; his failure to comprehend these allusions, reflections, and traits would be a failure of education and not of understanding. Can the contemporary reader with high literary competence also be expected to comprehend the allusions, reflections, and formal traits he finds in Modernist poets (at least at first reading)? Obviously, the answer is "no." This "failure" *is* a failure of understanding. No system of education—unless it be the Poundian *paideuma* itself—will prepare the reader to comprehend *The Cantos* at first reading in the same way that that reader would be expected to comprehend *An Essay on Criticism* at first reading (the fact that Pope's own self-contradic-tions may confuse the reader is beside the point).

In addition to the other prerequisites which the reader of Pope might have, he would possess the ability to abstract meaning as well. In fact, I may be accused of being a little disingenuous in my choice of a "traditional" poet in this regard: Pope's intent, at least in *An Essay on Criticism*, is clearly "abstract"; he wishes his reader to move from particulars to generalities in the progressive comprehension of the poem. The "abstraction" in the "abstraction of reference" which I attribute to Pound's poetry does not significantly differ in kind from abstraction of reference in Pope. I will remark at this point that when a reader abstracts references in a poem, he is not paraphrasing that poem. By "abstraction" then I am basically referring to the ability of the reader to experience the general in the particular without the mediation of intervening objective referents. Korg, once again, sheds a good deal of light on this concept:

> Art that strikes through particulars at universals . . . penetrates sense experience in order to grasp the necessary, unvarying relationships that exist independently of particular objects or events. If the poet is to feel the universal, recurring emotions of mankind as primary experiences he must also apprehend them conceptually, as forms, removed from the contingencies of actuality. (Korg, 1979: 154)

Such forms are embodied in the structure of *The Cantos*.

Another approach to Modernist abstraction involves consideration of the "organic," both as a formal mode and as a field of reference. It is rapidly becoming a commonplace among critics of twentieth-century literature that Modernist writers have employed "inorganic" structures more frequently than traditional, "organic" structures to articulate their works. Such inorganic structures may be defined as systems or codes which have little to do with the actual "subject" of the work; thus, numerology, the parts of the syllogism, "encyclopedia form," and a number of other arcane codes have all been attributed to the articulation of *Ulysses*. The proponents of main form in *The Cantos*, too, have argued that Pound's poem follows at least in broad outline the structuring of ritual (as in the *nekuia*) or of past literature (the *Commedia Divina*). I might note in passing that it is not altogether clear in what organic form might consist if inorganic form is defined as a structure inherently alien to the subject of the text: it is transparently obvious that the most realistic novels (for instance, the narratives of Robbe-Grillet) offer abundant examples of structures which have nothing to do with the field of reference of the work. At any rate, there is probably no literary period in which some writers did not occasionally make a conscious effort to draw attention to the form of works, and to slight those works' contents. Arguably, Modernist poets differ from earlier poets in this regard only in the thoroughness of the Modernists' attempt to use form to show, as Korg puts it, "the right road to immediacy."

Actually, I have argued both implicitly and explicitly that in Modernist poetry form is homologous with content and that, consequently, Modernist poetry *is* organic in the sense that form conforms to subject. Part of the conflict between organic and inorganic form arises out of the critical metaphors which have accreted around the terms. When we are told that in the organic work the form "grows" out of the work's subject, the metaphorical assumptions of such a statement often go unexamined. In fact, there is a good reason that metaphorical usages implying analogies between cultural objects and natural objects have been proscribed by post-structuralist theory. To repeat an argument which I have often forwarded here, and which is generally indebted to Riffaterre: a literary work is not *sui generis*; its origins are always complex and do not lie in the "originality" of the author but in the intricate network of conventions (only some of which are strictly literary). I have argued that Pound in *The Cantos* not only is aware of such profound conventionality in the structuring of his work but also uses such awareness as a central device in forwarding meaning.

In Modernist poetics, then, the text, not the world, creates coherence. Whether one adopts the openly polemic attitude of some twentieth-century writers and argues that earlier writers were self-deluded on this score, or whether one merely remarks the attempt in some traditional poetry to mirror order, the study of Modernism witnesses a shift in attitudes about the coherence of the world. This is a commonly observed fact about twentieth-century thought and one the reason for which is usually given as the decline of faith in divine providence, but, be this as it may, even Modernist poets, like Eliot, who detect a governed order in the universe still find, in the human world, order only in the text.

The text of *A Draft of XXX Cantos* is, then, synecdochic; any microcontext refers (as the dictum which opened this section stated) to all other microcontexts. I shall go further: any microcontext in the first thirty cantos possesses formal markers which not only "point to" other microcontexts but make that microcontext actually part of every other microcontext as the process of reading takes place.

Form as Chance/Chance as Form

I have until now assumed a continuous development of the formal devices in *The Cantos*, and I have written of the later cantos as if they were analogous to the later stages of a traditionally "coherent" epic like the *Commedia Divina*. Although we have only ex post facto evidence of Dante's intentions regarding the unity of his poem (in the celebrated Letter to Can Grande), it seems reasonable to assume that the poet was conscious of his final goal in the *Paradiso*. Again, it is obviously impossible for modern students to know exactly how much of the design of their works the great epic poets possessed before beginning the process of writing; nevertheless, Milton, Ariosto, and perhaps even Homer and Virgil must have obeyed a rough succession of events which had been conceived by them before or during the opening stages of composition. It is clear, on the other hand, from Pound's letters that he toyed with several possible organizational schemes for his epic and that he finally settled, in practice, on none (or perhaps all) of them. In support of this argument, I need only adduce Pound's adventitious introduction of various intertexts into *The Cantos*. Surely, no one would argue that Pound could have foreseen, for example, his later use of the *Sacred Edict*, de Mailla's *Histoire Générale*, or Paul the Deacon when he was in the process of writing the first thirty cantos.

But how applicable is the concept of plot as an organizational program to most forms of poetry? Although it is interesting to view lyric poetry *as if* it had a plot, even the most ingenious attempts to prove the actuality of plots in lyrics seem unconvincing. In some sense (that perhaps of a progressive emotional movement) poems like "Ode On a Grecian Urn" can be made to possess a plot structure. Be this as it may, few people would seriously cavil at the notion that epics possess plots in very much the same sense that novels do (or consciously do not) have plots. Critics may differ over "taxonomies" of plot, temporality of plot, or the relation of plot to reality, but most agree that something is being done in a poem like *Paradise Lost* which approximates the sequentiality of experience which most humans perceive as central to conscious life. Certainly, epics like *The Faerie Queene* exhibit plotting which is noncontinuous and episodic, but these episodes nonetheless contain plots, and, moreover, those episodes are related by more than the "paradigms" of imagery and symbol which relate the sections of a long lyric poem. Some readers in the course of this study may have objected to my terming *The Cantos* an "epic." I shan't take up the cudgel on this issue: I shall readily concede that Pound's poem does not fit any of a number of definitions of "epic," although the sheer number of those definitions and the fact that since Aristotle debate has been going on about what does and what does not constitute an epic should be enough to give anyone pause before calling nearly any poem an epic. What I should like to argue is that, whatever genre *The Cantos* may be, its length alone *a priori* implies cohesion.

I shall edge even farther out on my limb and say that length in literature, perhaps measured in terms of reading time, necessarily creates coherence. Now it very well may be that such coherence is merely created by the reader herself as she erects literary conventions which insist that length shall mean cohesion, but, nonetheless, whether coherence is imposed on form or whether extended form creates coherence, such cohesion must exist or the poem fails. Clearly, I am here employing "coherence" as an essential element of plot. Yet a lyric poem, too, attains coherence, so that this element cannot be the sole criterion of plot. Actually, it seems that there are two types of coherence in literature; the first involves coherence of paradigms—the systems of imagery, allusion, symbolism, and motif to which the text obsessively recurs; the second is syntagmatic coherence, a coherence in which objective events, among other things, are mirrored in the text. As long as one such objective event is reflected in the text's discourse, a plot in the second sense is present. Thus, if the reader wishes to point out that "The Solitary Reaper" has a plot, I shall readily occur. Some lyric poems are simply occasional.

Of course, there is an infinite number of ways to create mimesis; this number probably corresponds to the number of ways individuals witness reality, and, as Kermode argues, the human witness of reality makes reality human. There is neither space nor reason in the present study to rehearse the by-now creaky arguments over whether causality is a necessary property of the human mind.

The Cantos, as I trust I have demonstrated, possess the first kind of coherence, that of the paradigm; in Pound such paradigms comprise not only the traditional elements but also the production of models from matrices, the establishment of intratextuality, and the use of ideograms. Defenders of unity in *The Cantos*—the sort of unity readers find in the *Commedia Divina*—usually argue from the basis of some sort of paradigmatic unity. To do so, they often are pressed to contend that earlier epics— again, like the *Commedia Divina*—also cohere in a paradigmatic fashion. Rarely do these defenders contend that anything even faintly resembling syntagmatic coherence obtains in *The Cantos*. Of course, Pound's rather gnomic statements about his "failures" as he approached the end both of *The Cantos* and of his life lend support to both defenders and attackers of the poem's unity.

What then seems to be lacking in the structure of *The Cantos* the absence of which causes most readers to perceive the poem as "plotless?" Frank Kermode, in *The Sense of an Ending*, contends that "concord or consonance really is the root of the matter" of the sense of wholeness in narrative; "I think one can speak of specifically modern concord-fictions," Kermode argues, "and say that what they have in common is the practice of treating the past (and the future) as a special case of the present."[4] Kermode speaks of this situation in terms of the Heisenberg Principle, the principle of "complementarity" which seeks to reconcile conflicting accounts of the physical world. He continues: "It is not that we are connoisseurs of chaos, but that we are surrounded by it, and equipped for coexistence with it only by our fictive powers" (Kermode, 1967: 64). That the Western world in the last two centuries has been afflicted by this sense of chaos—as opposed to the ordered systems of Aristotle, Augustine, Aquinas, and Newton—is a commonplace; a commonplace, too, that the Modernists were the first artists to attempt accurately to reflect that chaos. But from the start, perhaps from the time of the Imagists, writers were brought up against the paradox that to mirror chaos is somehow to contain it, and that chaos contained is no longer chaos and thus no longer reality as the modern world knows it. The differences among Modernist poets and novelists will be found, I think, in the ways in which each resolves this paradox. My concern, however, is with how Pound especially confronts chaos; it is important for us to understand how he does this because Pound as an individual is inextricably bound up with modern history, and because *The Cantos* frankly confess the failures of individuals in trying to lend coherence to their allotted periods. My impression of Pound's letters during the twenties and thirties, after the publication of *A Draft*, is that his interest in the work becomes ever more exiguous; he seems less and less concerned with where his end is tending and more involved with problems arising from the section he is working on. Then, at some point during or immediately after his confinement at St. Elizabeth's, Pound begins to make statements counselling the reader to "wait a bit." And finally it seems as if he despairs of any order in *The Cantos* at all.

But *is* there syntagmatic coherence in *The Cantos*? Clearly not, if we define such coherence as linear unity; even after the reader has recognized the many unapparent, but firm, links between cantos and between sections of cantos, many portions of the syntagm remain which are disjointed from that which precedes and follows them. No portion of the syntagm, however (as I have repeatedly noted), is disconnected from *The Cantos* as a whole, and, in fact, a canto which at first seems disjointed from the section in which it appears often turns out to signify a canto elsewhere in the text, which will have great relevance to the "anomalous" canto's macrocontext.

But it is not clear why such "cross-referencing" should be enacted in the text at all. If one major purpose of *The Cantos* is heuristic (and there seems to be no doubt of this, given Pound's own remarks), then it would seem reasonable to group models of the same matrix together in the same portion of the syntagm. There are, of course, two reasons why Pound has not done this. The first obviously involves the simple fact that *The Cantos* were written over a long stretch of time, and individual cantos are separated *extratextually*; in other words, the objective world interferes in the world of the text, but not, however, by being a referent of the text, but by being an ontological *category* of it. If the initial motive behind disruption of the text is ontological, the second motive involves a reorientation of textual epistemology: It is merely a traditional convention of reading that states that elements of a narrative syntagm must be joined one to the other and not through the agency of a third element. Such a convention has always been a deception because *all* reading relies on a third term; that third term is reading itself. Put another way, I might say that the naive reader (the reader with low literary competence) perceives the text as a simple mimesis; the sophisticated reader until the twentieth century perceived the text as an esthetic whole removed from reference (one outcome of this, among many, is "art pour l'art"); the modern reader, schooled by the heuristic procedures of Modernism, however, perceives the text as *his own production*. In a very real sense (and not merely a figural one) Pound does not dominate *The Cantos*. His foregrounding of intertextuality initially alerts us to this situation, and the juxtaposition conditioned by the aleatory quality of life itself (Pound's life) confirms it. Thus the poet's remarks on the "failures" of *The Cantos*: at the end of his life, *The Cantos* had assumed an ontological status separate from that of their "creator" in exactly the same fashion as portions of *A Draft* (the Malatesta cantos, for example) had escaped from *their* origins. I might note that, in emphasizing the novelty of this situation in literature, one result of the text's complete autonomy is that it would be possible for an endless series of authors (thoroughly schooled, however, in the *paideuma*) to continue *The Cantos* endlessly.

These "authors" of course are the readers of *The Cantos*.

The Cantos thus call into question not only previous stylistic assumptions (the microcontext must manifest itself in syntactically and semantically "full" structures) but also supposedly "self-evident" assumptions about the literary triad itself. Curiously, it is the defeat of stylistic assumptions which suggests (or perhaps provokes) disruption of the relationships among author and reader and text. It is difficult indeed to determine where *The Cantos* originate. I might say that they originate with Pound since the poet "shapes" the text, or that they originate with the text since the formal properties of the text dictate how the text is to be read, or that they originate with the reader since only she will be conscious of a rereading which will cause the text to be understood. Readers of *The Cantos* have always known that the poem has no end. It is less evident, but no less true, that is has no origin either.

More important, then, than the enacting of new formal structures in Modernism is the movement away from the author's dominance of the text and his reader. It may seem paradoxical that a poet who is formally "difficult" is at the same time one who repeatedly abrogates his own textual authority. Yet, in reality, Pound's gesture of abdication can only be understood within a textual universe which, by its great formal difficulty, demands that the reader adopt responsibility for diminishing the difficulty. As a result, it may be that the most foregrounded aspect of *The Cantos*, when the poem is read "successfully," is the heuristic process itself.

Where, after all, does a reading of *The Cantos* stop? When the reader must have recourse to the intertexts informing the Malatesta, Adams, or Chinese cantos, he cannot truly be said to have interrupted his reading of *The Cantos*. Surely the binding together of intratexts across the vast textual spaces of *The Cantos* is not an interruption of a reading of the poem, even though "reading" has been halted. When the reader supplements the gaps brought about by extreme fragmentation, when he produces the multiple texts brought about by condensation, or when he suppresses intervening portions of the syntagm in order to join semantic equivalences in a coupling, he is at once "reading" the text (for without the text none of these operations would have been stimulated) and creating it (for without such creation the text would be unintelligible).

Therefore *The Cantos* represent a break with previous literature as fundamental as any in English literary history. Revolutions in literature doubtless manifest changes in each facet of the author-text-reader relationship, but each particular revolution may witness a particular emphasis in one of these facets; Romanticism may thus reflect an alteration in the link between author and text, while Modernism demonstrates a shift in emphasis toward text and reader. The logical outcome of adherence to the intentional fallacy is perhaps the disenthroning of the poet, at least in twentieth-century literature. Far from being the "legislators" of Romantic myth (via Shelley), poets have increasingly abdicated the authoritative legislation even of their own works. And concentration on the relationship between text and reader has been a willed decision in very many twentieth-century authors.

A vision of a future world conditioned by *The Cantos* is unsettling to those schooled in the traditional, and not-so-traditional, avenues of literature. In terms of poetry, it is a world which is, according to this traditional view, hopelessly fallen; its mourners, curiously, are not drawn from those careful workers who have labored early in the vineyard of sources and philological inquiry (who might be supposed to harbor the greatest resentment), but from the latecomers who, in the name of an "anti-formalism," of opposing the "anti-humanistic plain dreariness" of contemporary European criticism, labor to graft yet another ill-concealed critical impressionism onto the mainstem of poetry. It is this latter group which will reason darkly from the assumption that, as one of them puts it, "the great poets of the English Renaissance are not matched by their Enlightened descendants, and the whole tradition of the post-Enlightenment, which is Romanticism, shows a further decline in its Modernist and post-Modernist heirs."[5]

Pound, I feel, would have been greatly pleased with such grumblings, these genealogies tricked out with Nietzche (whose criticism is as "anti-humanistic" and plainly dreary as one could wish), which propose to demonstrate the "sterility" of the mainstreams of twentieth-century literature and criticism.

And a total revolution in sensibility and form, in consciousness itself, is likely to be disconcerting to those, like ourselves, who must experience it. *The Cantos* may indeed be a model on which is realized a network of Poundian scholar-poets, communicating via their home computers, entering anonymous bits of history, sequels to knowledge, lyric confessions, prophetic dreams, and masterly displays of prosody into the program which is *The Cantos* continued. Such a network would be the outcome of the abolition of space and time as they existed in 1900. Pound spent a lifetime on a "foreign" continent because that was where *paideuma* and *periplum* sometimes met; he spent a lifetime learning to traverse history so as to confine its typical moments to the pages of his text. Over the course of that lifetime, things changed utterly. Cut adrift from authority and completion, in the zero-g of formal upheaval, we moderns may well experience motion sickness. The antidote to such textual giddiness, the template and logarithm which locks the program of *The Cantos* in the axis of paradigm and syntagm, has been offered in these pages.

APPENDIX: TABLES

Table 1 shows the amount of fragmentation (of the types described in Chapter 1) in each of the cantos of *A Draft of XXX Cantos*.

Table 1. Fragmentation in the First Thirty Cantos

Canto	Fragments	V + ing	%	Canto	Fragments	V + ing	%
1	28	5	.37	16	67	26	.26
2	91	16	.58	17	109	11	.99
3	18	3	.43	18	6	0	.05
4	62	21	.48	19	16	7	.12
5	59	14	.48	20	133	10	.59
6	11	2	.14	21	58	8	.36
7	64	10	.51	22	13	1	.07
8	83	8	.47	23	17	8	.18
9	49	7	.20	24	55	4	.36
10	30	6	.18	25	69	9	.37
11	40	4	.29	26	69	2	.29
12	53	8	.38	27	27	3	.21
13	8	5	.10	28	30	1	.18
14	84	29	.95	29	65	9	.36
15	81	24	.77	30	18	2	.27

Column two indicates the number of lines which contain all or part of a fragmentation structure. I have been conservative in my estimation of lines containing fragments; lines containing any part of a "full" structure have been counted as "full," and no line has been counted as an NP-deleted subtype if a plausible subject may be inferred from the context of the canto. Only obvious examples of disintegrating sentences have been counted as such. Column three shows the number of appearances of a V + ing structure which may be said to supplant a full VP: consequently, this data gives a rough approximation of the quantity of the most common type of fragmentation in *The Cantos*. The last column designates the percentage of lines given over to fragmentation in a given canto. Overall, out of the 4,270 lines in *A Draft of XXX Cantos*, 1,453 are occupied by fragmentation structures: 34 percent of the first thirty cantos are fragments. Table two (based on Baker, 1967: 170–71) offers a rough scale of comparison with other poets.

Table 2. Comparative Fragmentation in Five American Poets

Authors	Emerson	Dickinson	Frost	Sandburg	Eliot
Percent of fragmentation	.19	.32	.11	.31	.41

NOTES

Chapter 1. *The Cantos* and Modernism

1. James Joyce, *A Portrait of the Artist as a Young Man* (New York: The Viking Press, 1959), p. 212.

2. The sense in which I shall be using the term "Modernism" here is defined in the Glossary. Unfamiliar or specialized words from the field of linguistics which are listed there will be henceforth followed by the notation "See Glossary" in parentheses.

3. J. H. Edwards and W. W. Vasse, *An Annotated Index to the Cantos of Ezra Pound* (Berkeley and Los Angeles: University of California Press, 1957); Carroll Terrell, *A Companion to the Cantos of Ezra Pound* (Berkeley, Los Angeles, and London: University of California Press, 1980). Hereafter, *"Companion."*

4. Walter Benjamin, *Reflections* (New York and London: Harcourt Brace Jovanovich, 1978), p. 158.

5. Christine Brooke-Rose, *A ZBC of Ezra Pound* (Berkeley and Los Angeles: University of California Press, 1971); R. J. Dilligan, James W. Parins, Todd K. Bender, *A Concordance to Ezra Pound's Cantos* (New York and London: Garland Publishing, Inc., 1981); Donald Gallup, *A Bibliography of Ezra Pound* (London: Hart-Davis, 1963); Hugh Kenner, *The Poetry of Ezra Pound* (Norfolk, Conn.: New Directions, 1951), and *The Pound Era* (Berkeley and Los Angeles: University of California Press, 1971); see for example the work of Kimpel and Eaves on the Leopoldine cantos in *Paideuma* 6 (Winter 1977), 7 (Spring/Fall 1978), 8 (Winter 1979); D. D. Paige, *The Letters of Ezra Pound* (New York: Haskell House, 1974); K. K. Ruthven, *A Guide to Ezra Pound's Personae, 1926* (Berkeley and Los Angeles; University of California Press, 1969).

6. Donald Davie, *Ezra Pound: Poet as Sculptor* (New York and London: Oxford University Press, 1964).

7. Michael Riffaterre, "Describing Poetic Structures: Two Approaches to Baudelaire's 'Les Chats,'" *Yale French Studies* 36–37 (1966):200–42.

8. Herbert Schneidau, *Ezra Pound: The Image and the Real* (Baton Rouge, La.: Louisiana State University Press, 1969), and "Wisdom Past Metaphor: Another View of Pound, Fenollosa, and Objective Verse," *Paideuma* 5 (Spring 1976):15–29.

9. Schneidau 1976, pp. 22–23.

10. For objections to Schneidau's argument, and for another view of metonymy in *The Cantos*, see P. H. Smith and A. E. Durant, "Pound's Metonymy: Revisiting Canto 47," *Paideuma* 8 (Fall 1979):327–33.

11. Christine Brooke-Rose, *A Structural Analysis of Pound's Usura Canto: Jakobson's Method Extended and Applied to Free Verse* (The Hague and Paris: Mouton, 1976).

12. Victor Shklovsky, "Art as Technique," in *Russian Formalist Criticism*, ed. L. T. Lemon and M. J. Reis (Lincoln, Neb.: University of Nebraska Press, 1965), pp. 3–24.

13. Michael Riffaterre, "Criteria for Style Analysis," *Word*, 15 (1959):154 ff.

14. Louis T. Milic argues persuasively for a dual perspective on this issue in "Rhetorical Choice and Stylistic Option: The Conscious and Unconscious Poles," in *Literary Style: A Symposium*, ed. Seymour Chatman (New York and London: Oxford University Press, 1971), pp. 77–78.

15. Riffaterre 1959, p. 162.

16. Michael Riffaterre, *Semiotics of Poetry* (Bloomington, Ind.: University of Indiana Press, 1978), pp. 48 and 63. All terms discussed here appear also in the Glossary.

17. William Beauchamp, "Riffaterre's *Semiotics of Poetry* with an Illustration in the Poetry of Emily Dickinsón," *Centrum* 1 NS (Spring 1981): 36–47.

18. Roland Barthes, *Elements of Semiology,* trans. Annette Lavers and Colin Smith (New York: Hill and Wang, 1967), 2, 1, 4. Hereafter, "*ES.*"

19. William E. Baker, *Syntax in English Poetry: 1870–1930* (Berkeley and Los Angeles: University of California Press, 1967); S. R. Levin, *Linguistic Structures in Poetry* (The Hague: Mouton, 1962); David Lodge, *The Modes of Modern Writing: Metaphor, Metonymy, and the Typology of Modern Literature* (Ithaca, N.Y.: Cornell University Press, 1977). See A. C. Partridge, *The Language of Modern Poetry* (London: Andre Deutsch, 1976) for an employment of Baker's terms and concepts. Levin's concept of "coupling" has gained fairly wide acceptance among a number of critics.

20. I have chosen this passage because it is the first salient instance of the use of these traits.

21. Ezra Pound, *The Cantos of Ezra Pound* (New York: New Directions, 1975), p. 4–5; all quotations are from this edition. There are a number of citation systems currently in use among Pound scholars: I have chosen simply to cite passages by page number in the New Directions edition with line numbers indicating order of lines on the page in question only (not, that is, beginning from the start of the canto). Passages which are extensively analyzed herein have been numbered by me in the left-hand margin.

Chapter 2. Metonymy, Imagism, and the Foundations of Pound's Style

1. James Thurber, *My World—And Welcome To It* (New York and London: Harcourt Brace Jovanovich, 1969), p. 169.

2. Roman Jakobson, "Two Types of Language and Two Types of Aphasic Disturbances," vol. 2 of *Selected Writings* (The Hague and Paris: Mouton, 1971), pp. 239–60.

3. Jakobson 1971, p. 255.

4. Peter Schofer and Donald Rice, "Metaphor, Metonymy, and Synecdoche Revis(it)ed," *Semiotica* 21, (1977):121–49; Group μ (J. Dubois, F. Edeline, J.-M. Klinkenberg, P. Minguet, F. Pire, H. Trinon), *A General Rhetoric,* trans. Paul B. Burrell and Edgar M. Slotkin (Baltimore and London: Johns Hopkins University Press, 1981). Metonymy is discussed in 4, 4, pp. 120–22.

5. Schofer and Rice 1977, p. 137.

6. Michel Le Guern, *Sémantique de la métaphore et de la métonymie* (Paris: Librairie Larousse, 1973), p. 28.

7. Joseph Riddel, "Decentering the Image: The 'Project' of 'American' Poetics?" in *Textual Strategies: Perspectives in Post-Structuralist Criticism,* ed. Josué V. Harari (Ithaca, N.Y.: Cornell University Press, 1979), pp. 322–58.

8. Riddel 1979, p. 345.

9. F. S. Flint, "Imagisme," *Poetry* 1 (March 1913):198–200.

10. Stanley K. Coffman, *Imagism: A Chapter for the History of Modern Poetry* (Norman, Okla.: University of Oklahoma Press, 1951).

11. Lodge 1977, p. 76.

12. Le Guern 1973, p. 25.

13. The most convenient collection of the *Lustra* poems is in *Personae: The Collected Shorter Poems of Ezra Pound, 1926* (New York: New Directions, 1949). "In a Station of the Metro" appears on p. 109 of that edition.

14. Schneidau 1969, p. 64.

15. *Personae*, p. 83.

16. Ezra Pound, *Gaudier-Brzeska: A Memoir* (New York: New Directions, 1970), p. 84.

17. Ezra Pound, "Mr. Hueffer and the Prose Tradition in Verse," *Poetry* 4, 3 (June 1914):112.

18. Ruthven 1969, p. 152.

19. Ruthven 1969, p. 132.

20. *Personae*, p. 92.

21. Kenner 1971, p. 367.

22. The nineteenth-century rhetorician Pierre Fontanier is often cited as providing a precedent for this classification. Fontanier, *Les Figures du discours* (Paris: Flammarion, 1968).

23. Baker 1967, p. 128.

24. Hugh Witemeyer, "Pound & The *Cantos*: 'Ply Over Ply,' " *Paideuma* 8 (Fall 1979):229–35.

25. Cf. the nearly identical view in Walter Baumann, *The Rose in the Steel Dust: An Examination of the Cantos of Ezra Pound* (Bern: Francke Verlag, 1967), p. 22.

26. Paige, *Letters*, pp. 385–86.

27. T. S. Eliot, *After Strange Gods: A Primer of Modern Heresy* (New York: Harcourt, Brace, and Co., 1934), p. 47.

Chapter 3. Deletion and Fragmentation

1. Dwight Bolinger, *Aspects of Language* (New York: Harcourt Brace Jovanovich, 1975), p. 171.

2. Baker 1967, p. 54.

3. See my "Larvatus Prodeo: Semiotic Aspects of the Ideogram in Pound's *Cantos*," *Paideuma* 9 (Fall 1980): 300.

4. Kevin Kerrane, "Phenomenology," in *Princeton Encyclopedia of Poetry and Poetics*, ed. Preminger, Warnke, and Hardison (Princeton, N.J.: Princeton University Press, 1974), p. 961.

Chapter 4. Condensation and Spatial Form

1. Joseph Frank, "Spatial Form in Modern Literature," *Sewanee Review* (1945): 223, 225, 227, and 229–30, respectively. Objections to the concept of spatial form are numerous; one of the most cogent arguments against Frank is Philip Rahv, *The Myth and The Powerhouse* (New York: Farrar, Straus and Giroux, 1965). Most of Frank's critics, however, have been answered by Frank himself in "Spatial Form, An Answer To Critics," *Critical Inquiry* 4 (1977):231–52. Further support to the theory is given by James M. Curtis in "Spatial Form in the Context of Modernist Aesthetics," in *Spatial Form in Narrative*, ed. Jeffrey R. Smitten and Ann Daghistany (Ithaca and London: Cornell University Press, 1981). As well as pointing out the weaknesses in Rahv's argument (pp. 177–78), Curtis offers an enlightening discussion of the relations of *langue/parole*, Gestalt psychology, and Lévi-Strauss to Modernist spatiality (pp. 176–77).

2. Sergei Eisenstein, "The Image in Process," in *The Modern Tradition*, ed. Richard Ellmann and Charles Feidelson (New York: Oxford University Press, 1965), pp. 163–69.

3. Ezra Pound, *Literary Essays of Ezra Pound*, ed. T. S. Eliot (London: Faber and Faber, 1954), p. 61.

4. Ernest Fenollosa and Ezra Pound, "The Chinese Written Character as a Medium for Poetry," *Little Review* 6, 6 (September–December, 1919): 59.

5. Lodge 1977, p. 76.

6. Ezra Pound, *The ABC of Reading* (New York: New Directions, 1960), p. 36.

7. Paige 1974, p. 355.

8. *Literary Essays*, p. 26.

9. Georg Lukács, *Studies in European Realism* (London: Hillway, 1950), p. 6. Actually, Pound was much interested in Lenin during this period.

10. It is interesting to note that handbooks to *The Cantos* serve as sources of what seems to be foregrounded to expert readers of Pound (but in this connection the reader will note the peculiar exegesis of passage two).

Chapter 5. Coupling

1. I am leaving out of account *early* speculations on Pound's part (which prompted, for instance, the "ur-*Cantos*," scraps of which now occur in Canto 3 and elsewhere).

2. The partisans of main form are legion, but the interested reader may find a representative spectrum of approaches in the following: Walter Baumann, *The Rose in the Steel Dust; An Examination of the Cantos of Ezra Pound* (Bern: Francke Verlag, 1967); Jacob Korg, *Language in Modern Literature: Innovation and Experiment* (New York: Barnes and Noble, 1979); William McNaughton, "A Note on Main Form in the *Cantos*," *Paideuma* 6 (Fall 1977): 147–52; Victor Reed, "Toward the *Cantos* of Ezra Pound," *DA* 12:824A (Berkeley); M. L. Rosenthal, "The Structuring of Ezra Pound's *Cantos*," *Paideuma* 6 (Spring 1977): 2–12; Hugh Witemeyer, "Pound & The *Cantos*: 'Ply Over Ply,' " *Occident*, 1 (1973).

3. The concept of coupling has a significant place in the *General Rhetoric* of Group μ, for example.

4. Samuel R. Levin, *Linguistic Structures in Poetry* (The Hague: Mouton, 1962). Hereafter, *Structures*.

5. W. B. Yeats, *Selected Poems and Two Plays*, ed. M. L. Rosenthal (New York: Collier Books, 1977), p. 115.

6. I am indebted to the *Companion*, page 93, for this attribution.

7. In fact, these three cantos may possess "self-sufficient" matrices.

Chapter 6. Prosody

1. *Princeton Encyclopedia of Poetry and Poetics*, p. 288.

2. T. S. Eliot, "Ezra Pound: His Metric and Poetry," *To Criticize the Critic* (London: Faber and Faber, 1965), p. 165.

3. Harvey Gross, *Sound and Form in Modern Poetry: A Study of Prosody from Thomas Hardy to Robert Lowell* (Ann Arbor, Mich.: University of Michigan Press, 1965), pp. 144 and 151, respectively. Also see William McNaughton's survey of Pound's prosodic techniques in "Ezra Pound's Meters and Rhythms," *PMLA* 78 (March 1963): 136–46.

4. Sally M. Gall, "Pound and the Modern Melic Tradition: Towards a Demystification of 'Absolute Rhythm,' " *Paideuma* 8 (Spring 1979): 36.

5. John Kuan-Terry, "The Prosodic Theories of Ezra Pound," *Papers on Language and Literature* 9 (Winter 1973): 55.

6. Wai-Lim Yip, *Ezra Pound's Cathay* (Princeton, N.J.: Princeton University Press, 1969), p. 158. Examples follow on p. 159.

7. Eliot 1965, p. 172.

8. James A. Powell, "The Light of Vers Libre," *Paideuma* 8 (Spring 1979): 6.

9. I am indebted to L. E. Guinn for this example.

10. *Princeton Encyclopedia of Poetry and Poetics*, p. 222.

11. *Literary Essays*, p. 169.

12. Charles Olson, *Selected Writings* (New York: New Directions, 1966), p. 22.

13. I am here discounting "shaped" poetry like Herbert's because such poetry is by no

means "irregular," and Mallarmé's *Un Coup de Dés* seems to me an anachronism (which is, moreover, a possible influence on twentieth-century experimentation).

14. *ABC of Reading,* p. 201.

Chapter 7. Macrocontexts: Speakers

1. Roger Fowler, "Commentary," *New Literary History* 12 (Spring 1981): 554.

2. Noam Chomsky, *Aspects of the Theory of Syntax* (Cambridge, Mass.: The M.I.T. Press, 1965), pp. 135–36.

3. Readers interested in this subject may refer to Chomsky, Chapter One.

4. T. S. Eliot, "Tradition and the Individual Talent," in *The Sacred Wood: Essays on Poetry and Criticism* (London and New York: University Paperbacks, 1960), pp. 58, 54, 56, 58, and 54, respectively. Also see my "Eliot, Tradition, and Textuality," *Texas Studies in Literature and Language* 27 (Fall 1985): 311–23.

5. Stanley Sultan, *Ulysses, The Waste Land, and Modernism: A Jubilee Study* (Port Washington, N.Y.: Kennikat Press, 1977), p. 62.

6. Joseph Riddel reaches a similar conclusion, contending that the "layers of textuality suspend . . . and immediately put into question the fiction of an original authorial voice"; *The Cantos,* according to him, "is a signifying machine, a machine producing signs out of an encounter of signs." *Georgia Review* 29 (Fall 1975): 588 and 590.

7. Albert Cook, "Rhythm and Person in the *Cantos,*" in *New Approaches to Ezra Pound,* ed. Eva Hesse (Berkeley and Los Angeles: University of California Press, 1969), p. 354. Cook's arguments concerning the scansion of *The Cantos,* by the way, are very similar to my own.

Chapter 8. Macrocontexts: The Historical Dimension

1. Michael F. Harper, "Truth and Calliope: Ezra Pound's Malatesta," *PMLA* 96 (January 1981): 97.

2. Ezra Pound, *Guide to Kulchur* (New York: New Directions, 1952), p. 159.

3. *Guide to Kulchur,* p. 194.

4. For an enlightening discussion of Eliot's complex attitude toward history and tradition, see Gregory S. Jay, *T. S. Eliot and the Poetics of History* (Baton Rouge, La.: Louisiana State University Press, 1983).

5. Lawrence Manley, ,"Concepts of Convention and Models of Critical Discourse," *New Literary History* 8 (Autumn 1981): 41–42.

6. *ABC of Reading,* p. 97.

7. Jacques Derrida, "Différance," in *Speech and Phenomena,* trans. David B. Allison (Evanston, Ill.: Northwestern University Press, 1973), p. 141.

8. *Guide to Kulchur,* p. 159.

9. Charles Altieri, "Objective Image and Act of Mind in Modern Poetry," *PMLA* 91 (January 1976): 104.

Chapter 9. Reading, Reference, and Chance

1. Alan Durant, *Ezra Pound, Identity in Crisis: A Fundamental Reassessment of the Poet and His Work* (Sussex: Harvester Press, 1981), p. 31.

2. For an opposing view see E. D. Hirsch, Jr., "Stylistics and Synonymity," *Critical Inquiry* 1 (March 1975): 559–80.

3. Frank Kermode, *The Romantic Image* (London: Routledge and Kegan Paul, 1957), p. 154.

4. Frank Kermode, *The Sense of an Ending: Studies in the Theory of Fiction* (New York: Oxford University Press, 1967), pp. 58–59.

5. Harold Bloom, *The Anxiety of Influence: A Theory of Poetry* (London and New York: Oxford University Press, 1975), p. 10.

GLOSSARY

Arbitrariness and motivation. Language is, generally speaking, arbitrary in its adoption of certain conventional forms to convey meaning: there is no "motivated" reason that the spoken or written signifier (q.v.) /dog/ should represent a four-legged mammal. On the other hand, some linguists doubt that syntax, as opposed to individual words, is altogether arbitrary; there may be a purely semantic quality to the ordering of syntactic chains. Onomatopoeia, too, is an example of "motivated" meaning (although linguists are beginning to question this assumption). Not all sign systems are, like natural language, arbitrary, however: various kinds of codes as well as a number of sign-types, like icons (q.v.) are systematically motivated.

Automatization and defamiliarization. First noted by the Russian Formalists, these two processes form a dialectic which is principally psychological in that both have to do with the way readers perceive features of the text. Conventional form and subject matter, for example, go unrecognized by most readers with literary competence (q.v.) and thus form and matter are automatized; conversely, formal experimentation and the use of unusual subject matter (the appearance of free verse in the early twentieth century, for instance) call attention to the text-as-text, thus causing defamiliarization.

Codes are explicit signifying systems, and, as such, they are the principal object of semiotic study. Generally, codes are considered to be simpler than natural languages, although Barthes (*ES* 1.1.6.) contends that, for most purposes, there is no reason to separate "language" from "code." The codes of mythology, comic books, boxing, the fashion system, and James Bond novels, among many others, have been investigated by semiotics.

Conversion and expansion. According to Riffaterre (1978: 48), "expansion transforms the constituents of the matrix sentence into more complex forms." Expansion is one of the two basic mechanisms of text production, the other mechanism being "conversion", which "transforms the constituents of the matrix sentence by modifying them all with the same factor" (Riffaterre, 1978: 63). Expansion, therefore, involves a "paratactic" movement of models (q.v.) by "addition," whereas conversion involves a "hypotactic" movement through internal transformation.

DIACHRONIC and SYNCHRONIC. These terms indicate the distinction made in linguistics between the historical level of language (diachrony) and the particular manifestation of language at any moment (synchrony). Since Saussure, linguistics has emphasized the study of synchronic structures, although the diachronic study of language development still plays a valuable role in understanding the state of language at any one time.

HYPOGRAMS are words or word groups to which a poem refers. Hypograms are "potential," and preexist in the linguistic competence (q.v.) of a speaker, or "actual," preexisting in particular texts known to the reader's literary competence. Hypograms, however, are not merely literary: they might consist of clichés, word "presuppositions" (and are thus nearly identical to traditional connotations), or whole "descriptive systems" which are metonymically associated with a word or group of words (see Riffaterre, 1978).

ICONS are signs (q.v.) whose signifiers "possess" some aspect of their signifieds. The term "iconicity," however, is used broadly in post-structuralism (q.v.) to refer to any signifier which in some sense "duplicates," or is analogical to, its signified. Consequently, many ideograms in *The Cantos*, although not strictly "synecdoches" of that which they represent, may be said to embody part of that which they represent.

IDIOLECT. In linguistics, the language as spoken by each individual speaker (the speaker's dialect, his verbal quirks, his particular vocabulary, and so on) is an idiolect; such a set of linguistic "habits" is open to formal definition. The importance of this concept to poetics is that a given writer's style may be likened to an idiolect; this stylistic idiolect is far more complex than the ordinary language idiolect.

ISOTOPY refers to the property of the text to cause various semantic fields (q.v.) to cohere. Isotopy, therefore, probably involves literary and linguistic competence (q.v.) in readers and listeners. Attempts to identify the exact operation of isotopy in the text (principally by Greimas) have been inconclusive, although the existence of such an operation seems indisputable.

LANGUE and PAROLE. The Saussurean dichotomy "langue/parole" is often translated as "language/speech" and Barthes defines *langue* as "language minus speech" (*ES* 1.1.2.). *Langue* then exists *in absentia* as an "institution" or "system," whereas *parole* exists as the individual embodiment of the system in spoken or written words.

LINGUISTIC and LITERARY COMPETENCE. Linguistic competence is generally equivalent to a speaker's possession of his *langue* (q.v.); thus such competence involves the embodiment of a speaker's vocabulary, his ability to use syntactic rules, and his recognition of various connotative strategies (among other elements). Competence is distinguished from "performance", which latter is the actual use of the *parole*. Literary competence is modelled on linguistic competence in that the former comprises a reader's understanding of conventions, figural systems, plot devices, and so forth: literary competence always includes linguistic competence.

MACRO- and MICROCONTEXT. These terms have no absolute value, but are defined by their relative positions within an actual text. In poetic stylistics, the microcontext is very often the individual verse line, and the macrocontext is the stanza; in a discussion of hemistichs, however, the line would be the macrocontext of the half-line's microcontext. Semantically, the microcontext may be viewed as a syntagm (q.v.) demonstrating isotopy (q.v.) from a restricted semantic field (q.v.). In *The Cantos* the following relationships are common: the line is the microcontext for the macrocontext of the verse paragraph; a group of verse paragraphs containing similar matrices and hypograms (q.v.) are the microcontext for the macrocontext of a particular canto; each canto is the microcontext of the macrocontext comprised by a section like *A Draft of XXX Cantos*.

MARKERS occur on all levels of language, from phonemes to semes (q.v.), and are used to confer meaning on some elements as opposed to others. Thus in the phoneme /p/ the sound feature "voiced" is marked, and in the seme /mother/ the semantic feature "human" is marked. Markers serve to "disambiguate" structures, and always occur in binary opposition to unmarked features ("unvoiced" being opposed to "voiced," "animal" being opposed to "human").

MATRIX. According to Riffaterre (1978: 19), the "poem results from the transformation of the matrix, a minimal and literal sentence, into a longer, complex, and nonliteral periphrasis." The matrix is "hypothetical, being only the grammatical and lexical actualization of a sentence." Matrices semantically "dominate" the text while, at the same time, they are never precisely realized within it.

MIMESIS as used here simply refers to the "representation of reality" in literature. "Reality" may further defined as a recognizable resemblance to persons, objects, and sequences of events as these are commonly met with in ordinary life. According to Riffaterre, all poetry is by definition a "deviation from a mimesis."

MODELS are "primary actualizations" in a specific poem of a particular matrix (q.v.). Variants are produced on the basis of such a model until, as Riffaterre puts it, "the paradigm of all possible variations on the matrix" is exhausted (1978: 19).

MODERNISM. Obviously, the aim of the present study is to forward a semiotic definition of Modernist poetry (as opposed to a purely historical classification). Thus, based on the formal properties defined herein, a number of authors outside the twentieth century may be seen as partly

Modernist (Smart, Blake, Sterne, Melville, Whitman, and Dickinson come immediately to mind). In the interest of simplicity, however, I have followed the lead of Kenner, Sultan, and others, and have defined as "Modernist" that period extending from the turn of the twentieth century to the onset of World War II. Consequently, *A Draft of XXX Cantos* is "Modernist" whereas *Rock-Drill* is not (a distinction which seems to be borne out by formal traits as well).

Paradigm and syntagm are the "axes" along which language is organized, paradigms indicating "links" in the "chain" which is the syntagm. A paradigm is constituted, simply, by a word and its semantic and syntactic associations. The paradigmatic axis is often said to exist *"in absentia,"* and thus paradigms have their reality in the mind of the listener or reader. The syntagm, on the other hand, exists in space, as print on the page or a phonic sequence, and is thus irreversible: syntagms exist *in praesentia*. If the paradigm is associative, the syntagm is combinatory. Although the most obvious syntagm is the sentence, other syntagms embrace the range from simple exclamations to blocks of many sentences.

Post-structuralism. With philosophy as its foundation and linguistics as its model, post-structuralism sees a common strain in the methodologies of the major disciplines of the twentieth century: psychoanalysis, Marxism, anthropology, systems theory, and of course structuralism itself. The key departure of post-structuralism from each of these disciplines individually is simply this interdisciplinary or transdisciplinary assumption of methodology itself. If the diverse "projects" of post-structuralists have any common aim, it is the "deconstruction" of textual duplicity; many post-structuralists are convinced of the text's tendency to offer its own reading (which often undermines the obvious reading it at first appears to offer).

Right- and left-branching structures. Simply speaking, these refer to the "branches" of tree diagrams which in transformational generative grammar represent the deep structure of a sentence. Very many sentences in English are right-branching in that they begin with an NP and continue with a VP in which subsidiary structures are generated to the right of the deep structure "tree."

Semantic field and semes. A seme in semantics designates the kernel oppositions which make up the meaning of a word; such kernels are usually represented as positive or negative features. In the word /mother/, for example, the semes + human, + female, + adult, + nurturing may be envisioned. Obviously, in the majority of words it is impossible to catalogue all possible semes because some semes involve connotations which may be peculiar to a speaker's idiolect (q.v.). A semantic field is made up of recurring semes in a text or a portion of a text.

SIGN, SIGNIFIER, SIGNIFIED. Although semiotics studies a variety of types of signs (and their associated systems), literary semiotics is chiefly interested in the verbal or written sign, the word. According to Saussure, the sign only has reality as the combination of signifier and signified: signifiers exist on the plane of expression and thus comprise sounds and visual "graphemes"; signifieds exist on the plane of content and comprise semes (q.v.), connotations, and conventions. As Barthes points out (*ES* 2.1.2.), there is a temptation to equate the sign with the signifier, but the sign can only exist in the relation between signifier and signified. Moreover, signifieds are always mental representations and are not to be confused with "referents" in the objective world.

TEXT and INTERTEXT. The recurrent use of the term "text" in contemporary criticism to refer to literary works foregrounds the artificial and "graphemic" nature of literature. Such emphasis may be the result of a reaction to a traditional criticism which dealt with literary works as if they were isolated, spontaneous effusions of the spirit. As used by post-structuralists, "texts," in fact, may be nonliterary as well as literary. Intertexts are texts inserted into an "original" literary work (here, *The Cantos*). Riffaterre employs a rather more generalized usage which seems to include the mere suggestion in one text of a previous text; thus the implication of a particular subgenre, such as the *blason* in French poetry, in a poem may be an intertext (see Riffaterre, 1978: 82–86).

WRITERLY and READERLY. These terms have to a certain extent a polemic intent in that they designate texts which encourage either passive consumption (the "readerly" work) or active "production" (the "writerly" work). Writerly and readerly texts are further distinguished by their general allocation to historical period; many "classic" texts (those written before the twentieth century) are readerly, while the Modernist "open" text, which requires "completion" by its reader, is writerly. Obviously, however, some classic texts, like *Tristram Shandy,* are writerly and many modern texts are readerly.

BIBLIOGRAPHY

Altieri, Charles. "Objective Image and Act of Mind in Modern Poetry." *PMLA* 91 (January 1976): 101–14.

Baker, William E. *Syntax in English Poetry: 1870–1930.* Berkeley and Los Angeles: University of California Press, 1967.

Barthes, Roland. *Elements of Semiology.* Translated by Annette Lavers and Colin Smith. New York: Hill and Wang, 1967.

Baumann, Walter. *The Rose in the Steel Dust: An Examination of the Cantos of Ezra Pound.* Bern: Francke Verlag, 1967.

Beauchamp, William. "Riffaterre's *Semiotics of Poetry* with an Illustration in the Poetry of Emily Dickinson." *Centrum* 1 NS, 1 (Spring 1981): 36–47.

Benjamin, Walter. *Reflections.* New York and London: Harcourt Brace Jovanovich, 1978.

Bloom, Harold. *The Anxiety of Influence: A Theory of Poetry.* London and New York: Oxford University Press, 1975.

Bolinger, Dwight. *Aspects of Language.* New York: Harcourt Brace and Jovanovich, 1975.

Brooke-Rose, Christine. *A Structural Analysis of Ezra Pound's Usura Canto: Jakobson's Method Extended and Applied to Free Verse.* The Hague and Paris: Mouton, 1976.

——. *A ZBC of Ezra Pound.* Berkeley and Los Angeles: University of California Press, 1971.

Childs, John Steven. "Eliot, Tradition and Textuality." *Texas Studies in Literature and Language* 27 (Fall 1985): 311–23.

——. "Larvatus Prodeo: Semiotic Aspects of the Ideogram in Pound's *Cantos.*" *Paideuma* 9 (Fall 1980): 291–307.

Chomsky, Noam. *Aspects of the Theory of Syntax.* Cambridge, Mass.: The M.I.T. Press, 1965.

Coffman, Stanley K. *Imagism: A Chapter for the History of Modern Poetry.* Norman, Okla.: University of Oklahoma Press, 1951.

Cook, Albert. "Rhythm and Person in the *Cantos.*" In *New Approaches to Ezra Pound,* edited by Eva Hesse. Berkeley and Los Angeles, University of California Press, 1969.

Curtis, James M. "Spatial Form in the Context of Modern Aesthetics." In *Spatial Form in Narrative,* edited by Jeffrey M. Smitten and Ann Daghistany. Ithaca, N.Y.: Cornell University Press, 1981.

Davie, Donald. *Ezra Pound: Poet As Sculptor.* New York and London: Oxford University Press, 1964.

Derrida, Jacques. "Différance." In *Speech and Phenomena,* translated by David B. Allison. Evanston, Ill.: Northwestern University Press, 1973.

Dilligan, R. J., James W. Parins, and Todd K. Bender. *A Concordance to Ezra Pound's Cantos.* New York and London: Garland, 1981.

Durant, Alan. *Ezra Pound, Identity in Crisis: A Fundamental Reassessment of the Poet and His Work.* Sussex: Harvester Press, 1981.

Edwards, J. H., and W. W. Vasse. *An Annotated Index to the Cantos of Ezra Pound.* Berkeley and Los Angeles: University of California Press, 1957.

Eisenstein, Sergei. "The Image in Process." In *The Modern Tradition,* edited by Richard Ellmann and Charles Feidelson. New York: Oxford University Press, 1965.

Eliot, T. S. *After Strange Gods: A Primer of Modern Heresy.* New York: Harcourt, Brace 1934.

———. *The Sacred Wood: Essays on Poetry and Criticism.* 1920. Reprint. London and New York: Methuen, 1960.

———. *To Criticize The Critic.* London: Faber and Faber, 1965.

Fenollosa, Ernest, and Ezra Pound. "The Chinese Written Character as a Medium for Poetry." *Little Review* 6, 5–8 (September–December, 1919): 62–64, 57–64, 55–60, and 68–72.

Flint, F. S. "Imagisme." *Poetry* 1 (March 1913): 198–200.

Fontanier, Pierre. *Les Figures du discours.* Paris: Flammarion, 1968.

Fowler, Roger. "Commentary." *New Literary History* 12 (Spring 1981): 547–57.

Frank, Joseph. "Spatial Form, an Answer to Critics." *Critical Inquiry* 4 (1977): 231–52.

———. "Spatial Form in Modern Literature." *Sewanee Review* 53 (1945): 221–40, 433–56, 643–53.

Gall, Sally M. "Pound and the Modern Melic Tradition: Towards a Demystification of 'Absolute Rhythm.' " *Paideuma* 8 (Spring 1979): 35–45.

Gallup, Donald. *A Bibliography of Ezra Pound.* London: Hart-Davis, 1963.

Gross, Harvey. *Sound and Form in Modern Poetry: A Study of Prosody from Thomas Hardy to Robert Lowell.* Ann Arbor, Mich.: University of Michigan Press, 1965.

Group μ (J. Dubois, F. Edeline, J.M. Klinkenberg, P. Minguet, F. Pire, and H. Trinon). *A General Rhetoric.* Translated by Paul B. Burrell and Edgar M. Slotkin. Baltimore and London: Johns Hopkins University Press, 1981.

Harper, Michael F. "Truth and Calliope: Ezra Pound's Malatesta." *PMLA* 96 (January 1981): 86–103.

Hirsch, E. D., Jr. "Stylistics and Synonymity." *Critical Inquiry* 1 (March 1975): 559–80.

Jakobson, Roman. "Two Types of Language and Two Types of Aphasic Disturbances." In vol. 2 of *Selected Writings*. The Hague and Paris: Mouton, 1971.

Jay, Gregory S. T. S. *Eliot and the Poetics of Literary History*. Baton Rouge, La.: Louisiana State University Press, 1983.

Joyce, James. *A Portrait of the Artist as a Young Man*. New York: Viking Press, 1959.

Kenner, Hugh. *The Poetry of Ezra Pound*. Norfolk, Conn.: New Directions, 1951.

————. *The Pound Era*. Berkeley and Los Angeles: University of California Press, 1971.

Kermode, Frank. *The Romantic Image*. London: Routledge and Kegan Paul, 1957.

————. *The Sense of an Ending: Studies in the Theory of Fiction*. New York: Oxford University Press, 1967.

Kerrane, Kevin. "Phenomenology." In *The Princton Encyclopedia of Poetry and Poetics*, edited by Alex Preminger, Frank J. Warnke, and O. B. Hardison, Jr. Princeton, N.J.: Princeton University Press, 1974.

Korg, Jacob. *Language in Modern Literature: Innovation and Experiment*. New York: Barnes and Noble, 1979.

Kuan-Terry, John. "The Prosodic Theories of Ezra Pound." *Papers on Language and Literature* 9 (Winter 1973): 48–64.

Le Guern, Michel. *Sémantique de la métaphore et de la métonymie*. Paris: Librairie Larousse, 1973.

Levin, S. R. *Linguistic Structures in Poetry*. The Hague: Mouton, 1962.

Lodge, David. *The Modes of Modern Writing: Metaphor, Metonymy, and the Topology of Modern Literature*. Ithaca, N.Y.: Cornell University Press, 1977.

Lukács, Georg. *Studies in European Realism*. London: Hillway, 1950.

McNaughton, William. "Ezra Pound's Meters and Rhythms." *PMLA* 78 (March 1963): 136–46.

Manley, Lawrence. "Concepts of Convention and Models of Critical Discourse." *New Literary History* 13 (Autumn 1981): 31–52.

Milic, Louis T. "Rhetorical Choice and Stylistic Option: The Conscious and Unconscious Poles." In *Literary Style: A Symposium*, edited by Seymour Chatman. New York and London: Oxford University Press.

Olson, Charles. *Selected Writings*. New York: New Directions, 1966.

Paige, D. D. *The Letters of Ezra Pound*. New York: Haskell House, 1974.

Partridge, A. C. *The Language of Modern Poetry*. London: Andre Deutsch, 1976.

Pound, Ezra. *The ABC of Reading*. New York. New Directions, 1960.

————. *The Cantos of Ezra Pound*. New York: New Directions, 1975.

————. *Gaudier-Brzeska: A Memoir.* New York: New Directions, 1970.

————. *Guide to Kulchur.* New York: New Directions, 1952.

————. *Literary Essays of Ezra Pound.* Edited by T. S. Eliot. London: Faber and Faber, 1954.

————. "Mr. Hueffer and the Prose Tradition in Verse." *Poetry* 4 (June 1914): 111–20.

————. *Personae: The Collected Shorter Poems of Ezra Pound, 1926.* New York: New Directions, 1949.

Powell, James A. "The Light of Verse Libre." *Paideuma* 8 (Spring 1979): 3–34.

Rahv, Philip. *The Myth and the Powerhouse.* New York: Farrar, Straus, and Giroux, 1965.

Reed, Victor. "Toward the *Cantos* of Ezra Pound." Ph.D. diss., University of California at Berkeley, 1963.

Riddel, Joseph. "Decentering the Image: The 'Project' of 'American' Poetics?" In *Textual Strategies: Perspectives in Post-Structuralist Criticism,* edited by Josué V. Harari. Ithaca, N.Y.: Cornell University Press.

Riffaterre, Michael. "Criteria for Style Analysis." *Word* 15 (1959): 154–74.

————. "Describing Poetic Structures: Two Approaches to Baudelaire's 'Les Chats.' " *Yale French Studies* 36–37 (1966): 200–42.

————. *Semiotics of Poetry.* Bloomington, Ind.: University of Indiana Press, 1978.

Rosenthal, M. L. "The Structuring of Ezra Pound's *Cantos.*" *Paideuma* 6 (Spring 1977): 2–12.

Ruthven, K. K. *A Guide to Ezra Pound's Personae, 1926.* Berkeley and Los Angeles: University of California Press, 1969.

Schneidau, Herbert. *Ezra Pound: The Image and the Real.* Baton Rouge, La.: Louisiana State University Press, 1969.

————. "Wisdom Past Metaphor: Another View of Pound, Fenollosa, and Objective Verse." *Paideuma* 5 (Spring 1976): 15–29.

Schofer, Peter, and Donald Rice. "Metaphor, Metonymy, and Synecdoche Revis(it)ed." *Semiotica* 21 (1977): 121–49.

Shklovsky, Victor. "Art As Technique." In *Russian Formalist Criticism,* edited by L. T. Lemon and M. J. Reis. Lincoln, Neb.: University of Nebraska Press, 1965.

Smith, P. H., and A. E. Durant. "Pound's Metonymy: Revisiting Canto 47." *Paideuma* 8 (Fall 1979): 327–33.

Sultan, Stanley. *Ulysses, The Waste Land, and Modernism: A Jubilee Study.* Port Washington, N.Y.: Kennikat Press, 1977.

Terrell, Carroll. *A Companion to the Cantos of Ezra Pound.* Vol. 1. Berkeley, Los Angeles, and London: University of California Press, 1980.

Thurber, James. *My World—And Welcome To It.* New York and London: Harcourt Brace Jovanovich, 1969.

Witemeyer, Hugh. "Pound & the *Cantos:* 'Ply over Ply.' " *Paideuma* 8 (Fall 1979): 229–35.

Yeats, W. B. *Selected Poems and Two Plays.* Edited by M. L. Rosenthal. New York: Collier Books, 1977.

Yip, Wai-Lim. *Ezra Pound's Cathay.* Princeton, N.J.: Princeton University Press, 1969.

INDEX

DATES